**Churches and Social Welfare
Vol. II**

The Changing Scene
Current Trends and Issues

Horace R. Cayton

Setsuko Matsunaga Nishi

**NATIONAL COUNCIL OF THE CHURCHES
OF CHRIST IN THE U.S.A.**

The Changing Scene

CONTENTS

List of Text Tables

List of Text Charts

List of Appendix Tables

This research was planned to meet the needs of the National Conference on the Churches and Social Welfare in Cleveland, Ohio, November, 1955. Because of the problem orientation of its approach, this study should prove particularly helpful to that body. The description of the actual problems facing the churches in their relationship to organized professional social work and those of the church-related agencies that occupy a dual position between the churches and the profession of social work is treated with insight. The background of these problems is located in the changes which have taken place in our society and are reflected in the new practices and organization of present social welfare. In addition to the benefit this study might have for ministers, church administrators, church social workers and church laymen, it should prove of importance to professional social work interests and some sections of the general public.

Horace R. Cayton and Setsuko Matsunaga Nishi have performed an excellent task in assembling the materials for the study in a field which presented difficult research problems. As this is the first attempt to develop an integrated statement on the diverse, involved and sometimes contradictory activities of the churches in social welfare, the fitting together of the mosaic of this involvement was not an easy task.

At a stage in the preparation of the study all of the resources of the Bureau of Research and Survey of the National Council of Churches were utilized. The excellent teamwork of the Bureau staff contributed largely to the completion of the work.

A word should be said about the conditions under which the study was made. Extensive research was planned which would have involved a considerable amount of money and an extended period of time. This was found impossible for a number of reasons, and the present statement was developed in a matter of a few months. Thus there is no assumption that this represents a comprehensive and exhaustive treatment of the subject. However, material presented not only defines problems of concern for program and policy but indicates large areas for further research.

The importance of the contribution of William J. Villaume and his staff in the Department of Social Welfare is difficult to fully acknowledge. During much of the entire process, he has added his criticisms and suggestions and made available staff and funds out of a most difficult budget.

1

The Research Committee of the Conference, Charles G. Cha-kerian, chairman, David W. Barry, Shelby Harrison, Merrill Krug-hoff, Almon R. Pepper, Francis A. Shearer, Arthur L. Swift, Wesley Hotchkiss, G. Paul Musselman, Alice Maloney, Howard Thomas, and John Shope, gave many suggestions and served to interpret the needs for research of the Conference.

The Bureau of Applied Social Research, Columbia University, through Peter Aptakin, contributed much to the development and analysis of the extensive study of church-related agencies.

The long experience and knowledge of such advisers as Shelby M. Harrison, F. Ernest Johnson, David W. Barry, and Charles Y. Glock were invaluable in the development of ideas for the frame-work of analysis.

Hard-working research assistants on the project have been Pauline Lewis and John J. Mullen, Anne O. Lively, Bertha Blair, Johannes H. Mol, and George P. Hermann gave brief but intensive assistance. Portions of the manuscript were written in preliminary draft by Inez M. Cavert, Benson Y. Landis, David W. Barry and the writer of this page.

A grant from the New York Foundation enabled the study to get underway. The major portion of the finances were derived from a special budget provided by denominations of the National Council for the Conference. In addition there are the countless, unnamed individuals and groups who have provided data, filled out ques-tionnaires and participated in interviews. For all help, we are grateful.

LAURIS B. WHITMAN, *executive director*
Bureau of Research and Survey,
National Council of the Churches
of Christ in the U. S. A.

————————————————

It is remarkable that in the voluminous literature both on the churches and on social welfare there should be so little on the interrelationship between churches and modern social work. The present volume, we believe, constitutes the first integrated effort to relate the social welfare activities of the churches to the development of professional social work.

One hears that there has been a trend toward secularization[1] in social work, but what this means in terms of actual changes in society is seldom made clear. This study addresses itself to this question by describing societal processes as they affect social welfare and the churches.

The approach of the book is historical in the first instance. It examines the traditional role and current involvement of the churches in social welfare. This is followed by a description of some of the changes in the field of social work which have come about in response to broad changes in society in the last fifty years —the growth and specialization of the field, the rise of social work as a profession and the development of federated and community-wide standard-setting and fund-raising organizations. Some of these developments have tended to widen rather than narrow the gap between the profession of social work and the activities of the churches.

The second approach of the volume is directed toward problems. The development of social work as a profession has created certain problems for the churches and for church-related agencies. There were problems related to the disparity between professional social work and the social welfare work of the churches. Some of the functions performed by social work impinge on the traditional functions of religious institutions. The church-related agencies also have some difficulties as they are identified with both the churches and their religious values and objectives, and with social work and its definitions of social values and objectives.

There have been attempts, however, to narrow the area of conflict and widen that of co-operation. Notable among these was that of the Church Conference of Social Work.

Finally, the study raises the question of the ultimate goals of the churches in the field of social welfare and those of social agencies under other auspices. The conclusion is that the goals are different but closer understanding will lead to better co-operation and will reduce the area of conflict.

An important contribution is the material on the present involvement of the churches in the social work field. For the first time, empirical data on the extent and nature of the churches' activities are made available upon which an evaluation and assessment of the role of the churches in social welfare can be made.

LEONARD W. MAYO

[1] In the sociological, not theological use of the term.

PART I

THE PERSPECTIVE OF SOCIAL HISTORY

There have been broad and important changes in our society. We have experienced wars, depressions, vast population movements, an expansion of our economy and a technological development which has been unparalleled in world history. In little over two centuries this country has changed from a small colonial settlement on the east coast of the continent to a mature and developed nation; during this short period America has come of age.

With this maturing process have come changes in the social structure of the country, changes in the institutional structure and in the type and nature of social relationships. These changes have affected the churches and the relationship of the churches to society. They have also altered the social work structure of the nation. Any analysis of the present role of the churches in the field of social welfare, then, must first be stated in the context of this development.

The churches have been historically identified with social welfare activities. Many writers, indeed, have referred to the church as the "mother of philanthropy." But the changes which accompanied America's coming of age resulted in a much more secular society. This process of secularization has affected the churches and has been reflected in the welfare activities of the churches. Therefore an examination of the present activities of the churches in this field reveals a confusing picture which represents their accommodation to social change. The pattern for these varied types of involvements and activities is to be found in the historical development of the country.

THE CHALLENGE TO THE CHURCHES IN SOCIAL WELFARE

The early importance of the churches in social welfare seems to have had no serious challenge. This applies to the churches' social services as well as to their active influence upon public attitude toward social need. The less complicated society of the past was more sacred; i.e., the churches, perhaps more than any other institution, defined values for and sanctified the actions of people, and this was not necessarily reflected in such an indication as church membership. The division of labor of this earlier, simpler social organization was not well developed into specialties, and fewer institutions performed more functions. The basic beliefs of the society were more uniform, there being constant reinforcement by the members of the more homogenous community. Serious challenge was hardly possible by a respectable member of the community—if he wanted to be a part of that community.

This small sociological digression is given in order that we might analyze the meaning of the mounting questioning of the churches' present involvement and position in the welfare field. Interestingly enough, it is not just the interested lay public or the social work profession that is calling for critical examination. The churches themselves feel the need to reappraise their role and function in this field. Understandably so, for the three are inseparably involved and a part of the same society that has undergone such tremendous change in the past century. It is apparent that it is no longer adequate for any of these groups to say that because the churches had a good deal to do with the initiation of social services and have laid the bases for the ideology that supports activities for the social welfare—that there is no responsibility to examine religious operations and influences in the welfare field.

Modern society, perhaps America especially, has developed too much regard for science, for technology, for efficiency, for man's needs to hold in further abeyance a candid and objective assessment of the churches' functioning in social welfare simply because it may not be quite proper or may seem disrespectful to question the sacred. Furthermore, there is a growing awareness that church-related social welfare is as influenced by secular interests as its sacred auspices.

It should be pointed out that the three elements of our society whom this research might concern—the churches, the profession of social work, and the interested public—would need to or perhaps would inevitably make their judgments in terms of their own particular framework of values or goals. That is, the church would assess in the light of its religious aims, the profession of social work, in terms of standards and concepts of the profession; and the interested public, in terms of its particular concerns in social welfare.

As recipients in the public of social welfare services, they would be making evaluations in the context of being able to get the kind of services they want most efficiently; as supporters in the public of welfare enterprises, either through voluntary contributions or through taxes, we should suspect that the primary interest would be in relation to economy and their conception of the appropriate functions of various institutions.

Of course, this is an oversimplification. The particular sets of values or goals which we have associated with these various elements rarely constitute their exclusive loyalties and all in varying degrees would enter into any one group's evaluation.

The highlights presented here of the Protestant (also Anglican and Eastern Orthodox) effort in social welfare are treated in more detail in Part III of this volume. The purpose of discussion at this point is to provide some guidelines for the consideration of changes and trends in the social welfare field in the chapters immediately following.

The most striking fact of the Protestant churches' involvement in social welfare today is its seemingly indefinite variation of expression. No matter what dimension is taken, there does not appear readily a pattern of what might be typical or of what might be generally true for protestantism, except for the fact of great range.

To describe even in outline the work of the churches in social welfare today is an effort that takes us into practically every realm of the churches' activities, for so much of what can properly be called social welfare is interwoven within the total functions of religious institutions in society. Much of the churches' contribution to the social welfare is of an intangible nature—not easy to measure. What can be empirically demonstrated without an elaborate and extensive research program, which we obviously do not have for this presentation, is the most obvious and manifest kind of social welfare activity.

Let us begin at the least empirically demonstrable point. It has long been simply understood that religious institutions laid the general ideological basis for society regardless of whether the members of the society consciously acknowledged this function. As keen a modern analyst of social ideology in America as Gunnar Myrdal has commented:

> . . . Apart from the historical problem of the extent to which church and religion in America actually inspired the American

Creed, they became a powerful container and preserver of the Creed when it was once in existence. . .

Religion is still a potent force in American life . . . American scientific observers are likely to get their attentions fixed upon the process of progressive secularization to the extent that they do not see this main fact, that America probably is still the most religious country in the Western world. . .

. . . The mere fact that there are many denominations, and that there is competition between them, forces American churches to a greater tolerance and ecumenical understanding and to a greater humanism and interest in social problems than the people in the churches would otherwise call for.

I also believe that American churches and their teachings have contributed something essential to the emotional temper of the Creed and, indeed, of the American people. Competent and sympathetic foreign observers have always noted the generosity and helpfulness of Americans.

. . . I cannot help feeling that the Christian neighborliness of the common American reflects, also, an influence from the churches. Apart from its origin, this temper of the Americans is part and parcel of the American Creed. It shows up in the Americans' readiness to make financial sacrifices for charitable purposes. No country has so many cheerful givers as America. It was not only "rugged individualism," nor a relatively continuous prosperity, that made it possible for America to get along without a publicly organized welfare policy almost up to the Great Depression in the 'thirties but it was also the world's most generous private charity.
. . .

These ideological forces—the Christian religion and the English law—also explain why America through all its adventures has so doggedly stuck to its high ideals. . . . [1]

Here, then, is the judgment of a competent social scientist. In church circles this has probably never been questioned, but in the last half century there has been a growing self-conscious effort on the part of the churches to influence the social atmosphere of society. Generally, this has been in the form of social pronouncements, and their implementing activity has been called social education and action.

The famous encyclical known as the *Rerum Novarum* of Pope Leo XIII on the condition of labor appeared in 1891. The Protestant Episcopal Church ten years later was the first Protestant denomination in the United States to take official recognition of the importance of the subject when its general convention appointed a commission to study the working conditions of the laborer. However, it was not until 1908 that a comprehensive set of resolutions were formulated in this country. In that year the General Convention of the Methodist Episcopal Church formulated a Social Creed that was later

9

adopted in substance by the Federal Council of Churches, and has been generally known as the Social Creed of the Protestant Churches. During the next few years various resolutions of a similar nature were passed at the general conventions of such leading denominations as the Northern Baptist Convention, the Methodist Episcopal Church, the Presbyterian Church in the U.S.A., and the Protestant Episcopal Church.[2]

Is this an indication that with the growth of influence of secular institutions the churches needed to formalize for public consumption their positions on social questions? Unlike the papal encyclicals and edicts of the Roman Catholic Church, the social pronouncements of the Protestant churches do not attempt to define *the* one right position to be taken by their constituency. Despite variation in the structure of authority that exists among Protestant bodies, it does seem clear that adherence to the positions of the churches' official pronouncements is almost entirely a matter of individual conscience and characteristically voluntary.

Furthermore, the initial interest of conscious church efforts in social problems was probably centered within "a small group of social reformers and theological students."[3] As the churches developed their programs in the atmosphere of the growing popularity of the social gospel movement, the efforts of the relatively small social-concern core of the churches came forth as denominational utterances. Until World War II, the number of pronouncements on a wide variety of general and very specific social conditions grew to large proportions. More recently, however, the number of such official utterances are fewer for whatever the reasons among other things 1) that the churches became more democratically representative of their constituency and thereby more responsible to them, who, after all, represent what is generally current thinking on social questions in the American public, 2) that their effectiveness in molding opinion and guiding action was being questioned, or 3) the seeming pressure from some sources to have the churches confine their activities to those that were exclusively spiritual in character.

In any case, the total expenditure in terms of special staff and funds for social education and action activities is exceedingly minor today in terms of the total financial outlay of the churches. However, an initial finding in a current study of the structures and resources of the member denominations of the National Council of the Churches of Christ in the United States of America, as relevant to social concerns is the following: Despite the fact that special organizations, staff, and funds for social education and action seem insignificant in terms of the total program of the churches almost all the agencies of the denominations in some way or other deal with such subjects as race relations, economic life, international affairs, religious and civil liberties, and social welfare. Religious education, home mission and sometimes foreign misson agencies; women's, men's, and youth groups; broadcasting and films; and publication organizations, all are somehow involved in the development of understanding of and Christian action regarding social matters. Social issues and interests are dealt with as an integral part of their respective programs.

Here then is an all too brief picture of the conscious efforts of the churches to influence the social welfare.

Some have suggested that this kind of contribution of churches to the social welfare and their general influence upon society's ideals are their most crucial role in this field. F. Ernest Johnson writes:

> As the institution pre-eminently responsible for teaching ideals and attitudes, keeping faith alive and inspiring to high endeavor, the church can function best by impregnating social work and all other community functions with its purpose, its vision and its courage through the instrumentality of members of is own fellowship who take up these tasks, some on a professional basis, some on a volunteer basis. This is, I believe a more valid theory for protestantism than the contrary theory to which the Catholic Church holds. The latter theory leads straight to the absorption of function after function by the church. . . . Community life cannot without danger be simplified by extending the control of one institution over it. This runs counter to the whole course of social development. . . . [4]

In any case, this function of churches in society as its primary definer of values and social conscience, is not an unimportant involvement of the churches in social welfare.

Perhaps the second major kind of present day involvement is the elaboration of social activities integrated within the churches' interest in religious education and missionary endeavor and pastoral care of their constituency—all distinctively religious institutional functions. Many of these activities, under any auspices other than churches, would be definitely included in anyone's conception of social welfare services. Brief mention has been made of the integration of social education and action activities within most of the agencies of the denominations. Something of the general growth of different means of accomplishing the churches' ends within their structures is described by C. Luther Fry in the 1933 *Recent Social Trends in the United States:*

> The great increase in the number and variety of subsidiary organizations within the Protestant church, chiefly for the various age and sex groups, marks an advance, on the one hand, over the exclusively formal type of religious instruction, and has required, on the other hand, to be related to the education aim and processes of the church. Church social

11

life has been greatly elaborated, partly in the attempt to substitute safe forms of social expression for worldly and danger-
ous ones, but also by reason of a greater recognition of group
life as a normal expression of religion. Cultural activities incidental to educational aims have taken such new forms as
dramatics and forums for discussions of public questions. All
these changes have added their demand for modifications of
organization, method and administration, and for additions to
staff, plant, and expenditures.[5]

A further expansion on the point of social services being a normal
part of the religious functioning of the churches is given by another
source:

By far the most numerous Protestant social welfare agencies,
either in country or in city, are the local churches themselves.
Even the more conventional ones make important contributions to this field. Their pastoral and fraternal assistance to
constituents has both a preventive and remedial aspect. They
render material aid, help in sickness, exercise vocational guidance and contribute to employment all as a matter of course,
without much consciousness that these are social ministries.
The church's contribution to social morale is essentially beyond measurement. It is entirely demonstrable, however, that
in the pre-depression era a full third of all the social welfare
funds, both public and private, expended in typical American
cities were expended for the support of leisure-time and char-
acter-building activities, entirely paralleling the normal activities of organized groups in the church often sponsored by
churches and generally supported by church people. The
share of the church in welfare work, as a by-product of its
religious value, is accordingly enormous. Its more highly organized groups for women, young people, boys and girls,
realize many, if not most, of the values found in the organizations undertaken for similar age groups in the name of social
work.[6]

In the rural churches, where this kind of elaboration of activities
is probably not so general, welfare services are very much a part
of their more informal and unspecialized activities.

The social welfare work of the rural churches . . . , professionally judged, is almost nonexistent. That, however, is not to say
that there is none of a sort. Few are the rural churches that
have not aided the poor or unfortunate among their own
number. But the average rural church member would be sur-
prised to hear that having the Boy Scouts take care of Widow
Jones's fires or that sending garments to tenant Smith's children after they were burned out, classified as social welfare
work. Rural people are neighborly and they are chiefly neighborly within the social groupings to which they acknowledge
allegiance. It is in such a way that a rural church moves to
relieve distress when confronted with it.[7]

But in both urban and rural churches there has been a growing tendency "toward the consolidation of little churches and the development of strong units. . . . The large church with a well equipped building and a staff of specialists is becoming more common. Many churches now have on their staffs a competent secretary, a director of religious education, a visitor, frequently a social caseworker, and part-time directors for boys' and girls' work."[8] Or, lacking such a staff, which is undoubtedly the more usual situation of local churches, the pastor himself possibly together with his wife must play all these specialized roles. "The increasing complexity of modern life demands that he be a combination pastor, administrator, counselor, priest, educator, organizer, and social scientist. He is a community leader—with problems ranging far beyond those of his immediate congregation."[9]

True enough, in the simpler past, the minister performed these functions without self-consciousness about playing all these specialized roles. But what is important here is that the modern conception of the specialist has changed the self-image of the minister— that, to be competent he must be trained to some degree in all these specialties. The tendency seems to be that since he cannot adequately pursue these specialties, he turns over these special responsibilities to someone else or to some other institution, but increasingly he feels the need to know enough about all of them in order to direct properly the problems with which he is faced as head of his congregation. This change has been noted in the following:

> Striking changes have come over the form and mood of pastoral ministries in recent years. The tendency toward impersonality and anonymity characteristic of urban relationships has left its mark upon the churches. Just as the visiting family doctor has given place to the specialist in the office, so the city minister has increasingly become a consultant to be visited by people in need rather than one who goes out to find them. Studies of the actual operation of the various professional functions reveal that the work of professional church visitors and social workers also registers a partial shift from the aggressively pastoral to the consultative form. There is a decreasing tendency for the pastoral worker to undertake the sole responsibility for cases and the much greater likelihood of reference to expert social agencies, and in general a greater recognition of the complexity of the problems of social and spiritual adjustment. A few churches have even undertaken serious professional ministries along the lines of vocational guidance and psychiatry.[10]

Not only the personnel of the churches reflects the growth and proliferation of specialized responsibilities subsumed under the normal functioning of local churches. The facilities that are now considered necessities for church buildings suggest a well equipped group-work center:

> Most new churches . . . are provided with departmental rooms for educational work, offices which are open daily, a large social room, club rooms for boys and girls, often a large assembly hall, dining hall and kitchen. . . . The tendency at present is to study the multiple use of rooms and combination uses of equipment for social and educational purposes.[11]

How apparent it is that as one author has remarked in speaking of church recreational activities:

> The church attitude has altered slowly from one of disapproval to one of noninterference, and finally to one of positive acquiescence and sponsorship. The modern recreation movement began to go forward only after play had "gained recognition" as a means to healthful living, and was no longer stigmatized as a form of idleness. The early years of this century saw not merely a marked decline in religious oposition to amusement, but also the promotion of recreational programs by churches and other religious organizations.[12]

We have been discussing the nature of social services that have become well organized as the normal functioning of local churches. Let us turn now to a brief consideration of the health and welfare services that stem out of basically missionary interest in certain social groupings that are somehow outside the mainstream of American life—Indian Americans, migrants, sharecroppers, defense communities, the underprivileged in cities, and racial and nationality groupings. As in the case of foreign mission endeavors, serving the social needs of the people goes hand in hand with the ultimate interest of bringing them to Christianity. And in most instances, it would be difficult to determine on the basis of the kinds of services rendered which might be the primary interest. Health services, child care activities, recreational work, family counseling, educational efforts, direct material relief, and liaison with and stimulation of responsibility by public and community agencies are an extensive and crucial part of the home mission enterprise.

In large cities, the missionary concern for disadvantaged racial and cultural groupings has expressed itself in social services that are usually intensely intertwined with a religious ministry. The city mission interests were given important impetus in their group work activities by the recurrent shifting of population groupings:

> The development of this particular type of activity was forced upon the church by changed neighborhood conditions. It was the movement of population incident to the growth of the modern city that presented this new problem. The normally Protestant church-going population moved out into the newer sections, leaving behind the church buildings surrounded by

religious control is strong without correspondingly strong assistance from the churches. The churches' influence is generally weaker in agencies which receive community chest or fund monies. Agencies receiving tax-supported funds also show some indication of this, but not as clearly as in the case of recipients of community-chest funds.

Church-related agencies are not indicated in the study sample to have any lower degree of professionally trained social workers than the general population of social workers in the United States. A definite relationship exists between the percentage of professionally trained social workers and the degree of religious control of an agency; that is, the stronger the religious control, the smaller the proportion of professionally trained social workers. This shows consistently to be true, not only for all church-related agencies, but for specific types of agencies such as homes for the aged, institutions for the care of children, hospitals, and neighborhood houses and settlements.

There is hardly an indication in the data that church-related agencies and institutions plan any retraction in their operations. Quite on the contrary, a good proportion of agencies report expansion plans.

We have in the above attempted to draw a summary picture of the present involvement of the churches in social welfare. The variation in types of expression of social welfare interests is evident. One further note should be added about the multiplicity of religious organizations which are involved. Mention has been made of local churches and denominational national organizations—but important also to be considered are the local, state, and regional denominational organizations; the local, state, regional, and national interdenominational groups; the local, state, regional, and national organizations of laywomen and men; and finally the non-denominational Protestant organizations. Thus, the organizational structure of participation of religious interests in social welfare is vastly complicated.

This organizational intricacy and the wide range of expression of church social welfare interests combine into a complexity that practically defies clarity of presentation of the churches' present involvement and position in social welfare.

Considered alone, the churches' activities in social welfare show no apparent pattern; but considered in the context of a changing society and the dynamics of trends in the social welfare field, it is believed that some meaningful analysis is possible to aid a consideration of the role and function of churches today in the field of social welfare.

With this perspective of social history of the traditional and current participation of churches in social welfare concerns, we now move to a discussion of the changes in the social welfare field that are relevant to the functioning of churches in this realm.

FOOTNOTES FOR CHAPTER 1

[1] Gunnar Myrdal and Others, *An American Dilemma: The Negro Problem and Modern Democracy* (New York: Harper and Brothers, 1944), pp. 10–12.

[2] Harry F. Ward, Editor: *The Social Creed of the Churches* (New York: Methodist Book Concern, 1914), p. 5f.

[3] C. Luther Fry, with the assistance of M. F. Jessup, "Changes in Religious Organizations," *Recent Social Trends in the United States*, President's Research Committee on Social Trends (New York: McGraw-Hill Publishing Company, Inc., 1933), p. 1014.

[4] F. Ernest Johnson, *The Church and Society* (Nashville: Abingdon Cokesbury, 1935), p. 145–146.

[5] C. Luther Fry, *op. cit.*, p. 1058.

[6] H. Paul Douglass and Edmund de S. Brunner, *The Protestant Church as a Social Institution* (New York: Harper and Brothers, 1935), p. 188–189.

[7] *Ibid.*, p. 187.

[8] F. Ernest Johnson, Editor: *The Social Work of the Churches* (New York: Department of Research and Education, Federal Council of the Churches of Christ in America, 1930), p. 37.

[9] Nancy Lawrence, "The Protestant Minister Today," *National Council Outlook*, (1955), No. 6, 12. This is a popular report of "A Study of the Functions of the Parish Minister," commissioned by the Russell Sage Foundation in 1953 and is being conducted by Samuel W. Blizzard in collaboration with Union Theological Seminary in New York.

[10] Fry, *op. cit.*, p. 1056.

[11] Johnson, *The Social Work of the Churches, op. cit.*, p. 37.

[12] Rex A. Skidmore, "The Protestant Church and Recreation: An example of Social Change," *Social Forces*, Vol. XX, No. 3, 1941–1942, p. 365. Inner quote from J. F. Steiner, *Americans at Play* (New York: McGraw-Hill Book Company, Inc., 1933), p. IX.

[13] *Proceedings of the Conference of Neighborhood House Work, June 10–12, 1925* (New York: Board of National Missions of the Presbyterian Church in the U.S.A.), pp. 22–23.

[14] F. Ernest Johnson, in his article, "Protestant Social Work," *Social Work Year Book, 1941* (New York: Russell Sage Foundation, 1941), p. 404, has stated:
"The more a religious group consciously differs from the prevailing religious pattern in the community, the stronger its tendency to maintain so far as possible its own social services. In other words, this is the sectarian pattern of action. The Mormons today illustrate this tendency to maintain social work as a part of a compact community life. When, however, as is true in America, the majority of the population belongs to communions which differ in relatively unimportant ways, the differences between prevailing ideals and standards of the churches and those of the community as a whole are narrowed. The fact that the great Protestant churches have far more than their numerical proportion of the well-to-do, who in one way or another must furnish the major support of social services no matter under what auspices they are conducted, tends to carry over into secular social work the ideals and purposes that are held by the church constituency. This tends to lessen the demand for distinctively Protestant social work."

[15] Refer to the discussion of a special study on church-related agencies in Chapter 10, from which the generalizations are made.

PART II

CHANGES IN THE WELFARE FIELD
AND THEIR RELATION TO
CHURCH ACTIVITIES

The American culture has become more and more complex. With its development from a rural society to an urban way of life, social relations have become specialized and segmented. This has resulted in new and altered types of social work to meet the changing concept of social responsibility. In the adaptive process which accompanied these social changes, three trends are evident. They are: the growth and specialization of social work, the development of social work as a profession, and the movement toward federation in the social work field. All three of these trends have had an important effect upon the churches' activities in the social welfare field.

One of the most striking changes in the field of social welfare in the past fifty years has been its great growth and specialization. Public welfare programs are responsible for the greatest portion of this growth. The huge expansion of public welfare funds has reduced the relative importance of the entire field of private welfare, including that of the churches.

The specialization of social work, too, has operated to make more difficult the former more dominant position of the churches in the welfare field. As society grew more complex, and with the growth in scientific knowledge, especially in the social sciences, a number of specialized agencies dealing with special problems and needing a personnel with new and extended training, appeared. For a number of reasons the churches were often unable to enter into all these specialties.

Closely allied to the growth and specialization of social work is the development of social work as a profession. The self-conception of the social worker as a professional person brought about changes in the social worker—in his idea of himself and of his role and position in society. Some of the drives which motivated the social worker in trying to achieve professional status tended to estrange him from the "dedicated" church worker. Religious interests found it extremely hard to give up the idea that the sincere desire to help people in distress was not sufficient reason for engaging in social work activities. The standards so enthusiastically fought for by the social work professionals were not always shared or thought necessary by the untrained, "dedicated" church worker. Today, however, the professional workers are the standard-bearers.

With the growth and specialization of social work and the rise of professionalism, there was a movement toward federation. Many new social agencies sprang up to meet the new demands of a growing and increasingly complex society. It became obvious that some sort of combining of efforts, of community planning and of federation for financial support, was necessary. In response to this need came the establishment of community councils—to prevent overlapping of services and the planning for the expansion of existing agencies and the creation of new services—and the creating of community chests for federated financing. Both of these movements, while helpful to social work in general, including church-related agencies, operated to take leadership in the field from the churches.

SOCIAL WELFARE EXPANDS
AND SPECIALIZES

2

One of the most striking changes in the field of social welfare in the past thirty to fifty years has been its rapid growth and specialization. When we consider the increasing complexity of social life, the rapid shift of much of our population from a rural to a more urban society, the tendencies toward specialization in industry and in the professions, and the rapid growth of specialized scientific knowledge—the growth and specialization in social welfare is understandable. What has gone on in social welfare is but a parallel to what has happened in society as a whole.

One indication of the growth of both private and public welfare programs is given in *America's Needs and Resources: A New Survey*. Here it is stated that total private welfare expenditures were estimated to be $1,278,000,000 in 1930, $1,419,000,000 in 1940, and $4,526,000,000 in 1950.

CHART 1

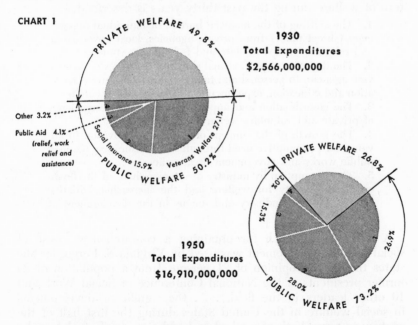

PRIVATE WELFARE 49.8%

1930
Total Expenditures
$2,566,000,000

Other 3.2%
Public Aid 4.1%
(relief, work relief and assistance)
Social Insurance 15.9%
Veterans Welfare 27.1%
PUBLIC WELFARE 50.2%

PRIVATE WELFARE 26.8%

0.0%
15.3%
26.9%

1950
Total Expenditures
$16,910,000,000

28.0%
PUBLIC WELFARE 73.2%

The expansion for public welfare programs was much greater. The estimated expenditures were $1,288,000,000 in 1930, $5,428,-000,000 in 1940, and $12,348,500,000 in 1950.

Thus, the estimated expenditure was approximately 250 per cent

21

higher in 1950 than in 1930 for private welfare; but public welfare expenditures were some 900 per cent higher in 1950 than in 1930. To elaborate further:

> Private welfare declined from 50 per cent of total outlays (excluding public health and medical service) in 1930 to 27 per cent in 1950. . .
> (Total) welfare expenditures were 4.1 per cent of the national income, (i.e. the total income of all the people) in 1930, 9.5 per cent in 1940, and 8.3 per cent in 1950. The growth in public programs is largely responsible for the vast increase in welfare expenditures. . .
> Church welfare expenditures were approximately 3.4 per cent of the total welfare expenditures of the United States in the years 1949 and 1950. They were about 13.5 per cent of all private welfare expenditures. . . Reliable data on welfare expenditures of religious bodies of all faiths are not available. . . The United Stewardship Council for 1949 has estimated that . . . total Protestant giving for welfare may be estimated at about $200,000,000 (there are no data for other years, with which the estimate may be compared).[1]

In the context of this financial development the changing pattern of welfare during the past thirty years is described:

1. The shifting of the financial burden of individual dependency (direct relief) from private agencies, local government, and religious groups to state and federal government;
2. The devotion of professional skill and resources of the private agencies to personal and family adjustment, group recreation and education, experimental programs and research;
3. The co-ordination and improved administrative efficiency of private and voluntary welfare agencies;
4. The growth of the concept of systematic provision in advance for presumptive need through social insurance, planned public works and government fiscal policy;
5. The assumption by industry of a major share of the financial responsibility for welfare and the increasing initiative exerted by both industry and unions in the development of private welfare.[2]

A different approach for obtaining a comprehensive view of social welfare development was used by Virginia S. Ferguson. She states that in the opinion of 21 persons from a population of 23 former presidents of the National Conference of Social Work and 10 other leaders in the field, . . . the significant developments in social welfare in the United States during the first half of the century in terms both of method and technique and of philosophy and theory [were in these major groupings]:

1. The Impact of Psychiatry on Social Work
2. The Professionalization of Social Work

3. The Effects of Specialization in Social Work
4. The Changing Concept of Community Organization
5. The Extension of Public Welfare Services and the Changing Role of Private Agencies.[3]

Here the effect of changing expenditures is implied, while the maturation of social work into specialized forms of service are of more specific concern. These differentiations in the field affected not only the separation of social work into casework, social group work, community organization, and medical and psychiatric social work, but naturally resulted in the emergence of specialized forms of program. These differentiations have focused attention on the interdependence of social agencies plus their need for a close relationship with complementary organizations and professions within the society.

> Specialization has also had an effect on our concept of social work in its broadest sense. An analysis of the growth of social work in the past fifty years must include recognition of the importance of the developments in the fields of health and education upon which developments in welfare have been in part dependent. . . Scientific advances in the fields of health, welfare, and education have tended to channelize them into communities, to deepen the channels, and to raise the barriers between the fields. The extension of social service into the schools, the hospitals, and the churches would, however, imply a close relationship between all agencies and groups concerned with welfare in its broadest sense.[4]

The multifarious specialized interests of social welfare may also be illustrated by a reference to the National Conference of Social Work, an agency for professional workers. At the 1954 conference the proceedings were organized in three sections: Services to Individuals and Families; Services to Groups and Individuals in Groups; and Services to Agencies and Communities. The 1950 Conference scheduled 350 meetings, and included the sessions of 47 associate and special groups. There was one assembly of 5,600 persons.[5]

The directories of agencies found in the *Social Work Year Book, 1954*, contains 387 voluntary national agencies, and 63 Federal government agencies having more or less responsibility for or relation with social welfare. It is estimated that about 100 of these national voluntary agencies seek support from the general public on a national scale.[6]

Mr. Rabinoff states that national voluntary agencies fall into the following general categories:

1. Foreign-service agencies that "raise funds here for service abroad." Church World Service of the National Council of the Churches of Christ in the U. S. A. is cited as an example.

2. The problem-centered agency, "which works on a national scale, and in which local units, if any, "are incidental."

3. "The local-agency-centered organization," serving humanity through local units; e.g., the National Traveler's Aid Association. (A few agencies fall into both the second and third category.)[7]

While it is true that voluntary efforts represent a relatively small proportion of the total welfare services in our country today one cannot overlook their significant contributions to the rapid growth and specialization of the field. The organization of voluntary services was a natural consequence of the industrial revolution and the growing dissatisfaction with the oft-times cruel and disorganized public efforts in the welfare field before the civil war. With the advent of urbanization such problems as pauperization, health, and sanitation, and child welfare were brought sharply into focus. Thus the crystallization of these problems of physical and spiritual well-being certainly led to the humanitarian sentiment of the nineteenth century which found its chief expression through the outlet which social welfare agencies provided.

The various private philanthropies arose quite separately during this period. Often, a certain group of individuals, seeing a particular need, decided to establish a philanthropy to take care of it. Other needs, however, still existed in the same community, and soon another group interested in these unmet needs proceeded to organize a new philanthropy. Often these groups represented natural groupings within the society.

> Among the earliest of the agencies that ministered to the inadequate or the unfortunate were the churches and the church societies. To them charity was intended for the deserving, meaning those of the right religious faith. Later this was supplemented by various nationality societies, such as St. Andrews for the English (1756), the German Society (1784) for the Germans, and the French Benevolent Society (1807) for the French.[8]

Dissatisfaction, however, regarding this multiplicity of effort and its failure of it to grapple successfully with the philanthropic needs stimulated the formation of more secular voluntary agencies. While church people have been credited with an influential role in the creation of associations for improving the condition of the poor in many cities, they were, primarily, nonsectarian agencies.[9]

> . . . (This) necessitated the organization of various nonsectarian agencies. An excellent example of the new type of agency was the New York Association for the Improvement of the Conditions of the Poor. It was organized in 1843 and immediately became a very useful organization. It endeavored not only to relieve poverty but to prevent dependency as well.[10]

24

While these associations, which appeared in many cities, had far-reaching influence over the type of service needed for assisting the city poor, they did not succeed in preventing the advent of numerous relief and aid societies. Many of these agencies gave little thought to co-operation with others and often a great deal of overlapping occurred. Usually the various agencies were quite oblivious of the functions and services of the others and the heads of the agencies were not acquainted. This led to mutual suspicion and reinforced the lack of co-operation both in respect to the handling of particular cases and a suitable division of labor in the field.

In an effort to relieve this increasingly confused pattern, the Charity Organization Society was introduced in America. It first appeared in Buffalo in 1877 and spread to many other large cities. A primary function, then, of Charity Organization Societies was the promotion of co-operation and the diminution of overlapping services. While these societies were originally patterned after a similar organization in London they were not long in adapting to an American setting.

> Within a few years (1897-1905) this society enlarged its activities by establishing a Tenement House Committee, A Committee on the Prevention of Tuberculosis. . . Other societies created similar committees, or undertook some kind of educational work as an adjunct to their original function. The charity-organization movement, in short, "Americanized" itself, ceased to look at poverty through the spectacles of a particular class movement in England, and began to deal with it in a more courageous spirit, by methods more harmonious with American resources and American traditions.[11]

The Charity Organization Society usually became the leader of philanthropic efforts wherever it was organized and was responsible for the initial development of many specialized services which are common in the welfare field today.

> Since there existed at that time few specialized agencies, such as day nurseries, legal aid bureaus, saving societies, the Charity Organization Society undertook many such activities. These when developed, were frequently cut loose by the parent organization and given an independent existence.[12]

Gradually, as specialized agencies became more common Charity Organization Societies limited their functions, and eventually a large proportion of them changed their names and became family welfare associations.

An example of a specialized voluntary service of this period (about 1885) was the development of state-wide children's home societies. They were organized specifically to provide care for children where no local child-care facilities existed and were a reaction against the evils of child maintenance in mixed alms houses and the abuses of the apprentice and indenture systems. They usually administered a receiving home for temporary care and facilitated placement with private families.

> They began with a distinct religious bias, and received much support from the churches. Although they were not directly a department of Protestant philanthropy it was Protestant leaders who were almost exclusively responsible for the development of these organizations. . . To begin with, these societies were managed largely by clergymen. And the churches throughout the state in which an organization was formed were expected to aid in the placing and the supervision of children. These societies were especially concerned with the care of children sent or committed from the smaller communities where no separate child-caring organizations were possible.[13]

Because of this historical involvement and emphasis by private agencies in the family welfare field one still finds a large proportion of private agencies active in this area of social welfare. This is especially true of the sectarian agencies. There is evidence that the existence of organizations supported by these special interest groups, maintaining their own identity, and their own services, is receiving increased criticism today.

> Social work in the family field is frequently complicated by a multiplicity of agencies representing the nonsectarian and, in addition, agencies representing Jewish, Catholic, Lutheran, and ex-soldier groups. Long strides have been taken already toward achieving co-operation, but I am about convinced that co-operation is not enough, and consolidation for operating purposes, in which group interest is conserved but sublimated to the general aim and purpose, can be effected with value to all concerned.[14]

Probably one of the most important new social institutions of the latter nineteenth century was the settlement. This was, of course, a distinctly voluntary effort which developed because of the recognition of the suffering caused by the industrial revolution.

> Philanthropy proving ineffectual, the experiment of living among the slum dwellers was tried, in the hope of raising the tone of the communities through neighborly service and friendship. Toynbee Hall, founded in 1884, was the first recognized settlement. As a result of the visits of Jane Addams and Robert Woods to England three pioneer American settlements were established in 1889. Hull House in Chicago, South End House in Boston, and the Neighborhood Guild in New York. . . Although the original motivation was religious the settlements soon became nonsectarian.[15]

While recreation was originally a predominant activity of the settlement, various other programs which were consistent with the restoration of neighborhood life were also promoted. These included such things as health work, clubs, forums, and adult education, which were indeed the forerunners of many of today's specialized services, both public and private.

While much of the specialization and initial growth within the social welfare field may be credited to private philanthropy, its workers, and supporters; today voluntary effort in social work is regarded as supplementary to, rather than as a substitute for, sound public welfare provisions. Thus in redefining their functions, private agencies have considered the need for expression of minority viewpoints and have recognized one of their functions as that of innovator and interpreter. Private agencies give flexibility to the expression of concern of citizens around new needs as they appear.

> In broad generalization, public agencies undertake to meet, more or less adequately, basic economic, health, and educational needs; in some cases for the whole population, in others for only certain specific classes of the disadvantaged. To voluntary agencies remain the important tasks of filling in gaps and inadequacies in these fields, of establishing standards and checking the work of public agencies, of covering many additional needs not now met by government, and of doing most of the exploratory, experimental, and research work. . .[16]

Undoubtedly there would be wide assent to a grand generalization that response to the needs of people in the great depression of the 1930's gave the impetus for the marked expansion of public responsibility for social welfare services. However, there were many citizens who dreaded the thought of Congress' voting money for the relief of individuals. The experience and attitudes of the past were not easy to overcome, and it was certainly the extreme emergency of the depression which helped such outstanding social work leaders as C. M. Bookman to revise their opinions on the subject. In 1931, as executive director of the Community Chest in Cincinnati, he stated:

> Unemployment relief can be handled best by local communities and I believe that national and state grants for direct relief, until all other sources are exhausted, should be discouraged. If we plan wisely in our local communities I do not believe it will be necessary to make or take national or state grants for direct relief.[17]

In 1932 Mr. Bookman was president of the National Conference of Social Work, and he said:

> . . . the local leaders . . . have found that back of the local community must stand the state and back of the state, the nation, if the emergency is to be met. . . Social workers . . . must accept the obligation of thought and study along the

broad lines of social and economic reconstruction. We can scarcely respect ourselves if we are content to limit our activities entirely to the ameliorative and casework aspects, of the social program.[18]

One of the actions of first importance in the development of public social welfare programs and federal participation was the passage of the Social Security Act of 1935, which authorized a number of Federal programs of national scope and of significance to the people in all the counties of the nation. The Act has been amended several times. We give below a brief résumé of the main aspects of these broad programs with a few figures concerning the extent of the recent activities and the amount of Federal expenditures resolved: (More recent data are from monthly issues of the *Social Security Bulletin*).

1. A national system of Old Age and Survivors insurance administered by the Bureau of Old Age and Survivors Insurance.

2. Federal-State systems of unemployed compensation and of employment services.

3. Federal grants to the states for public assistance.

4. Federal grants to the states for maternal and child health services, to enable the states to extend and improve their programs especially in rural areas.

5. Federal grants to the states for services for crippled children, administered by the Children's Bureaus.

6. Federal grants to the states for child welfare services administered by the Children's Bureaus.

The Public Health Service reported that state and local funds for their health departments amounted to about $215,000,000 in 1953. However, about 1,000 out of 3,000 counties did not have local full-time public health officers in their departments. These were largely in rural areas.

Among numerous other Federal activities, the following may be noted:

1. Railroad Retirement Board, established in 1935, which administers a system for payment of persons and disability annuities to railroad employees.

2. The School Lunch Program, consisting of grants to states for the benefit of pupils in both public and private schools.

3. Office of Vocational Rehabilitation. This office co-operates with the states in providing rehabilitation to persons in order to enable them to prepare for and take their places in remunerative employment.

4. Veterans Administration extends major benefits to numerous war veterans.

The strong organization of state departments of social welfare is one of the outstanding features of public social welfare in the nation. These are an outgrowth of the early history of public effort which concentrated on two methods: small grants in cash or kind, called outdoor relief; and placement of persons in local institutions known variously as almshouses, poor farms, county homes, or county farms.

Before 1929 public welfare agencies had been involved only nominally in these institutional services and in pauper relief since it was recognized that private agencies were outstandingly active, in these areas. Those public services which did exist were on a local community level, often only an appendage to an already operative public department such as a sheriff's office. Recognizing the deficiencies of such a program, a few states led the way in assuming responsibility for certain classes of their citizens who could be labeled as dependent, defective, or delinquent.

> Massachusetts was the first state to establish a state-wide organization. Created in 1863, the Massachusetts Board of State Charities was charged with the investigation and supervision of the entire system of charitable and correctional institutions and empowered to recommend changes directed toward the economical and efficient operation of such institutions. Furthermore the secretary was required to oversee and conduct the "outdoor business" of the state, i.e., relating to the unsettled poor who had residence in no county and hence were chargeable to the state. By the exercise of these powers the state was able to check on the reimbursements for the unsettled poor and to achieve some degree of control over a relief whether it was on a state or a local basis.[19]

The message from Governor Richard J. Oglesly, of Illinois, to the legislature of that state in January, 1869, is an excellent statement explaining the reasons for establishing state boards.

> It has been earnestly represented to me, in view of the separate organizations of our various charitable institutions under separate Boards of Management; the large number of inmates attending each and the constant demand for more room and accommodations for the large numbers necessarily excluded from the benefits of each; together with the important question of the means to be raised by taxation for the support and enlargement of the present or the construction of additional asylums; and to consider new questions arising out of experience as to the best modes of treatment and improvement of the various classes of patients and inmates of our several benevolent institutions, that our parental system ought to be thoroughly and carefully reviewed and revised, and the whole subject in its various bearings, placed in the hands of a Board, to be created, with full powers to investigate and re-

port on all these questions, to be styled the Board of Public Charities.[20]

By the early 1930's, there were sixteen state departments of public welfare, nine boards of control, fourteen supervisory boards and six state child-welfare agencies.

This recognition of the prostitution of state institutional services to the whims of partisan politics was an outstanding reason for the creation of state boards. As the movement of state-wide organization grew the public's attitude toward the responsibility of the state was modified, and by 1917 a positive approach was beginning to replace the negativism of the past three centuries. Public welfare was not only being regarded as necessary but also as a service with constructive possibilities.

A corollary is, of course, the creation of local public welfare offices, in cities and counties. It has been said that all ills tend to gravitate toward this office. In one county a visitor was told recently that the third most important source of income was the county welfare office, next to rice and cotton. These county offices generally administer the local programs of old age assistance, aid to dependent children, aid to the blind, aid to the permanently and totally disabled, general assistance, and child welfare. But there are many differences in the forms of local as well as of state administration. In June, 1952, there were some 54,054 positions in local offices, and 32,450 of these, or three-fifths were classified as executives and as social workers.[21]

Another significant and widespread development to note is that of workmen's compensation. All states and territories now have workmen's compensation legislation, the culmination of forty years of such activity. Yet these laws cover only three-fourths of the wage and salary workers in the nation. The laws vary widely, and most states permit an employer to insure with private carriers. Eighteen states have state insurance funds, in some of which the employer is compelled to use the state fund in insuring his risks. The laws and consequent systems created are designed to assure payment of benefits to insured employees or dependents of persons who suffer a disabling injury on the job, who contract industrial diseases or who die as a result of injuries sustained in their employment.[22]

We have attempted in this chapter to portray the growth and specialization of the field of social welfare under governmental and private auspices. The gigantic increase in public responsibility in the past twenty-five years has delineated the area of responsibility of private welfare. And in the process of adjustment between public and private responsibility there has been a definite reincorporation of social education and action interests in the sphere of nongovernmental social welfare functions. We therefore conclude this discussion of growth and specialization of the welfare enterprise

30

in America, with a note on the developing social work interest in social education and action since the great depression.

A renewed general interest in social action and in social reform is manifested in large sections of the social welfare enterprise. For a time "Social Action" was one of four sections of the National Conferences of Social Work. In 1934, for example, social action was regarded as "generally defined as covering mobilization of public opinion legislation, and public administration." The program for 1935 listed the following topics under social action:

Social workers and social legislation
Economic organization for social justice
Social work and industrial conflict
Charting a balanced economy
Incentives for economic rehabilitation
International labor standards.

Social action was a section of the Conference from 1935 to 1950.[23] Since then it has been treated as a method applicable to more forms of social welfare. In 1952 the conference had a committee on Methods of Social Action of Section III, "Services to Agencies and Communities." Donald S. Howard has commented on the relationship between social work and social reform.

> Social work, in principle and in tenet, is not separable from social reform; the very nature of the objectives of social work, as well as its place in a democratic society, commends it to working for the betterment of social living for all people.[24]

Howard continues:

> Reform has become the province of a number of citizen, political, and labor groups. As social reform came to be "everyone's concern," social work's responsibilities became less clearcut and more difficult to delineate. Structurally, therefore, social work is only one institution among many that have a stake in creating conditions that permit and foster positive social living. It is only in this structural sense that we can speak of social work and social reform.
>
> In spite of social work's commitment to the improvement of social conditions, and its heritage from the reform movement, it has taken on, in its institutional development, a highly ameliorative coloration. As mentioned earlier, social work organizations are established to render services, usually as a result of successful reform movements, and the service function then becomes paramount. This ameliorative function is challenged in many quarters and this questioning undoubtedly operates as a deterrent to the extension of welfare services.[25]

The social worker of today is certainly showing an increased concern in social reform and not only for purposes of amelioration.

The American Association of Social Workers, one of the outstanding professional organizations, as a registered lobbyist maintains an active interest and influence in legislation. New laws of social concern, which have been supported by this and other organizations. are studied after passage for sound methods of implementation. For instance, discussion on the recent bill outlawing segregation in public schools, as well as the total problem of desegregation, made up a substantial section of the 1955 National Conference of Social Work program. The combined voices of social workers today are perhaps stronger than ever and their strength will not go unnoticed.

FOOTNOTES FOR CHAPTER 2

1 The author defines his terms as follows: "Private welfare, under which come private philanthropy and employee health and welfare; and public welfare, which covers social insurance, including old-age and survivors insurance, public retirement systems, unemployment insurance, temporary disability benefits, workmen's compensation, and social insurance for railroad workers, together with veterans programs, public assistance, general relief, and social welfare services." John W. McConnell, "Welfare," *America's Needs and Resources, A New Survey* (New York: Twentieth Century Fund, 1955), p. 430.

2 *Ibid.*, p. 430.

3 Virginia S. Ferguson, "Fifty Years of Social Work," *Social Welfare Forum, 1950* (New York: Columbia University Press, 1950), p. vii.

4 *Ibid.*, p. x.

5 Lester B. Granger, Foreword, *Social Welfare Forum, 1950* (Columbia University Press, 1950), p. v.

6 " . . . co-ordination and planning are drawing increasing attention. The pace, the attitudes, and the results vary from place to place and between levels, and differences persist, but the process continues." George W. Rabinoff, "National Organizations in Social Welfare," *Social Work Year Book, 1954* (New York: American Association of Social Workers, 1954), p. 361.

7 *Ibid.*, p. 361.

8 Arthur E. Fink, *The Field of Social Work* (New York: Henry Holt and Company, 1949), p. 99.

9 Arnaud C. Marts, *Philanthropy's Role in Civilization* (New York: Harper and Brothers, 1953).

10 George B. Mangold, *Organization for Social Welfare* (New York: The Macmillan Co., 1934), p. 49.

11 E. T. Devine and Lilian Brandt, *American Social Work in the Twentieth Century* (New York: The Frontier Press, 1921), pp. 24–25.

12 Cecil Clare North, *The Community and Social Welfare* (New York: McGraw-Hill Book Company, Inc., 1931), p. 111.

13 Mangold, *op. cit.*, pp. 50–51.

14 Wayne McMillen, *Community Organization for Social Welfare* (Chicago: University of Chicago Press, 1945), p. 127.

15 Amos Griswold Warner, Stuart Alfred Queen, and Ernest Bouldin Harper, *American Charities and Social Work* (4th ed.; New York: Thomas Y. Crowell Company, 1930, pp. 461–62.

16 F. Emerson Andrews, *Philanthropic Giving* (New York: Russell Sage Foundation, 1950), p. 112.

17 C. M. Bookman, "Community Organization to Meet Unemployment Needs," *Proceedings, National Conference of Social Work, 1931* (Chicago: University of Chicago Press, 1931), p. 386.

[18] C. M. Bookman, "The Social Consequences and Treatment of Unemployment," *Proceedings, National Conference of Social Work, 1932* (Chicago: University of Chicago Press, 1933), pp. 10–13.

[19] Fink, *op. cit.*, p. 17.

[20] Frank J. Bruno, *Trends in Social Work as Reflected in the Proceedings of the National Conference of Social Work 1874–1946* (New York: Columbia University Press, 1948), p. 31.

[21] Ellen Winston, "Public Welfare," *Social Work Year Book, 1954* (New York: American Association of Social Workers, 1954), p. 435.

[22] Wilbur J. Cohen, "Social Insurance," *Social Work Year Book, 1954* (New York: American Association of Social Workers, 1954), pp. 487–8.

[23] *Proceedings, National Conference of Social Work, 1935* (Chicago: University of Chicago Press, 1935). Also see subsequent years.

[24] Donald S. Howard, "Social Work and Social Reform," *New Directions*, Editor: Cora Kasius (New York: Harper and Brothers, 1954), p. 159.

[25] *Ibid.*, p. 31.

SOCIAL WORK AS A PROFESSION 3

Social work as a profession grew mainly from the humanitarian movement of the nineteenth century which attempted to improve the desperate conditions of the poor, to achieve social reform by legislation and to awaken the social conscience of the public.

> Into a society largely disregardful of the welfare of others, new shoots of social consciousness gradually pushed their way. They flourished and in time grew into the movement of humanitarianism: a movement prophetic of the subsequent profession of social work.[1]

The growth of private charitable agencies flourished during this period and by the first half of the nineteenth century, they were established in considerable numbers. Many of these agencies combined moral goals with the relief of physical want. It was through the growth and establishment of these societies that large numbers of individuals began to be employed in the growing field of social work.

Very soon people working in the field began to raise questions about the training of others to carry on their tasks. Probably the first public recognition that professional training was necessary came through a paper read by Anna L. Dawes in 1893 before the International Congress of Charities, Correction, and Philanthropy.

> Miss Dawes raised the question why the men and women who were then departing from the field of active social work should not have an opportunity to transmit to their successors what they had learned during their years of service, so as to enable the new workers to take up the work where the older ones left off, without going through a long, hard period of learning by doing.[2]

Four years later, in a paper before the Civic Club in Philadelphia, Mary E. Richmond proposed that educational institutions should undertake the preparation of personnel, decrying the general lack of understanding regarding qualifications for social service:

> It seems sheer waste of time to say anything at this late day about the *need* of training in charitable work, and yet I have learned that philanthropy is still one of those disorganized branches of human knowledge in which he who takes anything for granted is lost. . . . "You ask me," wrote a clergyman, "what qualifications Miss —— has for the position of agent in the charity organization society. She is a most

34

estimable lady, and the sole support of her widowed mother. It would be a real charity to give her the place." Another applicant for the same position, when asked whether she had any experience in charity work, replied that she had had a good deal. She had sold tickets for church fairs. Though these particular ladies were not employed, is it not still a very common thing to find charity agents who have been engaged for no better reason, like one who was employed to distribute relief, because he had failed in the grocery business? And with our volunteer service it is no better. In no other field are good intentions permitted to play such havoc.[3]

Another outstanding paper entitled "Is Social Work a Profession?" was given by Abraham Flexner at the National Conference of Charities and Correction, in 1915. Here Dr. Flexner outlined his criteria of true professions. The challenge he expressed for attaining professional status provided further impetus for social workers in defining and developing their area of work and methods.

The self-conscious desire for professionalization combined with the demands of a twentieth century society, served to place much emphasis upon the great utilization of scientific knowledge. Developing knowledge in other fields produced material of use to social workers in defining their methods and philosophy.

Anthrapologists, and particularly the social anthropologists who had studied the life of contemporary primitive peoples, had been producing an enormous literature of the influence of custom, habit, and forms of social organization upon the behavior of human beings. Sociologists who studied modern society were equally impressed with the role of custom, habit and forms of social organization. Culture, which consists of ways of doing things, ideas, attitudes, habits, behavior, and the material objects attached to these, came to be regarded as the all important aspect of human existence and a determinant of all human behavior. Social workers in turn were affected by the discussion of these culture phenomena and incorporated much anthropological thinking into their own philosophy and practice of casework.[4]

Advances in other related fields such as medicine, psychiatry, and psychology also produced new concepts of use to the social worker.

While these pleas for training and the use of developing ideas in the sciences were being made, social workers were becoming an important occupational group in our country. In New York city alone, private agencies in 1915 were employing 3,968 social workers.[5]

Furthermore, the growing complexity of an increasingly specialized society made it apparent that more and better training for social work was necessary. Plans were developed under the supervision of experienced workers for apprenticeship training. A few agencies arranged lectures and courses in reading. Large national agencies like the Young Women's Christian Association and the Young Men's Christian Association established year-round schools to train their workers. Through the efforts of Edward T. Devine, secretary of the New York Charity Organization Society, a summer training course was organized primarily to provide supplementary education for "investigators" already employed. By 1904 this training course had become a one-year educational program of the New York School of Philanthropy which later became the New York School of Social Work. During the same period and to a large degree because of the scientific interest of the social workers themselves, other schools were formed.

> . . . an Institute of Social Science was established through the efforts of Chicago social workers as a part of the Extension Division of the University of Chicago. The Institute became the independent School of Civics and Philanthropy which was later incorporated into the University of Chicago as a graduate school of Social Administration. Similar developments were taking place in Boston where a school was established under the joint auspices of Harvard University and Simmons College . . . and in Philadelphia where a short training course expanded to become the Philadelphia Training School for Social Work (now the University of Pennsylvania School of Social Work.)[6]

In 1919 Porter H. Lee, director of the New York School of Social Work was instrumental in forming the Association of Training Schools for Professional Workers through his initiative in organizing a meeting for the heads of the seventeen known schools. Since the representatives of the various schools had such divergent views regarding the nature and content of professional training, it was not until 1927 that they were able to formulate requirements for admission. This association later became known as the American Association of Schools of Social Work.

In 1942 the National Association of Schools of Social Administration was organized to assist primarily in developing programs at the undergraduate level, although a few member schools also offered graduate training.

In 1946 the first meeting of the National Council on Social Work Education was held. Both of the above groups with professional standing joined the council to make studies and to develop methods of closer co-operation among them. In 1949, as a result of study, a committee on structure of the council formulated proposals for one national organization for social work education performing such functions as accreditation, consultation, research, and the issuance of publications. And in 1952 the functions of the two earlier groups were transferred to the council.

Thus we see the formalization of training requirements for social work, one of the criteria for the achievement of professional status. However, the zeal with which social workers pursued this goal can be further revealed by the rapid delineation of various fields of practice. Social classwork was the first of these to be defined as having a procedure based on science. Mary E. Richmond established the basis of casework method in her widely acclaimed *Social Diagnosis,* published in 1917. She presented a procedure in casework which could be used regardless of the agency setting in which it was practiced. Philip Klein describes casework as:

> . . . the introduction into social work of the scientific mode of thought and of the specific contributions of such social disciplines as sociology, economics, biology and political science . . . this brought a displacement of theological, religious and ethical principles.[7]

Soon casework came under a new influence. The scientific development and growth in the disciplines of psychology and psychiatry shifted the fundamental interest of social work from economic and sociological emphasis toward the psychological and emotional problems of the client.

> The coming of World War I was destined to strengthen even more strongly the dominance of social casework in the field of social work. The psychiatrists and psychologists who laid the basis of the first application of psychiatry to men in the armed services who were severely affected by the emotional shocks incidental to war found in the well-trained social caseworker just the assisting personnel necessary for the examination and treatment of those suffering from battle neuroses and psychoses; and because psychiatry was beginning to adopt the dynamic methods of the psychoanalysts, social caseworkers for the first time, had guidance in the treatment of their applicants, as well as more subtle diagnostic processes available for understanding them.[8]

The technique of social group work became a consciously defined method about twenty-five years ago. It developed in the framework of leisure time agencies which were providing recreation and informal education. These agencies built their entire programs upon a foundation of group organization and group leadership, and they have discovered that despite traditional differences they share a common function. Several schools such as George Williams College, devoted almost exclusively to training for group work, were established. However, because casework has always been considered the cornerstone of professional training, such schools have remained outside the traditional pattern and have usually not been eligible for membership in the American Association of Schools of Social Work.

Increasing social work emphasis is being given today to the process of community organization. Historically, one finds the beginnings of community organization in the charity organization movement of the nineteenth century which attempted to bring some order into the field of social welfare and to work out a community plan for co-operation among the various agencies in the field. Community organization has been described as "the social work" process of establishing a progressively more effective adjustment between the social welfare needs and the community welfare resources within a geographic area."[9] As a method it is used to some degree in all types of agencies and perhaps particularly in community welfare councils. However, it is the newest of the recognized processes.

> Although as a process it is as old as social work itself, as a professional area of practice it is relatively new. Only in recent years has the literature concerning community organization been sufficient to justify reference to it in professional terms.[10]

Another area of social work which concerns this discussion is that of social action. A perusal of the proceedings of the National Conference on Social Work seems to suggest that the great depression and its attendant growth in governmental welfare responsibility was an important stimulus to moving social workers out of their primary preoccupation with the achievement of professional status.[11]

By 1939, twenty-three of the forty-three papers of the Conference were published under the heading, "Current Sectors in Social Action." Ten others dealt in some manner with legislation and public policies. In the next annual conference, it was said that "social work tends logically to become a social reform movement,"[12] and definite acknowledgement of social action as a professional field of social work was given in a 1941 conference paper:

> With the explicit recognition of social action as the purpose of social work, social action itself became an area of specialized study, not with respect to its rationale but with respect to its technical problems.[13]

Additional professional specialties grew out of casework, requiring further technical training, that is, medical and psychiatric social work.

These fields, with their conceptual tools and technical requisites, are now being taught in fifty-two graduate schools of social work in the United States (including Puerto Rico and Hawaii). Seven thousand graduate students were enrolled in 1953.

Along with the growth of schools and the defining of methods of work came the organization of various professional associations. These associations, composed wholly or principally of individual social workers, were designed to assist these workers in professional development, to improve conditions under which work was done and to improve and extend the social services. The largest of these is the American Association of Social Workers. Others include the American Association of Social Group Workers, the American Association of Medical Social Workers and the American Association of Psychiatric Social Workers. These merged in 1955 in one organization known as the National Association of Social Workers. It has various sectional groupings for specialized interests.

The National Conference of Social Work (the National Conference of Charities and Corrections until 1917) has played a considerable role in the establishment of social work as a profession. An evaluation of its influence on American social work is almost impossible but probably its most conspicuous contribution is the holding of an annual conference or public forum.

However, while social workers have achieved their goal of professionalization, they are not without critics. Their goal being so intensely sought and so quickly attained (as contrasted to medicine, engineering, dentistry, etc.) has necessarily caused them to expend their energies where they were most useful to this end.

> It [social work] is intensely practical in its aim—so practical in fact that it has often been criticized for partially neglecting the search for general principles and the creation of a broad social philosophy which might form a solid foundation for practice. Its subject material comes, at least in part, from science and learning: from economics, sociology, biology, psychology, psychiatry, religion, medicine, law—all of these might possibly be utilized more extensively than they are—and from a literature which is gradually building for itself.[14]

Here, then, is the problem of specialization—as real and felt in social work as in any other field—even though some observers are more hopeful that the training program teaches the student "to arrive at some integrated perspective":

> The undergraduate program acquaints the student with the basic concepts and major findings of the social sciences, psychology, sociology, and economics. It also gives him an understanding of the importance of biology, genetics, history, and principles of government, social philosophy, public health, and family problems. The undergraduate student gains a broad background of present society and of man as an individual and as a member of various groups. He then learns to arrive at some integrated perspective of the relations between human behavior and the demands of our society.[15]

The work in the professional or graduate school, for the most part, familiarizes the student with the theory and practice of social work itself. The specialization of training required by the professionalization of social work poses a particular problem to the interests of organized religion.

No special place in the education for social work or in the principles of social work is given to religion except in the Catholic schools. The young student may or may not have religious training, but he would be quite unlikely to receive any as prescribed courses for training in the field. In view of the fact that churches are involved in social welfare activities for ultimately spiritual purposes, it can be understood why the professionalized social work schools without religious orientation and education are looked upon as not quite adequate from the aspect of some church spokesmen. One leader of church social welfare interests stated:

> The outlook as far as the Protestant forces are concerned, however, faces a dilemma. Either we must infuse into the secular schools of social work a Christian basis of social work, especially as it relates to a divinely changed life, or we must bring into being recognized schools where such a basis underlies the thorough training of the worker. For professional training we must have. And Christian bases for such training we also must have, with a definite commitment to the regenerated life as the necessity for the fullest and freest development of human personality. That way lies security for a Christian democracy. This emerges as our greatest unsolved problem.[16]

This may be a rather extreme point of view, and we should be aware that there is a range of attitude among Protestant leaders in this matter as well as in practically anything else. At any rate, it is an articulation of a crucial problem in the relation of the churches' welfare activities to professional concerns.

Part of the lack of Protestant church-oriented schools in this field lies in the philosophy and tradition of some Protestant groups. Another factor which might operate to inhibit sectarian schools in the development of a graduate level of training in social work would be the requirement of heavy financial resources and the need for field work training facilities.

Some of the schools which offer training in group work are definitely religiously oriented, but these are not eligible for accreditation and for membership in the Council on Social Work Education. There is Hartford Seminary Foundation's Institute of Church Social Service which offers much casework training on post-graduate level. As far as can be discovered it is the only such church school. One of the primary difficulties for accreditation has been the requirement for university affiliation. The problem arises in that universities generally do not favor a Protestant church approach in any of their schools except their seminaries.

40

Several accredited schools, however, are part of so-called "church-related" universities. The University of Denver, a Methodist-related school, has been accredited since 1933.[17] Boston University, also Methodist-related, has an accredited school of social work. The University of Tennessee, School of Social Work which was fully accredited in 1945 was founded originally as the Nashville School of Social Work under the combined auspices of Scaritt College for Christian Workers (Methodist), Peabody College, and Vanderbilt University. The present school was organized in 1951 by mutual agreement of the sponsoring schools and by act of the state legislature (six years after accreditation). Scaritt is a group work school, which permits its students to take courses at the University and use the credits for Scaritt's degree.

But with the secularization of education, the term "church-related" university signifies here only some formal or just historical relationship, and the character of the professional program offered is entirely secular, that is, without religious orientation.

The profession itself has not been without sensitivity in this regard. For example, the establishment of curriculum requirements for accreditation was a result of prolonged labor and reconciliation of many points of view which undoubtedly were compromised in the process. Furthermore, the teaching of religion in the public schools, having long been considered contrary to the traditional separation of church and state in our country, might well have inhibited the inclusion of religion in the curriculum of social work schools. This seems especially true since twenty-five of the fifty-two accredited schools in the United States (including Puerto Rico and Hawaii) are under public, that is, governmental auspices.[18]

The accrediting agency of the profession nowhere specifically excludes religion, and in the content of courses, matters of spiritual development might appear in the growth and human development curriculum sequences and occur as reference in a number of courses.

In light of the pressures which have affected professionalization, one can more easily understand the lack of formal incorporation of the vast knowledge, skills, and literature of religion and of the ministry. It is certainly to the credit of this profession that many of the questions regarding its relationship and use of religion are coming from within, indeed from the workers themselves who, in their functioning, miss the integrating functions of religion.

A social worker must have a philosophy of life that is based on faith. Many social workers, as educated men and women, have a sophisticated orientation to life. That is, they are willing to accept uncritically any explanation of life. This is, in many respects, admirable. Logical inquiry and an understanding of personality based on the findings of psychology should

41

enable them to substitute a humane but disciplined technique for the indiscriminate almsgiving of medieval times. The substitution of modern "isms" for traditional religious faith, however, has left many a social worker confused about the central problems of life. This obviously leads to confusion in the minds of clients of social agencies. It has also led to an overemphasis on the scientific method, with its dispassionate critical analysis, logical inquiry, and casual relationships, as important in the practice of modern social work. But the scientific method cannot solve problems which are basically ethical in nature.[19]

Undoubtedly there is today, then, this question of major concern to the churches and to at least some of the profession of how to include the resources of religion in training for the social work profession.

One trend in social work which is presently significant in terms of this problem and which is heightened by the dearth of trained workers and the increased need for them, is the development of interprofessional co-operation—the health team, the community team and so forth. In many of these, the ministry is being included as one of the complementary professions, and the churches, through their theological seminaries, are tending to give more attention to psychiatry and social work in their curricula. Some theological schools have emphasized the need for clinical training to provide better preparation for their students. One such program is described:

> The Philadelphia Divinity School (Episcopal) has completed its first three years under a reorganized plan whereby all students take clinical training. . . The first year's course centers in a general hospital, emphasizing contact with social work agencies; the second year's work in a mental hospital; and the third in a parish, in close co-operation with a family welfare agency. Students attend eleven months of the year, taking ten weeks' clinical work each year.[20]

The program in hospitals referred to above was initiated in 1937 under the direction of Seward Hiltner at Pennsylvania Hospital and constituted a training unit of the Council for Clinical Training of Theological Students. Incidentally, Hiltner was also responsible for establishing the Commission on Religion and Health in the Federal Council of Churches (now the National Council of Churches), which has brought selected pastors and psychiatrists together to explore common ground and has, in large part, been responsible for stimulating psychiatric interest in the seminaries.[21] This commission has also been influential in establishing standards of practice and education in the realm of pastoral counseling.

Placements from seminaries for training in welfare agencies other than hospitals have, in the main, been of special interest in the urban church movement.

Another pertinent development in the profession is a growing desire for re-evaluation of the entire professional education program. While there has been increased attention given to the recruitment of students for social work schools it is well known that a shortage of professional personnel will exist for many years. Recently, Ernest F. Witte, director of the Council on Social Work Education, reported that there were 10,000 vacant positions.[22]

Many welfare organizations have scholarships available for interested and qualified students. Several church bodies and denominationally sponsored institutions also offer such scholarships.[23]

However, there are approximately 100,000 positions classified as social work in the United States. Thus the need to align the educational program to meet the needs of varying job functions has become generally recognized. Although the following note is chiefly concerned with public agencies it may well have implications for private welfare agencies.

> It seems to me that we could cut through some of the fog of misunderstanding about what kind of personnel is needed in public welfare agencies if we determine whether or not a particular job—not the whole agency—requires the services a social worker can offer. Social insurance, for example, may have need of social workers in certain spots, while some phases of public assistance may not require the services of social workers as it moves toward noncontributory social insurance. . . Social workers have sometimes mistakenly tried to take over all the positions in many public welfare agencies and have found themselves bewildered and frustrated, as well as carrying the burden of public blame for what was a program defect.[24]

It may be said that as jobs and not agencies are defined there will develop a greater use of other professions and skills such as in music, handicraft, and homemaking. This might be an area in which the untrained worker would reappear in significant numbers.

Thus, while trends are still flexible and while concern is being expressed on a multitude of fronts, it seems opportune to explore the best direction and most appropriate method of relating the resources of religion and of the social work profession. For the problem of the need for religiously oriented training in social work from the point of view of some religious interests is but a part of the larger problem of the delineation of the total rule of religion and the proper use of its resources in the professional structure of the field. This may well be one of the most important challenges to this still youthful profession in our country.

In the last few decades, the churches—which after all preceded by centuries the profession in the rendering of social services and the laying of the ideological basis for social welfare—have seen this field newly defined in almost completely secular (nonchurch) terms with its own area of operation, a set of theoretical beliefs, and a method of training. And this has happened despite the fact that many of the vanguard in the drive toward professionalization were strongly and avowedly religiously motivated people.[25] It should not be surprising if it were found that a disproportionately large number of today's social workers are children of clergymen.

Furthermore, religious influences have never really been outside of the development of the social work profession, for the churches are a basic part of the larger society undergoing the changes which have affected both the churches and the profession. We have noted that many of the persons in the forefront of the movement toward professionalization were strongly religiously motivated and active church people. We have seen that as professional schools were established and accrediting standards and procedures developed, the Protestant churches seemed to go along with the general notion that these were properly the function of professional social work interests.

In the delineation of the fields of social work and their methods, many of the social welfare activities of the churches came under the influence of the profession in the utilization of standards of operation, knowledge, and personnel. Along with the organization of professional associations of social workers and social work interests, the churches, too, created complementary associations of church social workers and interests with the avowed purpose of a mutual enhancement of the work of the churches and of the profession in welfare activities. The record of the churches in relation to the profession is mostly a picture of co-operation and integration of the fruits of professionalization. But there is sufficient indication of interest for a fresh appraisal by churches, more self-conscious of their functioning in the welfare field, and by the profession, somewhat bothered by the awareness that specialized, technical attention often leads to a disintegrated and thereby inefficient approach to the ultimate ends of social welfare.

FOOTNOTES FOR CHAPTER 3

[1] Esther Lucile Brown, *Social Work as a Profession* (4th ed.; New York, Russell Sage Foundation, 1942), pp. 7–8.

[2] Frank J. Bruno, *Trends in Social Work as Reflected in the Proceedings of the National Conference of Social Work, 1874–1946* (New York: Columbia University Press, 1948), p. 138.

[3] Mary E. Richmond, *The Long View; Papers and Addresses,* Selected and edited by Joanna C. Colcord and Ruth Z. S. Mann (New York: Russell Sage Foundation, 1930), p. 86.

4 Arthur E. Fink, *The Field of Social Work* (New York: Henry Holt and Company, 1949), p. 121.

5 See Edward T. Devine and Mary Van Kleeck, *Positions in Social Work* (New York: New York School of Philanthropy, 1916).

6 Katherine A. Kendall, "Education for Social Work," *Social Work Year Book 1954* (New York: American Association of Social Workers, 1954), pp. 170–171.

7 Philip Klein, "Social Work," *Encyclopedia of the Social Sciences* (New York: The Macmillan Company, 1931), XIV, p. 167. Although the idea of "displacement of theological, religious and ethical principles" expressed here is rather extreme and may represent a personal viewpoint, it is nonetheless apparent that if "casework" is conceived of as based strictly on scientific principles and knowledge, "theological, religious and ethical principles" would fall largely into the category of scientifically untested principles. But they are influences that permeate society in reality, even though science has only begun to cope with them empirically. In the meantime, in the actual operation of casework, these "unscientific" principles are surely, consciously or unconsciously, a part of the equipment of most caseworkers.

8 Bruno, *op. cit.*, p. 187.

9 Walter A. Friedlander, *Introduction to Social Welfare* (New York: Prentice-Hall Inc., 1955), p. 187.

10 C. F. McNeil, "Community Organization for Social Welfare," *Social Work Year Book, 1951* (New York: American Association of Social Workers, 1951), p. 123.

11 Several articles in various editions of the *Proceedings of the National Conference on Social Work, 1932* (Chicago: University of Chicago Press, 1940), p. 13, about this time relate to this subject.

12 John A. Fitch, "The Nature of Social Action," *Proceedings of the National Conference on Social Work, 1940* (New York: Columbia University Press, 1940), p. 491.

13 Sydney Maslen, "Guideposts to Social Action," *Proceedings of the National Conference on Social Work, 1941* (New York: Columbia University Press, 1941), pp. 642–651.

14 Brown, *op. cit.*, pp. 21–22.

15 Friedlander, *op. cit.*, p. 623.

16 C. E. Krumbholz, "Basic Principles in Protestant Social Work and Their Application" (Paper prepared for, Church Conference of Social Work, 1939).

17 *Graduate Professional Schools of Social Work* (New York: Council on Social Work Education, 1955); *Education Directory, 1954–55, Part 3 Higher Education* (Washington, D. C.: U. S. Department of Health Education and Welfare. Office of Education, 1954).

18 *Statistics in Social Work Education as of November 1, 1954, and the Academic Year 1953–54* (New York: Council on Social Work Education, undated).

19 Arthur P. Miles, *American Social Work Theory; A Critique and a Proposal* (New York: Harper and Brothers, 1954), pp. 22–23.

20 F. Ernest Johnson, "Protestant Social Work," *Social Work Year Book, 1941* (New York: Russell Sage Foundation, 1941), p. 407.

21 Paul Hanly Furfey, "The Churches and Social Problems," *The Annals of the American Academy of Political and Social Science*, CCLVI (1948), p. 107.

22 *The New York Times*, June 8, 1955.

23 *Social Work Fellowships and Scholarships in the United States and Canada, 1955–56* (New York: Council on Social Work Education, 1954).

24 Arlien Johnson, "The Respective Policy of Governmental and Voluntarily Supported Social Work," *Social Service Review*, XXII, No. 3, September, 1948, p. 311.

25 Among them are Edward T. Devine the first director of the New York School of Social Work, who was an active member of the Commission on the Church and Social Service of the Federal Council of Churches; John Fitch, also a member of this Commission, who later taught at the New

York School of Social Work; Graham Taylor, who went from a professorship at Hartford Theological Seminary to the Chicago Commons and was a leader in the movement toward professionalization in that city; and Jane Addams, of Hull House, who broke with the church but acknowledged her religious purpose in her work. Shelby M. Harrison, Walter Pettit, Katherine Lenroot, Gordon Hamilton, and Eduard Lindeman ought certainly to be noted also.

THE MOVEMENT TOWARD FEDERATION 4

It is difficult in any social movement to indicate definitely the starting point of a new emphasis. Co-operative effort was, in some form, present from the beginning. However, the development of the chest and council movement, in the final analysis, sprang from the widespread and growing dissatisfaction with public social work in the late nineteenth century. Various groups of private individuals, instead of insisting upon improved legislation and more constructive administration, adopted the alternative of organizing private societies.

It was not long before a large number and wide variety of private organizations were in operation, all seeking funds for their support and independently driving ahead to meet the multiple social needs which they saw. Many who were connected with these social agencies both employees and laymen became acutely aware of the spotty character of the program. Thus, when the Association for Improvement of Conditions of the Poor was founded in New York city in 1843, one of its first objectives was the co-ordination of charitable and philanthropic effort. Some years later the charity organization society movement recognized this problem and attempted to deal with it, creating the district conference and the social service exchange.[1]

However, while Charity Organization Societies developed into functional agencies in the family welfare field and influenced greatly community organization, other methods of correlation and planning were also emerging as reported at the annual meetings of the National Conference of Charities and Correction (now National Conference of Social Work).

> The first meeting was in 1871. . . . It arose out of the desire of members of the state boards of charities and correction of New York, Pennsylvania, Illinois, Massachusetts, Michigan, Wisconsin, Connecticut, Rhode Island, and Kansas, to become better acquainted with one another, to meet for mutual benefit and encouragement, and to discuss questions in which they had a common interest.[2]

Numerous types of federations were being formed to represent special interests, such as the National Federation of Settlements, the American Prison Association, etc. While all of these efforts, to some extent, alleviated the problems of agency rivalry, quality of service, and duplication of programs it was not until the emergence of the council of social agencies movement that clear articulation of

47

organized methods for social planning was achieved. The move-ment spread slowly from 1909 when the first council in the United States was organized in Milwaukee until the time of the entry of the United States into the World War in 1917, when it was great-ly accelerated.[3]

Through representative participation of many, if not all, welfare agencies and institutions and the general public, community coun-cils endeavor to promote the general welfare through planning, re-search, co-ordination, education, and social action.

Each council maintains a distinctive program and structure which are related directly to the needs and resources of its com-munity. Thus, there is no universal council pattern. Some coun-cils are closely related to and financially supported through com-munity chests,[4] although in a few cities they remain autonomous.

Community councils are the dominant example of this type of collective activity. However, federations by other like-minded groups have also been established—especially since World War II. For instance, health councils were organized in numerous cities in order to co-ordinate and integrate all health services. Later many of these affiliated with the National Health Council, Inc. which was founded in 1921. The organization of the National Association for Mental Health, Inc. in 1950, the National Council on Agri-cultural Life and Labor in 1950, United Cerebral Palsy, Inc. in 1948 and United Community Defense Services in 1950 are additional ex-amples of this.[5]

Although such organizations are not structurally related to coun-cils of social agencies or community councils they are motivated by the same desire for co-ordination, for establishment of standards of education and practice and for inclusion of research regarding theory and techniques.

Simultaneously, with this trend toward community planning and co-ordination, there occurred the development of co-operative fund-raising. The birth of this movement may also be traced to charity organization societies. Along with recognizing the need to co-ordinate the work of the multiple private agencies, the charity organization movement also realized the need to pool devoted ef-fort spent on the financial support of those services. In many cities it was found that a handful of well-to-do and generous folk were being solicited over and over again by a host of organizations of every description.

> Every mail, it seemed, brought an appeal for funds. And per-sonal calls from those campaigning for specific agencies seemed to come with increasing frequency. This "multiple solicitation," as it was called, proved to be very confusing to lay donors. . . . Some of them came to be suspicious of all social workers. . . . A few began to rebel, and a good many

more were aware that something had to be done to bring order out of chaos.[6]

However, not only donors were suffering from the effect of multiple solicitation. Agencies, in some cases, became highly competitive among themselves in order to obtain as large an amount as they felt was necessary for their individual programs. They feverishly exploited potential sources of income, concentrating first on those which were most obvious. Today, in some large cities it is possible to find private agencies whose relationships with other community services still suffer because of this competitive drive for survival.

It was not until 1887 that a group of relief agencies in Denver formed the first federated plan in America. Twenty-three agencies joined in the first campaign which raised $20,000. The federations of Jewish charities began in Boston in 1896 and in 1909 the Federation for Social Service was created in Elmira, New York.[7]

It was common during these years preceding and during World War I to find many agencies under joint auspices experimenting in federated financing. Sectarian organizations provide noteworthy examples of this. The Brooklyn Federation of Jewish Charities was established in 1909. Eight years later, in 1917, a much larger program was initiated by the New York Federation for the support of Jewish Philanthropic Societies.[8] In 1920 the Catholic Charities of New York city was organized through the Archdiocese of New York.

> This group functions through ecclesiastical authority for its members. Like the Jewish Federation this Federation has professional leadership and organization for Catholics, and can represent its group in community work.[9]

The 1929 *Annual Report of the Federation of Protestant Agencies Caring for Protestants* (New York city) states that these agencies " . . . felt it was important to have some federated identity comparable to the Roman Catholic and Jewish groups." This federation was at first concerned primarily with co-ordinating and providing information services. In 1931 it expanded its services into financing when a Protestant Foundation was formed as a department of the agency "where funds may be entrusted, designated for specific use, or allocated for general use in the Protestant field."[10]

Many other "special interest" federations continued to be organized during the development of the community chest movement.

The first financial federation of a community type which achieved noteworthy success was organized in Cleveland in 1913. It is particularly significant since it introduced the principle of budgeting as a method of presenting to the community a picture of total needs and resources. It was created as the result of a study by the Cleveland Chamber of Commerce.

49

By the end of 1916, however, only fourteen similar financial federations were in existence, and their future was in great jeopardy.

A Committee of the American Association for Organizing Charities (now Family Service Society of America) was appointed to study the federation movement in 1915. While they reported gains in money-raising, their conclusions were somewhat unfavorable to the fund movement.

> . . . . in the social field, whether we agree or not regarding the economic field, there are spiritual and psychological factors which leave doubts as to the ultimate advantage to be derived from giving up a plan of work which has behind it the experience of more than one generation of social workers, in order to adopt one which, according to many who are in positions to know, is still in the experimental stage.[11]

World War I, which provided so much impetus to the entire field of social work, profoundly influenced the chest movement. The multiplication of a variety of appeals, including those for European War relief, induced some 400 communities to organize war chests for joint solicitation of funds.[12]

In 1918 the chests formed a national association known as the American Association for Community Organization, now known as the Community Chests and Councils of America, Inc. This represented a close affiliation of the so-called "functional" and "financial" federations.

Under the guidance of this agency, experience has been shared and the establishment of fairly uniform policies and standards have been achieved. Today chests are widespread and there are approximately 14,000 participating agencies of local chests across the country.

> It is estimated that the areas with community chests have a total population of 84,000,000, so that some 57 per cent of United States citizens are exposed to the chest-type of federated giving.[13]

Community chests and United Funds make up the greatest single voluntary fund-raising organization in the United States.

A community chest is usually considered to be a co-operative and representative organization of citizens and welfare agencies with two major functions. Its first responsibility is to raise funds for its affiliated agencies through a community-wide appeal and to distribute these monies according to a systematic budget procedure.

Secondly, it promotes co-operative planning, co-ordination, and administration of the community's social welfare, health, and recreation services.[14] In many communities direct responsibility for the second function of chests is vested in community welfare councils. Its programs are implemented by trained personnel under the

50

management and direction of a board of directors. The necessity for broad community representation on the boards of chests, to include important geographic, economic, and cultural interests, is emphasized as a corollary of the need and desire to solicit support from the total community. The work of a chest is usually accomplished through three committees: the campaign committee, the budget and admissions committee and the publicity committee.

The campaign committee has the primary responsibility for fund-raising. The campaign is usually conducted during one or two specific months of the year and utilizes a host of volunteers in addition to appropriate staff personnel. Kenneth Wood of the Research Department of Community Chests and Councils of America has said that about half or a little more of the 2,000 to 2,200 professional employees of chests, councils, and United Funds are engaged primarily in fund-raising (including year-round administration and collections) and that, in addition, 2,000,000 volunteers participate in the various campaigns. During these campaigns solicitation through businesses and corporations of their employees is emphasized in addition to the residential campaigns. The methods and techniques of promotion and publicity have been adapted from such commercial fields as advertising. Symbols such as the red feather have been introduced in addition to national co-ordination in timing. While chests have attempted valiantly to provide contributors with a sense of giving to a specific agency or need, the most universal criticism of federated giving, arises from the lack of identification by the giver to the cause.

> Philanthropies are good, but often too impersonal—just a question of taking money out of your pocket. It would be better for people, often, to do something physically, like helping in a hospital. The personal factor of helping people, although often a hit or miss, is more helpful for those who give than reaching in their pocket and giving a $5 bill or something.[15]

Some of the opposition comes from agencies who believe they can raise larger sums independently than they would receive through the chests. The American Red Cross was included, for a time but forbade its locals to join other organizations for federated fund-raising.[16] This policy was changed early in 1955 to permit affiliation.

While corporations have in most cases welcomed combined appeals—primarily because it reduced the number of requests for solicitation and therefore reduced budget expenditures in terms of accounting and loss of work time—the employees of these businesses express quite different attitudes.

> In our study of corporations we found that 65 per cent of all the companies sampled—and 100 per cent of the large ones —permitted employee solicitations in the plant. In some cases

these were limited to one or two a year, in others there were few limitations. About half the companies permitted payroll deductions for charitable contributions. Wage and salaried workers are now contributing large amounts to welfare funds from their work places.

In this survey the final questionnaire asked no direct opinions on shop solicitation, but questions about Mark, who chose to pay his debts rather than support his shop's 100 per cent contribution record, and several general questions, inspired comments on this subject.

Not one respondent expressed enthusiasm for payroll deductions or collections in the office and workshop. A few recognized the advantages for the agencies, or "never got mad" about being asked to contribute. Others were shamed into giving. Still others felt that undue pressures were being exerted, amounting sometimes to absolute compulsion; they particularly resented the 100 per cent type of drive.[17]

Community Chests and Councils of America have long recognized many of these issues and have listed four "hazards" in community chest organization. These are: (1) membership in the chest may tend to diminish the agency's sense of responsibility and initiative; (2) in exceptional cases control of social services may become vested in a small group, and tend to be arbitrary and dominated by the dollar; (3) immunity from specific appeals may lessen the giver's personal interest and personal knowledge concerning individual organizations and their special programs and (4) pioneer efforts for new or more effective services may be discouraged.[18]

Another important area of consideration for chests, which is a corollary of their successful development of community support, is the growing pressure for greater representation on the policy-making boards and on the various lay committees by special interest groups. Labor has often been cited as a recent example of this and in recent years, chest boards have included more union representatives than previously.

The budget and admissions committee usually makes recommendations regarding special appropriations and the admission of institutional members. It also studies the budgets of all participating organizations and makes recommendations regarding allowances, budget increases or reductions and payment to the agencies. Each chest usually develops a standard contract which all agencies must sign before affiliating.

Such a contract will often limit an agency's independent fund-raising efforts in terms of time of the year, and also in terms of the type of business or organization from which it may solicit. This is of course meant to prevent overlapping and to protect the contributor from multiple solicitation. Member agencies are usually expected to make their services available to the entire local community needing such service rather than to a specific group of the agency's preference. This is consistent with the chest's conception of itself as a community-wide organization but often creates problems and leads to misunderstandings by member agencies and their boards and the chests.

Agencies who are often anxious to affiliate with a chest as a method for achieving more stable financing, in many cases do not sufficiently evaluate their goals in relation to chest goals before affiliating. In many cases the agencies feel that the adjustments which are necessary for eligibility are less important to them at the time of application than they are later. In addition, it is often difficult for a small local agency to withdraw its chest membership and therefore resume the total responsibility for its own financing.[19]

The publicity committee supervises and directs a continuous educational and publicity program which is designed to inform the community of local social needs and to describe the services of the chest and its member agencies.

The Community Chests and Councils of America set up a National Budget Committee in 1946 after the dissolution of a similar committee which it had formed in 1942 to consider war appeals (since 1947 the National Budget Committee has also been sponsored by the National Social Welfare Assembly). It was obvious that, while one goal of community chests was the distribution of funds in relation to need, the budget committee of a local community chest was often in no position to determine (1) the national need for cancer research and treatment, (2) how that need would be related to requirements for heart disease, and (3) what proportion of either was the equitable share of the community's citizens. The facilities of the National Budget Committee are available on a voluntary basis to:

> national agencies that wish to submit their detailed budgets, programs and other financial data for evaluation, and to local communities which generally are unable to undertake detailed evaluation for themselves.[20]

An active and important subcommittee is the National Quota Committee which is responsible for determining the proportion of each affiliated agency's budget which should be raised in each of the states. State ratios are based on thirteen factors such as number of households, passenger car registration, telephones and effective buying power. The recommendations of this committee are totally advisory since the National Budget Committee is without enforcement powers.

While supporters of chest organization face many unresolved problems it is evident that the agency which raises its own budget through its own campaigns, through private endorsement, through service fees and charges and through income from investment, is becoming increasingly rare indeed. While chests are troubled by the number of independent drives, usually by national agencies, it is likely that the pressure exerted by highly industrialized communities—which find single plant solicitations a convenient and efficient device—may influence increased affiliation to some degree.[21]

The organization of a fund-raising campaign, which has been so highly developed in Community Chests, is often imitated, refined and adapted by other independent organizations in their separate drives. The typical organization of this "short-term campaign" has been described by Aileen D. Ross:

> The short-term campaign . . . involves a volunteer executive committee comprising an honorary chairman, chairman, vice-chairmen, secretary and treasurer. One of the vice-chairmen is generally a woman who is in charge of all female canvassers; the others are in charge of teams of volunteer canvassers assigned to different areas of the business world, such as "industry" and "finance." The duties of the Special Names Committee are particularly important; since they canvass all the largest subscribers, whether male, female, or corporation, the success of the campaign largely depends on their efforts. Therefore, this committee must consist of people who are influential in the business and/or social world who will be able to use personal influence with their prospects. Besides the volunteer executive, a paid professional organizer is now an essential part of any large campaign. His function is to see to the careful organization of the whole campaign. For an important city-wide campaign this may call for a year or more of work with the assistance of a large staff. The professional organizer is therefore the backbone of present-day campaigns, but, as his status in the community is not equal to that of the executive, he remains in the background, out of sight of the general public.[22]

It is significant to note that some churches now also employ professional fund-raising organizations to assist them. Such organizations generally pattern their campaigns in a fashion similar to that described above.

> Churches are often hampered by tradition. If the scales tip on the side of clinging to casual, outmoded methods in giving, it is well to interject a catalytic agent—a Christian fund-raising specialist—into the local situation fairly early in the planning stage.[23]

While many studies have attempted to determine the motivation for giving, there appears to be no possible agreement on any dominant motivation. Donors are influenced by many factors. Arnand C. Marts has said that "the church is the chief agency which systematically tries to teach people to give, starting this unique

54

process even with its youngest children. It teaches cradle roll chidren in the Sunday schools of Protestant churches."[24] This theory is supported by interviews such as this:

> I prefer to give to church charities, and I'll tell you why. At the beginning, hospitals, care of orphans, all these originated in the church, then they were taken by secular organizations. But still these don't take care of all the needs. Child care in other countries, medical care in other countries, our secular organizations don't reach. . . . Also in church charities there is more personal contact and more spiritual feeling, which is extremely important to everybody, especially in our civilization, where people tend to be treated as a mass, and not as individuals.[25]

Some people are motivated by a personal experience or particular sympathy for organizations concerned with specific needs, such as cancer or tuberculosis. Others give because they are solicited by a friend and express little if any desire to give because of the purposes or services of the agency.

But beyond the motivation to give because of friendship is the pressure exerted through social-status organizations. The case of John Smith, which appears in *Social Class in America,* is typical.

Mr. Smith, a newly rich man in a far western community, wanted to get into a social club of some distinction and significance in the city. His name was submitted by friends. It was then noted, however, that he had not contributed the expected amount to a philanthropy headed by Abner Grey, an influential club member. When Mr. Smith finally challenged Mr. Grey about the failure of the club to consider his membership application, the following conversation took place:

> Finally Mr. Smith said, "Ab, why . . . am I being kept out of your club?"
> "But, John, you're not. Everyone in the X club thinks you're a fine fellow."
> "Well, what's wrong?"
> "Well, John, we don't think you've got the kind of money necessary for being a good member of the X club. We don't think you'd be happy in the X club."
> ". . . I could buy and sell a half dozen of some of your board members."
> "I know that, John, but that isn't what I said. I did not say the amount of money. I said the kind of money."
> "What do you mean?"
> "Well, John, my co-workers on the charity drive tell me you only gave a few dollars to our campaign, and we had you down for a few thousand."
> For a moment Mr. Smith was silent. Then he grinned. So did

Mr. Grey. Smith took out his fountain pen and checkbook.
"How much?"
At the next meeting of the X club Mr. Smith was unanimous-
ly elected to its membership.[26]

It is obvious that this depersonalization of philanthropy has done
much to change its character. The urge to help fellow human beings is often lost in the pressure-campaigns of most organized
money efforts.

There is evidence of growing resistance to voluntary philanthropy. People object to such things as the still too numerous solicitations and to the apparent waste of money on overhead. The
future of voluntary philanthropy rests on a complicated fabric.

> It lies . . . in the attitude of the average citizen toward the
> purposes and techniques of professional and volunteer leaders
> in the fields. In the final analysis, the attitude of the citizen,
> and the statesmanship of the health and social work profes-
> sions will determine the price to be paid for the conservation
> of human resources. . . . Above all, he (the citizen) is con-
> cerned about costs. He wants to know "where it is all going to
> end," how far agencies intend to develop their programs and
> whether we should be serving a relatively few people well, or
> more people less expertly.[27]

We have attempted in the above to describe the tremendous development of community organization for social welfare. We have
seen in outline how the structure for co-operative planning and
fund-raising for social welfare in the private field came to consist
in general of local agencies and their national functional federations, and local councils of social agencies and community chests
and their national organization. As this movement toward federation developed, the former autonomy of agencies became subject
to community controls in the interests of co-ordinated planning of
services and financing to meet community needs.

As part of the social welfare structure, many church-related
agencies, too, have turned over some of their independence in
planning services and fund-raising to community controls. In this
process, the influence of church interests in their organized welfare programs needed to be adjusted to community standards and
goals.

The special problems that have arisen for church social welfare
interests are discussed elsewhere, but we make brief mention of
them here.

With the systematization of community-wide co-ordinated fund-
raising for welfare, pressures for giving came to be defined in
many forms other than religious, and displaced—for many persons—
the idea that contribution for welfare purposes was an expression
of their Christian charity.

Church interests in social welfare, confronted with the increasing problem of competing for funds from the community, the members of which were largely their ultimate constituency, often had no alternative but to join in the federated financing organizations. Such community-wide support often was associated with the necessity of nonsectarian service in which the religious character of agency programs was de-emphasized or at least neutralized. Evangelistic interests in welfare activities particularly became limited.

Protestant social agencies had early adopted, for the most part, the principle of community-wide services even before there was community-wide support. What was once voluntary on the part of Protestant agencies, now became an obligatory rule of the social work councils and community chests.

Many church agencies found that their goals and objectives were being redefined in nonreligious terms and raised the question as to the appropriateness of these new conceptions as the functioning of church interests.

There arose, also, the problem of standards of operation which were enforceable under most community council-community chest systems. Standards, being established on certain value bases, were sometimes conflicting between church and professional interests.

Thus, the churches' distinctive role and contribution to social welfare as part of the federated planning and financing structure of welfare programs has become of serious concern to both religious and professional interests.

FOOTNOTES FOR CHAPTER 4

[1] See Amos Griswold Warner, Stuart Alfred Queen and Ernest Bouldin Harper, *American Charities and Social Work* (4th. ed.; New York: Thomas Y. Crowell and Co., 1930), p. 522.

[2] Miriam Van Waters, "Philosophical Trends in Modern Social Work," *Proceedings of National Conference of Social Work, 1930* (Chicago: University of Chicago Press, 1931), p. 4.

[3] See Wayne McMillen, *Community Organization for Social Welfare,* (Chicago: University of Chicago Press, 1945), Footnote 4, p. 416. Discussion of founding date of Pittsburgh Council.

[4] Table T-7, p. 101, refers to the Community Chest relationships of Councils reporting.

[5] Edward T. Devine and Lilian Brandt, *American Social Work in the Twentieth Century* (New York: The Frontier Press, 1921), pp. 30–31.

[6] McMillen, *op. cit.,* p. 415.

[7] See Herbert Hewitt Stroup, *Community Welfare Organization* (New York: Harper and Brothers, 1952), pp. 367–86.

[8] Leonard A. Stidley, "Protestant Welfare Federation, New York," *Religion Functioning Socially,* Editor: Leland Foster Wood (New York: Church Conference of Social Work, Federal Council of the Churches of Christ in America, 1938), p. 21.

[9] *Ibid.,* p. 22.

[10] *Thirty-first Annual Report of the Federation of Protestant Welfare Agencies, Inc.* (New York: Federation of Protestant Welfare Agencies, 1951).

[11] *Financial Federations,* by Special Committee of American Association for Organizing Charity (New York: Family Welfare Association of America, 1917), p. 67.

[12] See Frank J. Bruno, *Trends in Social Work as Reflected in the Proceedings of the National Conference of Social Work 1874–1946* (New York: Columbia University Press, 1948).

[13] F. Emerson Andrews, *Philanthropic Giving* (New York: Russell Sage Foundation, 1950), p. 141.

[14] *Organizing and Operating a Community Chest* (New York: Community Chests and Councils of America, Inc., 1949), Bulletin No. 143, p. 3.

[15] F. Emerson Andrews, *Attitudes Toward Giving* (New York: Russell Sage Foundation, 1953), p. 24. (Interview)

[16] *Ibid.,* p. 152.

[17] Andrews, *Attitudes Toward Giving, op. cit.,* pp. 61–62.

[18] *Organizing and Operating a Community Chest, op. cit.,* pp. 4–5.

[19] McMillen, *op. cit.,* p. 428.

[20] *Manual; National Budget Committee* (New York: National Budget Committee, 1954).

[21] Andrews, *Philanthropic Giving, op. cit.,* pp. 158–59.

[22] Aileen D. Ross, "The Social Control of Philanthropy," *The American Journal of Sociology,* LVIII, No. 5, March 1953, pp. 451–52. Also see: Aileen D. Ross, "Philanthropic Activity and the Business Career," *Social Forces,* Vol. XXXII, No. 3, March 1954.

[23] Harl Russell, "Observations on Fund Raising," *1955–56 Stewardship Facts* (New York: Joint Department of Stewardship and Benevolence, National Council of the Churches of Christ in the U.S.A., 1955), p. 41.

[24] Arnand C. Marts, *Philanthropy's Role in Civilization* (New York: Harper and Brothers, 1953), p. 79.

[25] Andrews, *Attitudes Toward Giving, op. cit.,* p. 87. (Interview)

[26] Relating this incident to the class structure of American societies the authors go on to say: "Mr. Smith translated his money into philanthropy acceptable to the dominant group, he received their sponsorship, and finally became a participant in the club. The 'right kind' of house, the 'right' neighborhood, the 'right' furniture, the proper behavior—all are symbols that can ultimately be translated into social acceptance by those who have sufficient money to aspire to higher levels than they presently enjoy." W. Lloyd Warner, Marchia Meeker, and Kenneth Eells, *Social Class in America* (Chicago: Science Research Association, Inc., 1949), pp. 21–23.

[27] Leonard W. Mayo, "Who's to Pay for Social Work?", *The Survey* and *Survey Midmonthly,* LXXXVI (1950), p. 59.

THE ADJUSTMENT OF THE CHURCHES   5

In the thirty-year period 1900-1930 which saw the formalization of the social work structure of the country—the growth and specialization of its agencies and fields of work, the rise of professionalization, the federation of its service agencies and the emergence of national co-ordinating and professional bodies—there is little to suggest that the churches had any particular anxiety about the relation of their welfare activities to these developments.

In the first place, that these changes ultimately resulted in organized social work from its earlier primary dependence on the churches was not recognized by many church people. Indeed, the extent to which the process of secularization has taken place in the social field today may have been obscured by the notion that the social service activities of the community and of the Protestant churches, representing the majority populace, were the same and shared similar goals.

But there was a large group of people interested in the churches who were aware of the changes. Many members of this group were active in bringing them about. There were several reasons for their accepting the growth of a community-wide welfare pattern.

Protestantism accepted very early the idea of community responsibility for general social conditions and developed a pattern of establishing service agencies to serve the entire community. Perhaps because these agencies were to a large part run and controlled by Protestant staffs and boards of directors, and perhaps because society was predominantly Protestant in numbers and control, the churches generally have not resisted a number of these agencies' becoming nonsectarian. Many large welfare agencies and child care organizations had their origin in the churches and have gradually, over a period of time, moved from Protestant-sectarian auspices to a nonsectarian status. Indeed, this movement became so marked that in the councils of social agencies of many cities there was no group recognized as constituting Protestant agencies, which were lumped together with the nonsectarian group.

There were, it should again be noted, large numbers of persons interested in and connected with the churches who were actively working for these agencies undergoing this process of secularization. Within the various councils of social agencies these people were working toward the unification of the social welfare pattern on a community-wide basis.

59

Another reason for the acceptance of the new pattern of social work was the disunity of protestantism due to denominationalism. This acted as a stimulus to the development of secular social work.

> The disunity of the Protestant church made the secularization of social work imperative. There are enough limitations in a religiously inspired institutional charity to justify the conclusion that secularization is a desirable end. . . . The anarchic disunity of protestantism makes the secularization of social work inevitable, even if it were not desirable. It is quite impossible, in grappling with the increasing complex problems of urban civilization, to use an instrument as divided as the Protestant church.[1]

Still another reason the churches were willing to allow many institutions they founded to become secular was the matter of finance. As the social problems in an expanding society became greater and more complex, the agencies serving an entire community necessarily had to expand their programs to meet the new needs. Many Protestant churches and Protestant leaders realized that such expanded agency programs would be too heavy a load for the churches to manage both financially and administratively. As they had the security of being the majority group in the community—culturally, financially, and religiously—there was little fear on the part of these church groups of letting the support and administration of these agencies become community wide.

Early there developed, then, a pattern of Protestant participation which has been described by F. Ernest Johnson as one "in which the Christian motive tends to find its social expression through individual voluntary participation by members of the Protestant churches in activities and agencies that are conducted under secular auspices." These agencies, Dr. Johnson believes, furnish a channel of Christian benevolence and vocational outlet for ideals of Christian service.

However in some places, notably New York, Protestant groups began to feel that they were in a disadvantageous position in the social welfare structure in relationship to the two other faith groups.

In New York, perhaps because the population was almost equally divided among Protestants, Catholics, and Jews, some of the problems which were present in the adjustment of the churches to the new pattern of social welfare throughout the country came into sharp focus.

New York's attempt to federate Protestant agencies on the same basis as that of Catholic and Jewish agencies illustrates the unique position which Protestants occupy in the community and within the social welfare structure. Federation was difficult because the

Protestant philosophy allowed many independent approaches to the welfare problem and made central representation difficult. Many nonsectarian agencies which had been organized under church auspices had become so secularized that they no longer wished to be identified as Protestant. These reasons, combined with the fact that there was not a clearly defined Protestant community in the sense that there were Catholic and Jewish communities, made the attempt to organize a Protestant federation nearly impossible. An examination of the New York experience illuminates this point.

The New York Protestant Federation was organized in 1920. In describing the position of this federation the dilemma of the movement in protestantism is described:

> This federation is not clearly sectarian, nor does it have a sharply defined constituency; it has no closely knit organization, since it is not representative of all Protestants; it has neither centralized financing nor a financial lever for standard raising; and it is not aligned with the churches, as is the Roman Catholic Charities. . . . The Protestants have been continually influenced in their thinking by the types of organization, motivations, and accomplishments of the other sectarian welfare federations. The Protestants have sought to increase their strength through adopting methods similar to those employed by the Jews and Roman Catholics. At the same time they have sought to retain their own identity; to develop a federation in keeping with the Protestant tradition and the Protestant faith.[2]

At first much attention in the federation was devoted to the caring for Protestant children where sectarianism was more possible, but in the period from 1925 to 1931 the issues became more sharply defined. Then the organization asked itself the following questions:

1. Are more than children to be the concern of the Protestant welfare federation?

2. If the scope is enlarged what will be a satisfactory title for the agency?

3. What is to be the relationship of the Protestant Federation to Protestant churches, as the latter works through the Greater New York Federation of Churches?

4. Is it desirable for the Federation to seek to become a financial federation for Protestant agencies, as the Jewish Federation and the Roman Catholic Charities have been for their respective constituents?

5. What form of organization can best make articulate a Protestant position in social work?[3]

Soon the proper financial function and responsibility of the fed-

61

eration to Protestant welfare agencies became a paramount issue. The fact that the Jewish and Roman Catholic boards were both fiscal agencies caused the board to state:

> No work of value could be done until the Protestant Federation became as strong as the Jewish and Roman Catholic Welfare Federations.[4]

But the federation ran into the difficulty of the Protestant agencies who had or were becoming secularized in their outlook.

> A repercussion of the proposal to form an all-inclusive Protestant financial federation came from the nonsectarian family welfare organizations. They were not in favor of the proposed Protestant charities. They did not want to be classified as Protestant organizations. Many of the nonsectarian social welfare organizations may have admitted that they were Protestant in origin, control, and support, but they did not want to be known as Protestant social welfare agencies. They were chartered as nonsectarian. Also, the proposed set-up seemed, from the point of view of social workers and social work executives, "a form of autocratic control which was not justifiable under the circumstances."[5]

The attempt to establish a Protestant financial federation failed. There was not enough cohesiveness among the agencies to make possible what would be primarily a fiscal agency. The membership of Protestant agencies had ties which were different from those that held together the Jewish Federation and the Roman Catholic Charities, which had no definite link with nonsectarian welfare agencies. Secular Protestant agencies and nonsectarian agencies, although they might have Protestant origin and control, did not have strong common bonds.

In 1931 the federation was reorganized under the name of the Federation of Protestant Agencies. Later the word, "Welfare," was added. The term, "Protestant Agency," was used as meaning non-Jewish and non-Roman Catholic. In order clearly and accurately to limit the constituency of the federation and to clarify the relationship between nonsectarian and Protestant agencies the board defined as a Protestant agency:

> An agency which is Protestant in origin, control and support, and which is admittedly Protestant, although the service of such an agency may reach Jews and Roman Catholics, constitutes a Protestant agency.[6]

This definition excluded the nonsectarian agencies, which, although in most instances Protestant in origin, did not wish to be designated as Protestant. It created four groupings of private agencies: Protestant, nonsectarian, Jewish, and Roman Catholic. It gave definition for membership in the federation but not of ecclesiastical authority—as in the case of Roman Catholic Charities—or on the religious-cultural ties as in the case of the Jewish Federation. The Federation of Protestant Welfare Agencies now became, both by constitution and in fact, the co-ordinating agency inclusive of all Protestant welfare agencies that desired federation.

Difficulties later developed regarding the federation and its role in the Welfare Council, the central co-ordinating agency of New York city which illustrate the difference between the relationship of Protestants to the welfare structure and that of Catholics and Jews. The Welfare Council recognized sectarian welfare federations but it co-ordinated welfare services through functional divisions. In the case of the federation its sectarian recognition would have meant the further division of welfare on sectarian bases. The Welfare Council then raised the question as to whether the federation really represented all Protestants as did the Catholic Charities or the Jewish Federation. No settlement was made and the federation continued its sectarian approach and the Welfare Council its functional approach.

Difficulties also continued with the nonsectarian family welfare agencies. Almost from the beginning what amounted to a state of tension existed between the federation and these agencies. Both appealed to Protestant groups for financial support. Where Jewish and Roman Catholic constituencies were called upon to support definitely sectarian social agencies, the Protestants were appealed to by both. When community funds were distributed to the faith groups the Jewish Federation and Roman Catholic Charities received the share allotted to their respective constituencies, and the nonsectarian family welfare agencies the share allotted to the community as a whole.

> But the federation included no recognized Protestant family welfare agencies in its membership, it received nothing. The fact that Protestant groups were operating family welfare agencies, however, caused many Protestants to feel that they were not getting their share, and gave rise to considerable agitation to change the situation.[7]

When the Greater New York Fund was launched in 1937-1938 the federation was uncertain of its role. The Greater New York Fund was committed to the distribution of funds on a functional basis. On the basis of co-ordinating and advisory relations with its members the federation was accepted only as an advisory group.

In general the federation was thwarted in its ambitions by the individuality and independence of Protestant agencies and resistance of nonsectarian agencies.

> The will, on the part of Protestant agencies, to assert individual independence weakened the federation, so that many members have retained loose and limited ties. When, in the

development of the federation, there was agitation for centralized financial co-ordination, the looseness of the bonds of membership limited such possible development. Likewise, when community welfare funds were distributed to other sectarian welfare federations, there was a feeling on the part of the federation and some of its members that Protestants were not getting their share of the allotments, but the voluntary membership ties did not enable a strong Protestant position to express itself readily. Also, when the Federation, by action of the Board, defined a Protestant agency and excluded nonsectarian agencies from membership, it was found that a Protestant federation enjoyed a special relationship with nonsectarian agencies that other sectarian welfare agencies did not have. Although the federation defined a Protestant agency, it did not work out a clear-cut relationship with nonsectarian groups. In each of these situations, there resulted uncertainty of function on the part of the federation.[8]

In general throughout the country no attempts were made to establish Protestant federations and the churches adjusted to the community organization of social welfare. The interdenominational council of churches was accepted as the agency through which adjustments between the social work structure and the churches would be worked out. Many of these councils had divisions of social welfare and, in these, problems affecting Protestant and nonsectarian agencies were worked out.

Recently, however, there has been an upsurgence of concern on the part of many Protestant groups again about the role and position of nonsectarian agencies which formerly were Protestant organizations. There has been the feeling that in spite of the fact that some agencies, especially in the child care field, have been organized and are supported largely by Protestants, there is no assurance that Protestant children would be looked after. Such a situation arose in Chicago, for example, where the children's agency working with the courts had become nonsectarian. Jewish children were looked after by the Jewish agency as were the Catholic children, by the Catholic Charities. All others—Protestants and those not connected with any religion—were left to the nonsectarian agency. Often, then, as the agency could not meet the demand, Protestant children could not be handled. This led to self-consciousness on the part of many Protestants and even criticism on the part of the other sectarian groups that Protestants were not looking after their own.

Indeed this situation, as well as the continued feeling that Protestants were in a disadvantaged position in the general welfare organization in relationship to Catholics and Jews, has led to a rethinking of the Protestant position.

There were, in addition, other irritants in the relationship with other faith groups under the welfare system which made many Protestants restive. The Catholic Charities in each community dealt in effect with the councils of social agencies and the community funds as a group. This meant that for the most part the councils of social agencies were limited in their standard setting function in relationship to Catholic agencies.

In dealings with the various community funds the usual pattern was for the Catholic Charities to be guaranteed a certain fixed sum. Protestant groups often felt that this procedure did not always work out fairly.

Another point of irritation was that the Catholic Charities, working as a united group, would sometimes force their will on the councils at a price of refusing to participate if they did not get their way. The controversy over the Planned Parenthood Council is a case in point. In New York the Catholics opposed the admission of Planned Parenthood to the Welfare and Health Council because of their opposition to birth control. When there was some chance that they would be overridden and the agency would be accepted for membership, the Catholics threatened in a group to resign from the Welfare Council.

This rather arbitrary behavior on the part of the Catholics was irritating to all Protestant groups and added to the feeling that protestantism should have a more distinctive role in the welfare system. This position was held by many Protestants who had no desire to form a Protestant federation but wished a more democratic arrangement within the present system.

Recognition of this concern on the part of many Protestants has bothered people in the secular welfare field. At an important conference held by the Community Chests and Councils of America in 1948 which discussed social service under the Catholic, Jewish, and Protestant auspices in the opening address it was stated:

> . . . there has been in recent years a growth of sectarian influence in social work. In the area of auspices the trend is toward a growth of sectarian influences. Such a growth gives rise to problems for the casework, the group worker, and the community organizer. In the casework field there is a division of family and child care services on strictly sectarian lines. There is a growing insistence that the sectarian background be recognized and client referred accordingly. In the group work field we see demands that church settings be used. Agencies are expressing fear of excessive control of programs by the church. In community organization we find ourselves concerned over a further fragmentation of social work. We have the problem of unifying the community and we see division being created. Such fragmentation complicates an already complicated job. Particularly, the observable trend as it relates to protestantism is disturbing to the community organ-

izer. The development of unity among Protestant groups has given rise to a demand to establish Protestant services. This development in the Protestant field reverses the earlier pattern of releasing agencies to nonsectarian auspices.[9]

The question of the role of protestantism—its relationship to the agencies formerly Protestant which have become nonsectarian, the question of Protestant federations to parallel those of Catholics and Jews, the continuation of the pattern which allows the process of secularization or the emergence of another pattern which emphasizes Protestant agencies—must be more completely thought out. This constitutes a group of problems which must be dealt with in any discussion or deliberation to determine how protestantism will, in the future, operate in the welfare field.

FOOTNOTES FOR CHAPTER 5

[1] Reinhold Niebuhr, *The Contribution of Religion to Social Work* (New York: Columbia University Press, 1932), p. 15.

[2] Leonard A. Stidley, *Sectarian Welfare Federation Among Protestants* (New York: Association Press, 1944), pp. 24–25.

[3] *Ibid.*, pp. 33–34.

[4] *Ibid.*, p. 36.

[5] *Ibid.*, pp. 37–38.

[6] *Ibid.*, p. 45.

[7] *Ibid.*, p. 58.

[8] *Ibid.*, p. 72.

[9] *Social Services Under Catholic, Jewish, and Protestant Auspices in the Total Welfare System* (New York: Community Chests and Councils of America, Inc., 1948), p. 2.

PART III

THE PROTESTANT EFFORT

There is no single Protestant approach to the field of social welfare. There are philosophies within the Protestant heritage and experience, but no philosophy. Protestants have emphasized individual responsibility and voluntary effort for the support of social welfare, and denominational administration of most of the varied enterprises. There exists today the feeling among the various churches and groups in the various churches that churches should not engage in social work; that Protestants should have a distinct position in the field approximating that of Catholics and Jews; that the churches should supplement the social work structure by meeting new needs and by experimentation; and that Christian motive finds its social expression through voluntary participation by members in activities and agencies that are conducted under secular auspices.

The social welfare program of the churches is extensive. The activities are much wider than the area covered by the formal professional social workers, and find expression in most of the activities of the churches. There have developed then, a number of organizations—local and national, denominational and interdenominational—through which this concern is expressed. The present volume will deal with these interdenominational efforts and with the church-related agencies. The companion volume will discuss the denominational efforts.

The National Council of Churches is important in the interdenominational effort both because of its co-ordinating function and its program of social welfare. Its Department of Social Welfare co-ordinates and stimulates the varied activities of the churches. The Council's organized efforts are in such fields as service to migrants and to Indians, Church World Service, and Pastoral Services.

State and local councils of churches operate on those levels to implement the welfare program of the churches. The councils of church women relate the activities of lay women to the formal and informal welfare activities of the churches' welfare programs.

In the church-related agencies there is a varied expression of the churches' concern for social welfare. A statistical analysis of the present involvement is presented in this section.

PROTESTANT APPROACHES
TO SOCIAL WELFARE

6

"This important group of religious bodies has no generally accepted philosophy of social work under religious auspices, or of relationships to community agencies and public welfare services."[1]

This observation is found in a *Survey of Protestant Social Service in New York City*, which reveals that the kinds of work under Protestant sponsorship are dominantly institutional, including such projects as hospitals, homes for the aged, homes and services for children, neighborhood houses, day nurseries, institutional churches, the Christian Associates, and the Salvation Army. But there is "no generally accepted" Protestant philosophy.

Rather there are philosophies within the Protestant heritage and experience. The current theories of social welfare work come out of a long and diverse experience. Current Protestant theories in the United States draw upon and have been influenced by such factors as the charity of the ancient church, the early social welfare work of the churches of the Reformation, and the situations faced by the churches in numerous American communities.

> From the very beginning (of the Christian community), not only did its members, each in his own sphere, recognize compassion for the distressed as one of the necessary duties of their new life, but the community as such from the very outset accepted as a task laid upon it the practice of charity by means of its different organizations. . . . The Christian Church can never be conceived of as without charity; it was inherent in it from the very beginning. And it was so, not only because its Lord and Head taught love and commanded love, but because he himself practised it.[2]

Reinhold Niebuhr has commented on the philanthropic spirit of the church.

> The philanthropic spirit of the early church was in part due to a natural sense of solidarity in a numerically weak community living in a hostile world. The emphasis upon hospitality, for instance, was no doubt due to the natural fellow feeling of members of a small sect living in a none too sympathetic world. . . . Naturally there was never a thought about the more basic causes of the poverty which incited the church to good deeds. The social situation was taken for granted. But within terms of it heroic efforts were made to relieve human suffering. Chrysostom answered a critic, who thought he spoke too much about charity, "Yes, every sermon is about alms and I am not ashamed of it." Augustine de-

69

clared: "The true sacrifice of a Christian is alms for the poor."[3]

Under the influence of the Reformation, Protestant churches and many communities made varied responses to the needs of the handicapped, the weak, the oppressed. Marie Kamphuis, a Dutch social worker, has recently traced some of these developments.

> In 1523, in Leisnig, Germany, the responsibility for assistance of the needy was shared by the local government and the church. In 1525, in Yyperen, the Netherlands, there took place the secularization of charity. [There] local authorities felt that because the church had failed to meet social needs, they should assume the responsibility. A third movement, in the Calvinistic churches was the appearance of the deaconages, especially in the Netherlands. The deaconage movement spread, and with it a methodology for the individual contact, and at the same time, the humane way in which helpless persons, be they poor, disabled, sick, or orphaned, are approached. . . . The Calvinistic Reformation looked upon the deaconages as an essential part of the church. . . . Assistance under secular auspices was rejected. However, this was often unrealistic because many towns had already secularized their relief work.[4]

Here we have presented three points of view, persisting to this day:

1. The town and the church should share responsibility.
2. The church failed to meet social needs; hence the town should act.
3. The church administered charity through an office of its own; it rejected the idea of secular auspices; but this was unrealistic because many towns had already effectively organized assistance to the needy.

Almon R. Pepper listed various motivations for the "age-old concern of the churches for the welfare of their own people and of those in the general community.

   a. Christian charity, and the pastoral concern of the church for its own people;
   b. An evangelistic hope that the religious life of the individual cared for will be nurtured and strengthened and that he may be encouraged to join the church if not already a member;
   c. A broadly humanitarian and democratic concern for the needs of people and the improvement of society, which provides service surely in terms of need; and
   d. The professional attitude of performing a given service or function in the way most satisfactory and beneficial to the client and the community."[5]

Such motivations are applied differently in specific situations and govern, in varying degrees, the actions of contributors, clients, boards of directors—staffs.

Probably there would be wide assent that Protestants have emphasized individual responsibility and voluntary effort for the support of social welfare, and denominational administration of most of the varied enterprises.

> Inevitably protestantism bred an individualism (in its reaction against the medieval church, which had developed vast institutional charities). Luther's ideal was that love should be spontaneous and not be under either the guidance or the coercion of an institution.[6]

The Protestant emphasis on the priesthood of all believers, on the minister as only the "first among equals," on private judgment, has, of course, colored its participation in social welfare activities. The placing of responsibility on the individual conscience is widely regarded as one of the positives in Protestant experience. This has been manifested in many practical ways.

Might we say that a wide search is now going on, in Protestant social welfare enterprises, for some sort of integration of the individualism that has been inherited with the social spirit and the social responsibility that are needed in an age with many social problems and crises and human needs?

Somewhat the same types of problems present themselves in connection with denominational control and administration. Much social welfare is somehow related to the denominations. Through local councils of churches, and more especially their social welfare committees and offices, varying degrees of co-operation are being attempted. In larger cities, this degree of co-operation is probably more highly formalized than in smaller cities.

But, as in other aspects of community activity, it is often observed that no one denomination can adequately meet community need, and that this interdenominational co-operation has become a necessity. This is being achieved only slowly. The situation is often confused by the great variety of relationships that social agencies have with their denominations, by the tendency of some agencies to become somewhat unofficial, and by the tendency of others to become altogether independent.

Might one sum it up in much the same terms as in the discussion of individualism, by observing that a wide search is going on for a reconciliation of the advantages that accompany denominational control with the necessities of community co-operation and of interdenominational activity? Apparently in these latter days there has been more emphasis than previously on the practical problems of interdenominational co-operation.

Another area presenting dilemmas is found in the movements

during recent decades toward the assumption of community-wide responsibility.

> In the early history of welfare federations and community funds, some of the church agencies found it difficult to seek membership in and support from these organizations. They feared a kind of control which might interfere with some of their policies, especially in regard to religious ministry. More recently many of these church agencies have found it to their advantage to become members of the federation and to receive community funds. It has helped them to keep in touch with the changing needs of individuals and groups so that they can accommodate their programs to these needs; and the supervision and co-ordination involved has helped them to improve their programs on a level with other community agencies.[7]

Dr. Pepper observes: "The basic theological teaching of the churches has caused their members to support, financially and morally, not only their own church agencies but also those of the general community." Churchmen serve on boards of directors of community agencies. He also finds evidence that the general community favors the support of religious social welfare agencies, "as a demonstration of the basic relationship between religion and democracy."[8] Again, in many circles, there goes on a sincere inquiry concerning the maintenance of religious auspices in an era in which there is wide acceptance of the idea of community responsibility.

Comparison with other faiths in the field of social welfare yields experience that bears heavily on the development of a philosophy of Protestant social welfare. All too briefly put, it may be said that, in contrast to the multifarious ideas and activities of the Protestant world, one finds much more coherent and consistent policies in Roman Catholic and Jewish social welfare work.

The Roman Catholic theory has called for relatively complete services under church auspices. The parishes, the diocesan bureaus, the specialized institutions and agencies, have had the responsibility of meeting the social welfare needs of the members. It is a theory that "breaks down," particularly in times of depression, when unemployment has mounted. Also, Roman Catholic members avail themselves of certain of the standardized services of the government, e.g. social security. But, compared with protestantism, Roman Catholic theory is more uniform and thorough, and it consistently places more responsibility upon the church as such.

When Jews first came to America, the needy were usually given relief by the religious congregations.

> Early social work was largely sectarian ... (But around 1870) under the impetus of the charity organization society movement, there was a tendency to combine the congregational

ladies aid societies into the United Hebrew Charities. . . .
Finally, about 1900, there evolved the federation form of
community organization.[9]

Thus Jewish social welfare becomes a series of agencies of the
Jewish community within the American community. Social agencies among Jews tend to parallel community-wide agencies. Recognition has been made of the great advance in publicly supported
social welfare service. Thus the Jewish agencies tend to supplement
government services. "The bonds to religious groupings are casual,"
Rabinoff concluded. And the Jewish agencies are confronted with
the same set of problems and issues as private agencies generally.

With this as background, we may now state certain of the schools
of thought that one encounters in Protestant circles with respect to
philosophies of social work. These cannot be stated simply in terms
of denominational polity or policy, even though in some denominations there is more complete acceptance of thorough theory than
in others. A Lutheran clergyman recently remarked: "There is no
one Lutheran school of thought when it comes to social welfare."
Since in a companion volume authoritative statements are made
concerning what many denominations are doing and why, the consideration here will be limited to concise statements of schools of
thought that are found in a number of denominations, or that "cut
across" denominational lines.

1. There is some concurrence among Protestants with the Roman
Catholic theory of relatively complete church handling of social
welfare needs, outlined above.

> The more a religious group consciously differs from the pre-
> vailing religious pattern in the community, the stronger its
> tendency to maintain so far as possible its own social services.
> . . . there is in evidence a disposition to make Protestant
> social work a more distinct entity than it has been in the
> past.[10]

2. A Protestant pattern calls for participation of Christian individuals in secular agencies.

> . . . protestants could adjust themselves to the passing over of
> social work to secular, nonsectarian auspices, in the same
> fashion as they did with respect to the secularization of ed-
> ucation. The process effected a distribution of the financial
> burden and created a common pool of professional and tech-
> nical resources within a cultural setting in which Protestants
> are at home, and with respect to which they perhaps feel
> some sense of group proprietorship.
> Thus, partly from sheer necessity and partly because of the
> diffusion of a common religious spirit among secular agencies,
> there has grown up in America a Protestant pattern of social

work in which Christian motive tends to find its social expression through voluntary participation by members of the Protestant churches in activities and agencies that are conducted under secular auspices. These agencies furnish a channel of Christian benevolence and also a vocational outlet for the ideals of a service that Christianity has fostered.[11]

3. There are those who say that social welfare under religious auspices should be emphasized because this makes possible the rendering of services with the "plus" element. Those who hold to this view stress such matters as personal interest, religious motivation, or willingness to render the unusual service that is often not possible in a public institution. Others stress the sacrifice and the devotion of the religious worker as carrying with them distinctive elements in church social work.

> We know that the Christian faith—with its glorious gospel of a God who cares—is essential for real health of mind and body. We know that the Christian emphasis on the importance of relationships has the answer to loneliness, and to family problems, and to race relations. We must, in our church agencies, be demonstrating this plus the quality of Christian service.[12]

Roswell P. Barnes has observed that:

> Charity and welfare work are not synonymous. It is possible to have either without the other. A charitable intent expressed in a charitable deed does not necessarily result in a contribution to welfare. . . . On the other hand, social welfare may be promoted by means which are provided without a charitable intent. . . . charity needs guidance in its expression lest it be wasted or worse, and that social welfare work needs the spirit and quality of charity lest it degenerate into mere professionalism or into a factor of group conflict contributory to community tension. . . . The resources are found in our Christian faith and experience. First of all, the Christian knows that he is not alone in caring, because he knows that the Creator and Father of all men cares infinitely. Second, the Christian knows that there are limitless resources of inner strength and security. One who follows Christ understands what he meant when he said, "My yoke is easy and my burden light."[13]

4. Another emphasis is on "The Whole Man." The churches should co-operate with an institution even if independent, if it gives evidence of meeting the needs of, or of ministering to "the whole man." If an agency denies the need of such a comprehensive service and ministry, then the churches would be justified in setting up their own organization.

5. The churches should encourage the community to take steps

to meet special need. This may involve several important steps. The first will be to call attention persistently to the need—stir up the people.

After the churches have aided in stirring up the community, they should then offer to co-operate with others in meeting the need. If this process is successful, the churches' mission would be largely accomplished.

If co-operation with others does not result in meeting the need, then the churches would be justified in setting up their own agencies.

In approaching the Protestant effort in terms of concrete manifestations in the form of organizations and areas of work, then, the fact that there are Protestant approaches rather than a Protestant philosophy must be kept in mind. Protestants, unlike Catholics and Jews, do not have a single approach to the welfare problem. If this is not understood, it is difficult to comprehend the complex and involved form which the Protestant effort takes in the welfare field.

FOOTNOTES FOR CHAPTER 6

1 *Survey of Protestant Social Service in New York City.* Foreword by Worth H. Tippy (Mimeographed; New York: Brooklyn Church-Mission Federation, Greater New York Federation of Churches, Queens Federation of Churches, Federation of Protestant Welfare Agencies, 1936).

2 Gerhard Uhlhorn, *Christian Charity in the Ancient Church* (New York: Charles Scribner's Sons, 1883), p. 56.

3 Reinhold Niebuhr, *The Contribution of Religion to Social Work* (New York: Columbia University Press, 1932), pp. 5–6.

4 Marie Kamphuis, "Distinctive Elements in Protestant Social Work," *Christian Social Welfare*, Vol. II, No. 4, April, 1955 (New York: National Council of the Churches of Christ in the U. S. A., 1955).

5 Almon R. Pepper, "Protestant Social Work," *Social Work Year Book, 1945* (New York: Russell Sage Foundation, 1945), pp. 304–5.

6 Niebuhr, *op. cit.*, pp. 9–10.

7 Pepper, *op. cit.*, p. 305.

8 *Ibid.*, p. 306.

9 George W. Rabinoff, "National Organizations in Social Welfare," *Social Work Year Book, 1954* (New York: American Association of Social Workers, 1954).

10 F. Ernest Johnson, "Protestant Social Work," *Social Work Year Book, 1954* (New York: American Association of Social Workers, 1954), pp. 378–9.

11 *Ibid.*, p. 378.

12 Mrs. Theodore O. Wedel, "Health and Welfare Needs of the Nation and the Place of the Church Agency" (Department in Social Relations, Diocese of New York, Protestant Episcopal Church, 1954).

13 Roswell P. Barnes, "Charity and Welfare Work," *Christian Social Welfare*, Vol. I, No. 1 (New York: National Council of the Churches of Christ in the U. S. A., 1953).

NATIONAL INTERDENOMINATIONAL PROGRAMS

7

In this chapter and those following we make note of the major current organized welfare efforts of Protestants. Denominational programs—their nature and organization—are described in a companion volume, and the interest here is primarily on the level of interdenominational co-operative effort, although there are several chapters given to a description of the extent, nature, and problems of denominationally related health and welfare agencies and institutions.

The National Council of Churches

The National Council of the Churches of Christ in the U. S. A., formed December, 1950, has general responsibility for such conciliar functions as its thirty constituent bodies authorize or commit to it. The objects, as stated in the Constitution, include the following:

> To manifest the common spirit and purpose of the co-operating churches in carrying out their mission in the world.
>
> To do for the churches such co-operative work as they authorize the Council to carry on in their behalf.
>
> To continue and extend the work [of the various agencies merged in 1950].
>
> To foster and encourage co-operation among the churches for the purpose set forth in [the] Constitution.
>
> To promote co-operation among local churches and to further in communities, states, or larger territorial units the development of councils of churches, and councils of church women. . . .

The main responsibilities for implementation of these general objectives, in the area of social welfare services in the United States are borne by the Department of Social Welfare, the Division of Christian Life and Work, and the Division of Home Missions.

Department of Social Welfare

The Department of Social Welfare, in accord with the objectives of the Council and of its Division of Christian Life and Work, expresses the co-operative concerns of the churches in matters affecting social welfare and seeks to advance these services and the influence of the churches in these areas. The department has been interested in such matters as unmet social needs; the adequacy of health and welfare standards, including the standards of the church-related agencies; public policies in social welfare; and all the spiritual, moral and social forces making for the good society that offers opportunity to all persons to live the Christian life.

The functions of the department include the promotion of co-operation in social welfare among the constituent bodies of the Council; the development of co-ordination with other units of the Council in respect to social welfare interests; work with the churches in development of their own standards in social welfare; co-operation with state and local councils of churches; representation of the churches with voluntary organizations and government agencies; study and interpretation of social needs of the nation; and others as noted in its rules of procedure and annual reports.

Among recent activities reported by the Department of Social Welfare, Division of Christian Life and Work, are the following excerpts from the *Biennial Report 1954 of the National Council*.[1]

The department sponsors a membership organization, the Christian Social Welfare Associates, of which both professional and lay persons are members.

The Church Conference of Social Work is carried on as "the forum of the Associates." It is an affiliate group of the National Conference of Social Work and meets annually in conjunction with it. Here Christian social workers are given an opportunity "to discuss such subjects as the role of the church in strengthening family life, the church and social work education, the chaplain as an essential part of the welfare team."

A periodical, *Christian Social Welfare*, issued five times yearly, is distributed to the Associates and to others that subscribe. It offers cross-fertilization by sharing philosophy and program in social service, education, and action, and by noting social trends."

The Department has shared responsibility with the Division of Home Missions for preparations for the National Conference on the Churches and Social Welfare, called by the General Board of the Council in 1954, being convened in Cleveland, Ohio, November 1-4, 1955. This Conference is to "consider the role and function of the churches in relation to rapidly changing needs in social welfare." The Conference will report its findings to the constituent communions. It is hoped that those attending "will be led of the spirit to a common mind so the churches may give more dynamic leadership in meeting the nation's welfare needs in this generation."

The staff of the department endeavors to express the mind of the churches when serving on the board of directors of the National Social Welfare Assembly and its host of functional committees, the board of the National Housing Conference, the citizens advisory group of the Federal Housing and Home Finance Agency, the National Health Council, the Council on

Social Work Education, American Social Hygiene Association, and many similar agencies of national significance. But what is the mind of the churches?

Although a common approach to the churches' responsibilities in social welfare is not yet in sight, this department has been a corporate venture undertaken *by* the churches and *for* the churches. The partnership has been evident in joint publication and distribution of material, such as the recent folder on recruitment of personnel for church social work and the distribution of approved statements on matters of common concern.

Three statements prepared by the department and adopted by the General Board were:

The Churches' Concern for Housing

Confidentiality of Assistance Records

Standards and Licensing of Church-Related Institutions for Sheltered Care.

These declarations "may seem to indicate that in some areas the churches have a common mind, but more accurately a concensus among elected representatives."

"To make the churches and church agencies aware of common problems and opportunities and to encourage exchange among Christian groups is insufficient unity in the field of social welfare."

Division of Home Missions

"The Committee on Home Missions Institutions provides an opportunity for national administrators of home mission schools, hospitals, and community centers under the various home mission boards, to share information and experience and to plan together and to study areas of common concern," reads the report for 1953-54, presented to the Biennial Assembly of the National Council, December, 1954.

This Committee is "concerned with criteria for difficult types of church-supported institutions. Criteria for community centers are being developed and the Committee is working with the Department of Social Welfare of the National Council in developing" these criteria and others for other types of institutions.

The Committee has co-operated with the Department of Social Welfare in preparing for the National Conference on the Churches and Social Welfare, noted above, and this has been one of its major activities in recent years.

Other projects which the Committee has undertaken include a complete listing of all home mission institutions of various types in all fields . . . , a study of principles and practices in the transfer of mission projects to public agencies; and a study of opportunities for training for church social work.

78

The National Migrant Committee which is a part of this division functions with the following purpose:

> In the migrant ministry the churches are united to serve men, women, and children who are following the crops. The program is centered in the Christian faith and seeks to share that faith with the migrant, and to develop in him a sense of his personal worth, belonging, and responsibility. It seeks to awaken the community to the opportunity and obligation of sharing equally all the protective benefits and warmth of community life. It challenges the local churches to include these seasonal neighbors in their concern and full fellowship. It calls on the state and nation to apply Christian principles to the economy in which migrants live and work.

Activities of the division include the following:

The Extension Unit of the Department of the Town and Country Church ministers to sharecroppers and low-income families through services rendered to their pastors. Six full-time field workers have been employed.

The Department of the Urban Church has administered the work of the Committee on Ministry to Defense Committees. More than 300,000 contacts with migrant industrial workers and their families have been reported by the field staff, co-ordinated by "minister-directors" of the committee in three areas. The department has continuing responsibility in this field.

Both these departments encourage co-operative planning of their constituents in the meeting of human needs, and both co-operated in planning the National Conference at Cleveland, 1955.

The Committee on Indian Work has assisted in various recent new efforts to meet the social needs of Indian people, especially among Indians who have gone to cities. Directly under the committee's supervision is a Christian center in Rapid City, South Dakota. The committee co-operated in setting up a center in Minneapolis and St. Paul, Minnesota. Many other details will be found in the *Biennial Report, 1954*, National Council of Churches.

We have, in the preceding description of the National Council of Churches, made reference to some of the interdenominational structures which exist to implement the churches' concern in social welfare. Some are developed in terms of services to particular groups of people, others around particular kinds of services.

We turn, then, to a description of some of the major functional areas of concern. These programs, although welfare in nature, are closely interwoven within the churches' spiritual ministry and generally fall outside the usual concern of the professional social work structure.

These descriptions, though selective and brief, may be sufficient to indicate some important and distinctive expressions of the churches' interest in social welfare.

Migrants

Perhaps one of the best examples of a distinctive, highly organized social service activity of the churches is the ministry to migrant labor. It has grown up as an area of work reaching from the level of national church organizations and has caught the imagination of many church people and of many people outside the church.

No one, including the U. S. Government, knows exactly how many migrant workers there are in the nation. It is estimated there are between 1,000,000 and 2,500,000. In composition they range from Southern Negro to Bahamians, Puerto Ricans, Mexican "wetbacks," and poor native whites. Their homes, if such they can be called, "are where the crops are ripe."[2] Their attitude toward themselves is poignantly stated in the utterance of a New Jersey tomato picker who told a newspaperman in 1952: "Of all the forgotten men, I guess we're the most forgottenest."[3]

That attitude is changing rapidly, for a study of the activities and results achieved by the Migrant Ministry of the Division of Home Missions of the National Council of the Churches of Christ in the U.S.A. reveals an ever-broadening scope of activity, not only to convince the migrant he is not "forgotten" but to get him to "remember" he is a human being.

In 1920 the Council of Women for Home Missions began working with agricultural migrants. When the Council of Women merged with the Home Missions Council in 1940, men began to contribute important support to the task, but church women remained dominant in the field. Approximately three-fifths of the funds for this purpose are raised by offerings gathered in Protestant churches the first Friday in Lent. The balance of the funds come from twenty-three Protestant home missions boards.

Concretely, among the accomplishments brought about by the years of work by the National Council in this field—by acting as a "spark plug" to ignite national and local authorities into action—the following have been accomplished since 1950:

1. The appointment by the President of a Federal Committee on Migratory Labor, to aid various federal agencies in mobilizing and stimulating more effective programs for migrant workers, and to provide services to state and local areas.[4]

2. The U. S. Children's Bureau, the U. S. Office of Education and the U. S. Public Health Service organized a conference in May, 1954, of representatives of public and private agencies on the East Coast to plan and provide for services to migratory workers. This was followed by a broader conference in September.

3. As a result of the above action, the Farm Placement Service has started a program to stimulate local communities to extend local services and facilities to migrants, heretofore refused or excluded from such services.

80

4. The U. S. Bureau of Labor Standards has started a program to aid states in establishing Migrant Labor Bureaus.

5. The National Council was instrumental in helping liberalize the Social Security laws to extend to migrant labor the right to collect Social Security benefits nationally after the worker has worked for one grower long enough to earn $100.00. There are efforts under way to further liberalize Federal welfare laws to cover migrants.

It had been long recognized by home mission workers in the migrant field that before much could be done regarding the over-all plight of the migrant, a big hurdle to be overcome was bringing local citizens of farming communities to a more friendly attitude toward the annually appearing migrants.

> The public acknowledges the existence of migrants, yet declines to accept them as full members of the community. As crops ripen, farmers anxiously await their coming; as the harvest closes, the community, with equal anxiety, awaits their going.[5]

Big strides have been made in this respect. Communities now are changing their attitudes, due principally to the slow, painstaking efforts of home mission workers. Some communities have learned to welcome the annual influx of field workers and their families.

One of the potent weapons of the home mission workers in coping with the seemingly insurmountable problem of helping a floating, rootless, and in the main, illiterate population is the use of the "Harvester"—a station wagon carrying a folding organ, a communion service and folding altar; craft materials, books, first aid supplies, sports equipment, a motion picture projector and movies, and a record player. Wide areas are covered by the Harvesters each year, especially as their numbers increase (there were twenty-two in February, 1955). Three hundred thousand miles are covered and scores of thousands of migrants are reached annually.

While these methods are highly effective, the basic approach is through the local church, the local minister (who is given the migrant area to administer to during the harvesting season) and, of course, the field workers and volunteers of the Division of Home Missions. A perusal of reports submitted to the National Council by staff workers from farming areas throughout the country reveals that with each passing year as the crops ripen, more and more church people are turning up as volunteer workers, and importantly, more public agencies and officials are taking a constructive attitude toward the migrant. This is a drastic change from the picture a magazine writer presented in 1952:

> Social Security, child labor laws, medical care for the indigent, collective bargaining, minimum wage laws, housing standards and sanitation codes—none of these apply to him. . . . His

children remain uneducated, and his illiteracy rate is 60 per cent. He is usually at the mercy of the labor 'contractor' who often cheats him; the gambler, the prostitute, and the dope peddler dog his wanderings. Despite his vast contribution to our economic welfare, he is not accepted as a member of any community.[6]

True, according to surveys conducted by the Division of Home Missions, many of the basic ills still persist; there is much mistreatment; generally there is still a plague of bad housing. The minimum wage laws do not protect the migrant. But, on the other hand, conditions have measurably improved through the efforts of the church workers. The labor "contractor," for instance, has been dealt a harsh blow through the actions of the U. S. Farm Placement Service, which now watches the labor supply situation closely and each year estimates how many workers will be needed in a given area—thus acting as a buffer against the kind of contractor who in the past used to overload a region for his own purposes.

Child labor is still a thorn in the side of the field workers of the Division of Home Missions. In many instances it is the man and wife of the migrant family that has to be "worked on" to keep the children away from the fields. In other instances it is the calloused grower who closes his eyes to children toiling under the hot sun during harvest. Another big problem that adds to the difficult situation is the lack of strong child labor laws in many states; while the general child labor laws prohibit regular employment of children, there are sufficient "seasonal" laws that allow children to be sent into the field through the large existing loop holes.

> . . . I have seen children as young as seven laboring all day under the torturing heat of the sun—110 degrees heat—which I thought I could not endure for an hour. This is done to about 1,000 underaged children in Pennsylvania each summer in known violation of a state law. . . . The children's sweatshops in the sun have to be seen and felt before the horror of them can be believed.[7]

While disappointing reports reach Home Missions headquarters from field workers in some areas, sharp improvements are constantly recorded elsewhere, more than offsetting the negative conditions. The Division of Home Missions reported last February these developments:

1. Six states have established commissions or committees on migrant labor—New York, New Jersey, Pennsylvania, Wisconsin, Michigan, and Colorado. (Some of the worst offenders were among these states).

2. New York has a new law which provides that crew leaders (often merciless toward their crews) must be registered and certified. The state Health Department has adopted more rigid stand-

ards for camps. The state also took over child care centers handling 800 children which had been started by the Home Missions Council of North America years ago.

3. New Jersey now inspects several thousand migrant camps each year—as does Pennsylvania—and both conduct migrant clinics. Pennsylvania launched its first state-operated child care program in 1953.

These are impressive results in this different field. A field report to the Migrant Committee, quite typical of the work being performed nationally, reveals in figures and facts what some of these accomplishments are in the central states' region.

> Work was carried on in 52 different communities each having its own local committee with a combined membership of 689 people. Eight of these projects were new. Helping them and the staff were 1,116 volunteers who gave time and energy to direct work with the migrants. The combined expenses of the work in these local communities was $41,000. Added to this were duplicated expenditures by the Division of Home Missions of nearly $39,000, making a total of $80,-000 expended. The work was carried on in ten states, with developing work in four more. There are nine active state committees with a membership of 80 people. Used in this region were five Harvesters, one staff car, and twenty-nine additional temporary Harvesters owned and operated by local projects. . . . On the whole here in the central states this has been a year of real problems and great progress. (The central states region of the Home Missions program include Arizona, Illinois, Indiana, Michigan, Minnesota, New Mexico, North Dakota, Ohio, Texas, and Wisconsin.)

Manifestly, even if the staff of the migrant industry were a hundred times its present size and the number of volunteers increased tenfold—the tremendous areas involved, the number of migrants involved and the difficult social problems encompassed could only be scratched on the surface. So the church workers in this field have adopted the policy of what amounts to "encouragement by example," and it has been fruitful, indeed. This policy is one of establishing pilot projects, such as child care centers, schools, improvement of housing conditions, etc. and by demonstrating to growers, public authorities, and migrants that there is a better way of living—and that everyone fares better for living better. These pilot projects are increasingly being taken over and sponsored by growers, communities, and states.

The role of the churches in social welfare appears here to be above all that of the initiator and stimulator. As in the past, the church has often stepped into the breach to meet unmet needs, the migrant program today continues that tradition.

Indian Americans

Another specialized welfare effort of the churches has been the ministry to Indian Americans. On the whole, it is well known to the people in the churches, having been the subject of periodic mission study books.

It is very difficult to separate the welfare services from the other activities of the church program for Indians. It can be said that, in general, the entire program has been aimed at the welfare of the Indian, with emphasis upon meeting both his spiritual and material needs. To see this over-all approach of the churches to the needs of Indian Americans it seems desirable to look at the total Indian work in brief summary form.

Essentially, the Protestant churches work among the 400,000 Indians of the nation and perform the role of counsellor and spiritual guide to them. Missionary work among the Indians dates back literally to the discovery of the continent by Christopher Columbus. On his second voyage in 1493 he brought twelve missionaries under Bernardo Buil, a Benedictine, to bring Catholicism to the Indians. Later explorers brought priests with them. The colonials at Plymouth used the ministry effectively in establishing peaceful relations with surrounding Indians and brought many of them into the church.

The Division of Home Missions has a full department devoted to Christian work among Indian Americans. Corey estimates that one-half of the nation's 400,000 Indians have "been reached by the church," while on the other hand, the 1952 government census estimated that 97 per cent are "connected with Christian churches."

That latter estimate seems to be over optimistic, according to experts among the missionary workers, but it is generally agreed that the church constitutes one of the greatest single influences upon the lives of these original Americans.

G. E. Lindquist, in a factual study of church work in this field, reported 215 church projects, ranging from church buildings, sanctuaries, parish halls, plus 107 Sunday schools, "and others" in existence in 1950 under the auspices or guidance of the Division of Home Missions.[8]

Approximately 15,100 Indians attended these church functions. Meanwhile, Christian training is provided for 5,000 Indian students in off-reservation government boarding schools in Alaska, Arizona, California, Kansas, New Mexico, North Dakota, Oklahoma, Oregon, South Dakota, and Utah. The Home Mission organization conducts important activities in its Indian Christian leaders training program, training young Indians of all denominations. The Cook Christan traning school at Phoenix, Arizona, is open to all young adult Indians for this special schooling.

In 1950, there were thirty-six different denominations

engaged in some form of missionary work among the Indians in the nation. Of these, 15 were constituent members of the Home Missions Council. These do not include separate societies within some denomination where special units responsible for mission schools, hospitals, women's work, etc., have been set up. These figures can be contrasted to a survey conducted in 1930 which showed 23 denominations listed and six nondenominational groups working among Indian Americans . . . (Today, 1950) These various denominations and societies carry on some form of missionary activity in 375 communities, including reservations and tribes.[9]

From what can be gathered from various surveys conducted by those engaged in this field of missionary work, the multitude of projects, ranging from Indian Protestant denominational churches, to hospitals, schools, etc., the total number of Indians reached by some form of contact is in excess of 200,000.

The perspective of the Division of Home Missions in the realm of Indian work, according to I. George Nace, executive secretary of the division, is a gradual shift of church interest from church-established and church-conducted projects toward more concentration on religious training. The aim is to have community and government agencies assume responsibility for established projects so that missionary workers can concentrate more effectively upon Christian education work. Meanwhile, the Division of Home Missions is directing its attention toward a campaign among public officials who propose to "sever" all government responsibility for the Indians and integrate them more completely into the body of the U. S. population. Generally, there is little or no opposition to this "severing" proposal called for in the laws passed and others in the congressional hopper—but there is concern as to how this is to be brought about.

> The church has stood for justice in the face of exploitation. It stands today in a unique position to urge full participation on the part of the Indians themselves in the preparation of the legislation affecting them.[10]

It is apparent that the role of the churches in social welfare activities for Indians has been closely related to their missionary interests. Missionaries have tried to provide for meeting health and welfare needs as well as providing opportunities for worship and religious instruction. Hospitals, clinics, schools, and homes have developed as part of the efforts to reach the Indian with the Christian gospel.

Now the whole missionary approach to the Indian Americans must be reappraised and perhaps reshaped in view of the changing situation confronting the Indians. It is not the task of this summary to predict the changes which will develop in social welfare.

85

Perhaps the future will find the churches concentrating on "religion" with assignment of welfare activities to other than religious agencies, as has been intimated above. On the other hand, the churches may discover that any attempt to redefine their role in this period of change will call for increased social welfare concern. At least, it can be said that any redefinition of role cannot overlook the social welfare aspects of the church program for Indian Americans.

Church World Service

Church World Service is an important, specially organized co-operative welfare effort of the churches. It is an expression of the social concern of the churches which, literally, reaches around the world.

Material relief and spiritual assistance to the needy on an international scale is the prime function of the Department of Church World Service of the National Council of Churches.

CWS was supported by eighteen member denominations and seven co-operating communions according to its latest official Board of Managers Report, issued for the year 1954.

Reporting on developments in CWS during the period 1950-54, the Board of Managers stated in its summary for 1954:

> During these four years, practically every denomination related to CWS has completed the process of incorporating within its denominational structure provision for raising and administering relief and reconstruction funds. The patterns vary, but the common fact gives reasonable stability to CWS.

The report states further:

> Because relief and reconstruction have been a comparatively recent concern of the denominations and CWS was established by them very early in the postwar period, a larger proportion of total denominational expenditures for such purposes is channeled through CWS than is the case with any other large unit of the National Council. Of reported total contributions of $7,592,555 for this purpose received by the denominations in their budget years in which the 1953 One Great Hour of Sharing occurred, $1,468,000 was channeled through this department [CWS].[11]

As to further expenditures, the report states " . . . in 1954, out of a total of $8,099,176 spent by the various units of the National Council of Churches, $1,897,794 or over 23 per cent was spent through Church World Service. . . . "

With the passage of the Agricultural Trade Development and Assistance Act of 1954, CWS became one of a group of relief organizations which undertook to ship and place in the hands of the needy of Europe, Asia, and other trouble spots of the world, some $150,000,000 of government surplus commodities over a three year period. This called for a drastic expansion of CWS personnel and a widening of its program.

CWS undertook as part of its immigration services program for 1954 (1) service to persons already resettled in this country needing medical, rehabilitation, or other assistance,[12] (2) resettlement of persons eligible to immigrate to the United States under the regular immigration quotas and Section 3 (c) of Displaced Persons Act of 1948, (3) service to orphans who came under CWS sponsorship, (4) co-operation with persons in the United States in the migration to South America of their friends and relatives from China, and (5) participation with the voluntary agencies in migration, refugee, and related matters.

Specific accomplishments in this vital field were reported to the migrant committee as follows:

> During 1954 we initiated or reactivated 10,202 applications for immigration covering approximately 21,000 persons, bringing our total case load to 12,549 for approximately 24,000 persons. Our first Assurance was forwarded to Washington in April and by the end of the year we had secured and endorsed 2,613 Assurances covering 5,148 refugees and, in addition, began processing 440 cases (covering 650 refugees) for whom Assurances were filed directly with the Government by sponsors or organizations relying on CWS-NCC for processing and transportation, making a total of 3,053 Assurances for 5,798 refugees. During 1954 we received a total of 1,051 arrivals of whom 115 were visaed under the RRA.[13]

The material relief program of CWS totaled shipments in 1954 of 15,324 tons of clothing, bedding, medicines, vitamins, cotton, and other relief goods valued at more than twelve million dollars. Through CROP (Christian Rural Overseas Program), needy in fourteen nations were aided.

On virtually every front, ranging from the vast material shipments, to securing refuge and transportation for resettlement for thousands of displaced persons or refugees, CWS reaches out and brings spiritual aid and physical comfort to countless persons. Small but significant projects include sanitoriums and hospital treatment in Switzerland for pastors and church workers from countries where adequate medical facilities are not available. Others in this category receive special grants toward treatment in their countries of residence. Travel expenses and scholarships are provided for theological students and fellows from Europe, Asia, and Africa. Churches, church institutions and missions of Asia and Europe likewise receive help through CWS.

Like the migrant program, Church World Service provides an illustration of a program initiated to meet special needs. It has come to provide an example of efficient service in its areas of service and is now recognized and used as a service channel for many nonchurch agencies.

Pastoral Services

The Department of Pastoral Services of the National Council of Churches provides another example of specialized organization with social service interests which has developed within the churches.

This department's chief concern is to assist ministers in being more effective in their professions. It is recognized today that individuals are living under increased tensions and strains, and are more generally in need of competent advice and assistance. Ministers are being called upon to counsel persons in crisis situations. The department is constantly seeking ways to make the services of the pastor more effective to his parishioners and to his community.

The department does not sponsor, in the strictest sense of the word, any direct service program. It considers its chief function to be advisory and educative. This generally takes two forms. The first would be one of sitting down with the staff of a council of churches to assist them in clarifying their role in a problem which would be concerned with the Council's effectiveness in an area of pastoral services. The second would be the dissemination of information for the churches' guidance in working in areas of need where the spiritual assets and other resources are valuable. Since the department does its most extensive work in these two areas, it will meet, or provide material, upon request, to a wide variety of organizations including appropriate private groups and public agencies. Since the department is an integral part of the National Council, it usually works through a state organization when assisting a local organization of that state.

The department functions through three commissions. The first of these is the General Commission: The Department of Pastoral Services. In this area the department has exercised leadership in the provision of specialized forms of education and training in pastoral counseling. It has also conducted and published studies on special subjects of concern to the churches and of concern to theologians doing pastoral counseling. Along with their interest in developing standards for training in pastoral counseling, an annual catalogue is published, which lists courses offered in theological seminaries in the United States on pastoral psychology, pastoral counseling, group dynamics, clinical pastoral training, clinical psychology and guidance.[14] In order to provide a more critical basis for determining necessary training, the department is supervising a special research project in pastoral counseling. It also works closely with the Council for Clinical Training and the Institute for Pastoral Care. The department co-operates with professional schools engaged in the study of problems which are of concern to the churches. This would include such things as problems relating to the use of alcohol, sex education, and narcotic addiction. Often the department will act as a nominating agent in clearing applications of clergy for attendance at these schools. For instance, the department serves as the clearing agency between the churches and the Yale School of Alcohol Studies.

The second unit is the Commission on Religion and Health. The department is most often called upon to provide consultant help in the area of religion and health since most church organizations have already incorporated this interest in their structure. Due to the increasing awareness of the relevance of spiritual assets in dealing with problems of mental health, the department has supervised the writing and publication of *The Church and Mental Health.* The department also did an extensive and comprehensive study in both the United States and Europe in the field of spiritual healing. The findings of this study have been made available to the ministry. Another valuable contribution is the sponsoring of programs and conferences dealing with the interpretation of the relationship of pastors to other professions. For example, the department was instrumental in organizing the St. Louis Conference of Ministry Students and Medical Students.

The third unit is the Commission on Ministry and Institutions. This area of work is becoming increasingly important since 25 per cent of the population receives some type of institutional care every year. The department feels a growing obligation to alert people of the churches to the size of the institutional population in the United States, to the consequent acute needs that these people have, and to the effect of this total problem on our society.

The department meets this challenge in two ways. It uses all mass communication media available to it to explain the situation and to demonstrate the ways that church people can be effective in their relationships with institutionalized persons. In working with the institutions, the department often serves as an adviser in the method of incorporating spiritual guidance into the program. In connection with this, it has established specific standards for chaplaincy in institutions.[15] The department is asked to recommend ministers to serve as chaplains in a variety of institutions. It frequently advises on methods of initiating chaplaincy services in institutions. An outstanding example of its influence in providing chaplaincy service is its co-operation with the U. S. Department of Justice, Bureau of Prisons. The Bureau of Prisons recognized the important service of chaplains in its penal institutions, but, to be effective certain specific standards were needed. It was felt that chaplains could provide help to people while in prison, and because of the high rate of recidivism, to prepare these people for their return to everyday life.

Upon request, therefore, the Department of Pastoral Services reviews applications for all chaplains of federal prisons, and makes recommendations to the Bureau of Prisons for hiring chaplains. The chaplains in this way can relate both to the Bureau of Prisons and, by use of a monthly report system, to the Department of Pastoral Services. This pattern has proved so successful that the department is now often asked to participate in the development of more effective penal systems in state institutions and the institutions in foreign countries. In addition, the department has a concern for the increased rate of juvenile delinquency. Here it concerns itself with the dynamic structure of delinquency and demonstrates this interest in the promotion of chaplaincy service in specialized institutions.

The important role of this department appears to be that of helping professional church leaders render more valuable service not only in their churches but in co-operation with existing social welfare agencies. While increasing the effectiveness of the minister, it also enables him to know and utilize available resources in the field of social work. It also seems to provide liaison between the churches and numerous organizations in the total field of social welfare.

We have, in this chapter, described some of the interdenominationally organized interests in welfare on the national level. Now we turn to a discussion of interdenominational organizations on the state and local level.

FOOTNOTES FOR CHAPTER 7

1 *Biennial Report, 1954;* National Council of Churches (New York: National Council of Churches, 1954).

2 Paul Marcus, "The Ladies Had an Answer," *The Saturday Evening Post,* October 4, 1952.

3 *Ibid.*

4 The General Board of the National Council of Churches, upon recommendation of the Division of Home Missions, proposed Presidential appointment of such a committee in a statement issued in September, 1951. *Biennial Report, 1952,* pp. 26–27.

5 *Migratory Labor in American Agriculture* (Washington, D. C., U. S. Government Printing Office, 1951).

6 Marcus, *op. cit.*

7 Cyrus H. Karraker, chairman of the Pennsylvania Citizens Committee on Migrant Labor, "Life Off the Academic Manor," *Friends Intelligencer,* Vol. III, No. 14, April 3, 1954, p. 2.

8 Gustavus E. F. Lindquist, *Indians in Transition* (New York: Division of Home Missions, National Council of the Churches of Christ in the U. S. A., 1951), p. 35.

9 *Ibid.*

10 E. Russell Carter, Editorial, *National Council Outlook,* Vol. V, No. 2, Feb., 1955 (New York: National Council of Churches of Christ in the U. S. A., 1955).

[11] Report of Executive Director to Board of Managers, CWS, 1954, (Mimeographed), p. 9.

[12] In the main, this service is rendered through the denominations but frequently the direct co-operation or assistance of Church World Service is required.

[13] *Ibid.*, p. 34.

[14] See *Opportunities for Study, Training, and Experience in Pastoral Psychology, 1955* (New York: The Department of Pastoral Services, National Council of the Churches of Christ in the U. S. A., 1955).

[15] "Standards for Chaplaincy Service in Institutions" (New York: 1950. Commission on Ministry in Institutions, National Council of the Churches of Christ in the U.S.A., 1955).

From the very beginning, councils of churches have been interested in social welfare work. In the early days of the councils, many opportunities for social service were open to them. In fact, it has been pointed out that social reform and meeting social needs were major factors in the development of church councils. H. Paul Douglass said:

> It thus turned out that these leaders of the co-operative [church] movement made a recognized place for themselves among the pioneers of the American social thought. . . . In such hands, social motive was the primary dynamic of co-operation. So great a challenge could be met only by united effort. It was simply assumed that a socially motivated church could not be sectarian. . . . The difference was that these leaders were primarily concerned with unity for the sake of power to meet the social challenge of the city and the nation. This they sought without waiting for an organic union of churches; and this they anticipated most hopefully from the various forms of a federative co-operation of churches culminating in the historic church federation movement.[1]

The very rapid growth of the council movement with many new councils and many new workers has put the councils of churches in a position to exercise an important function in social welfare. There are now over 700 state and local councils with volunteer leadership and over 200 with paid staff. The council has become the accepted means of operating co-operatively at the local level for most Protestant churches. There can be no question as to the potential for social welfare activity that exists within the councils.

The social welfare role is recognized and materials are made available to help the councils with the development of their programs. An example is a pamphlet entitled, "The Social Welfare Department of the Local Council of Churches." This pamphlet includes a statement of the objectives of a local council department of social welfare which is quoted here.

1. To provide qualified leadership for guiding the Protestant churches in their total social welfare interests and responsibilities in the community.

2. To supervise such direct social service activities as the council of churches may already have or may later develop. (The purpose here is to co-ordinate the services in the council under one director.)

3. To provide the opportunity for closer co-operation and support of the social service agencies under Protestant auspices.

4. To provide professional social work assistance to denominations and Protestant agencies in matters of welfare policy and planning.

5. To assist local churches and denominations in their Christian social relations (social education and action) programs by interpreting social welfare needs and services.

6. To provide a liaison service between Protestant churches and the public and private social agencies of a community. To help the churches and social agencies make use of one another's services in assisting families and individuals with their problems.

7. To interpret to social agencies, public and private, the resources of the churches and the reconstructive values in the Christian religion for personal growth and development.

8. To provide a means for social workers in all types of agencies to think through the implications inherent in the concept of Christian vocation.[2]

The above list can be considered as representative of the thinking of a large group of council leaders and would still reflect the basic purpose of the councils in the field of social work.

It is also of interest to note in the same pamphlet a statement of the functions of the department of social welfare in a council of churches. No claim is made that this is an exhaustive list of functions, but it is indicative of the type of activity that church council leaders think is important and that they recommend to councils at the local level. The statement of functions follows:

INFORMATION AND REFERRAL SERVICE

This service may be carried by the director of the department, along with his other duties. Usually, however, a full-time church social worker, trained in casework, is in charge. A major part of the service is in assisting churches to make use of the social services in the community for people who come to them for help. Likewise, the social agencies are assisted to make use of the religious and social resources of the churches for persons who are clients of the agencies.

In addition the Information and Referral Service:

1. Assists churches in planning meetings by providing factual information on local social problems.

2. Provides help to the churches in understanding the problems in their own parish and assists them in co-operating with other churches and agencies in working for improvements.

3. Helps to secure speakers on welfare problems and agency programs.

4. Arranges "Go-and-See" tours to agencies.

5. Assists in developing social education projects of a constructive type, particularly to meet the social service interests of churches at Thanksgiving and Christmas.

6. Helps the churches keep clear of charity rackets by providing information on all social agencies requesting financial contributions from churches.[3]

The pamphlet also indicates the fact that not all aspects of the social welfare role are clearly defined for the councils. There are arguments presented on both sides of the question of direct sponsorship of social service functions. By direct social services, the authors mean "such programs as juvenile court work, Big Brother and Big Sister programs and social service institutions." It is apparent that the two series of arguments reflect basically different points of view. Since the role of the councils in the social welfare field cannot be fully understood without recognizing this conflict as to functions, the following quotation is included here.

Some arguments that have been advanced favoring direct social service activities by councils of churches are as follows:

1. The council should carry on social service activities to demonstrate a need. The purpose of such a program is to have it taken over by the community after it has proven its value. Examples: a casework service for children and youth that has as its goal the development of a professional casework service in the probation department, or a visiting teacher program with the public schools.

2. The council should have direct social service programs as major social education projects for the churches of the city. They thus become a medium for interpreting modern social work programs to church members and thereby help to develop understanding and support for other programs public and private.

3. Such a program gives the churches an active part in social services and makes possible participation and representation in community planning along with civic groups and other religious faiths. (For example: membership in the Council of Social Agencies.)

4. This program provides an opportunity for using the resources of religion in the readjustment of individuals and should stimulate the use of the resources of the churches by other community agencies.

The following are arguments that have been given against social service activities in a council of churches.

1. The direct social services of the council are a competitive factor with other agencies in the community for the interest of church members.

This may limit the council in giving leadership in the total welfare field.

2. The function of the church is in the field of social education and action rather than in administering social services.

3. The church's primary task is to motivate people to support community services, serve on boards of directors, and assist in community chest drives, etc.[4]

This statement of purpose and function, together with the arguments for and against "direct social service" presents a background against which to consider the actual role of the councils in social welfare today.

In order to study the social welfare and social education and action activities of church councils a questionnaire was sent to all state and local councils of churches. The questionnaire was developed to parallel the instrument used in studying the councils of church women.[5]

The questionnaire, which appears in the appendix, consisted of two parts. The first part, dealing with more general aspects of the councils social welfare activity, was filled out by the general secretary. The second section was answered by the staff executive of each department or unit of the council with primary responsibility in social education and action or social welfare.

While the questionnaire was sent to all councils, including those with volunteer leadership, analysis is limited here to the councils with paid staff. There are several reasons for this limitation. The per cent of returns from the councils with volunteer leadership was

Table T-1

TOTAL NUMBER AND RESPONDING NUMBER AND PER CENT OF COUNCILS OF CHURCHES BY GEOGRAPHIC DIVISION

	Total number of Councils	Responding Councils	
		Number	Per cent
United States	212 (40)*	107 (22)	50
New England	32 (6)	15 (4)	47
Middle Atlantic	44 (4)	18 (2)	41
East North Central	47 (5)	20 (2)	43
West North Central	19 (7)	12 (4)	63
South Atlantic	19 (6)	6 (3)	32
East South Central	7 (2)	4 (1)	57
West South Central	11 (2)	9 (1)	82
Mountain	7 (3)	5 (2)	71
Pacific	26 (5)	18 (3)	69

* Numbers in parentheses indicate state councils.

unsatisfactory. Furthermore, a survey of those returned appears to indicate that the councils of churches with volunteer leadership parallel the councils of church women in their pattern of social welfare and social action programs. Therefore, in the following analysis, councils of churches refers to councils with paid staff.

There was a return of 50 per cent of the mailed questionnaires. Of the 212 sent out, 107 were returned completed. These were fairly well distributed geographically as is shown in Table T-1. The smallest return was from the South Atlantic division while the highest was from West-South Central with return from 82 per cent of all councils.

The present report is a preliminary analysis prepared in a limited period of time for inclusion in this document. Only the analysis which will describe the nature and scope of the social welfare role of the councils in a very broad manner are included here. More extensive analysis will be possible on the basis of data available but was impossible in the time available.

Furthermore, it should be pointed out that the possibility of generalizing from the data available from the questionnaires returned is limited. A very brief check of the councils returning questionnaires and those failing to do so indicates the possible presence of certain selective factors. It appears, for example, that larger councils with more adequate staff resources were more apt to complete the questionnaire. This is easy to understand but poses a real question as to the wisdom of broad generalizations. It seems best to say that the findings apply for the councils reporting and may be fairly typical of all the councils with paid staff.

It is of interest to note first of all that most of the councils deal with subjects of social concern in their regular programs. This was true of all the state councils and most of the local councils. Ninety-nine of the 107 councils reporting indicated such concerns. This represented 92 per cent. There is some indication of relationship between the size of the community in which the council is located and the presence of a program of social concern but the percentage is too high in all size categories to make this really significant. Table T-2 presents a summary of this pattern.

There is, of course, no way to relate this high rate of social concern to the history of the particular councils reporting. It would be interesting to know whether these councils, or some of them at least, came into being as the result of a desire on the part of churches to co-operate in solving social problems as was said to be true of many councils in the H. Paul Douglass quotation, which appeared earlier in this chapter. (p. 92) On the other hand, it may simply indicate that churches working co-operatively in councils seek to express their common concerns in attempts to implement the Christian gospel in areas of social education and action and social wel-

Table T-2

NUMBER OF COUNCILS WHICH DEAL WITH SUBJECTS
OF SOCIAL CONCERN BY SIZE OF COMMUNITY

	Number replies	Dealing with subjects of social concern		Not dealing with subjects of social concern	
		Number	Per cent	Number	Per cent
State Councils	22	22	100	—	0
Local Councils					
Population under 25,000	3	2	67	1	33
Population 25,000-100,000	20	17	85	3	15
Population 100,000-500,000	44	42	95	2	5
Population 500,000 or more	16	14	88	2	12
Population not given	2	2	100	—	0
	107	99	92.5	8	7.5

fare. It can at least be said that councils of churches definitely seem to express social concern pretty generally.

Furthermore, it is almost equally true in all parts of the country that the councils have the concern for social issues (Table T-3).

Table T-3

COUNCILS DEALING WITH SUBJECTS OF SOCIAL
CONCERN BY GEOGRAPHIC REGION

	Number replies	Dealing with subjects of social concern		Not dealing with subjects of social concern	
		Number	Per cent	Number	Per cent
New England	15	11	73	4	17
Middle Atlantic	18	17	94	1	6
East North Central	20	20	100	—	0
West North Central	12	12	100	—	0
South Atlantic	6	5	83	1	17
East South Central	4	3	75	1	25
West South Central	9	8	89	1	11
Mountain	5	5	100	—	0
Pacific	18	18	100	—	0
Total United States	107	99	92.5	8	7.5

New England and the East-South Central regions show the lowest percentage with an affirmative answer to the question about social concern, but even in these regions, three-fourths of the councils replied that they dealt with such concerns.

It should be mentioned here that the questionnaire was designed to make it easy for councils which do not deal with social concerns to submit their negative answer. This question came on the first page preceded only by a few identifying questions. If the council had no social education or action or social welfare program, the negative answer was checked and the form was returned without further work. A brief check of a sample of councils not returning questionnaires indicated that a very high percentage of these councils dealt with social concerns.

The councils reported that they employ 202 paid staff members who have primary responsibilities in the social education and action or social welfare field. These included both full-time and part-time staff members. Of these 202 individuals, 35 were employed by state councils, and the remainder at the local level. The larger the community, the more people are employed in social service activities, as would be expected. No councils in communities with less than 25,000 population reported that they employ workers with primary responsibilities in the field.

Of this group of council employees it was reported that 129 or about 64 per cent were ordained. There is no way of telling how many were women and ineligible for ordination, but it can be assumed on the basis of general observation that some of this group are women and, therefore, an even higher per cent of the men in the field are ordained. It is known that in some cases, ordination is a requirement for a position of this type.

Relatively few of the council workers in areas of social concern have social work degrees. Twenty-five, or 13 per cent, were so listed. While the absence of a social work degree does not mean an absence of training in the field, it is true, nevertheless, that the degree would be required by many professional agencies, and obviously is not a requirement with the councils.

It should be pointed out, however, that many of the staff members without social work degrees, and even without much specialized training in the field, become highly skilled technicians in their work and render very effective service. For better or for worse, their basic orientation is, however, usually toward the church and religious rather than professional welfare concepts.

Incidentally, there seemed to be little overlapping between ordination and social work degrees in the reports. In other words, it appeared that most of the holders of social work degrees employed by the councils were not ordained.

A wide variety of positions was indicated by the replies (Table T-5). The councils are employing staff members with primary social service responsibility in positions ranging from council executive to caseworker.

The largest single group is the group employed as chaplains. This seems to indicate a tendency on the part of the councils to try to deal directly with individuals in areas of social need.

Table T-4   NUMBER OF PAID PROFESSIONAL OR EXECUTIVE STAFF WITH PRIMARY RESPONSIBILITY IN SOCIAL SERVICE OR SOCIAL EDUCATION AND ACTION, BY POPULATION OF AREA SERVED

Area Served	Number Employed								Ordained		With social worker's degrees	
	Full-time		Half-time or more		Less than half-time		Total employed					
	Total number	Per-centage	Total number	Per-centage	Total number	Per-centage	Total number	Per-centage	Total number	Per-centage	Total number	Per-centage
State Councils	25	19.4	5	27.7	5	9.1	35	17.3	28	21.7	3	12.0
Under 25,000	—	—	—	—	—	—	—	—	—	—	—	—
25,000-100,000	6	4.7	3	16.7	5	9.1	14	6.9	9	7.0	—	—
100,000-500,000	16	12.4	3	16.7	22	40.0	41	20.3	22	17.0	1	4.0
500,000 or more	82	63.5	7	38.9	23	41.8	112	55.5	70	54.3	21	84.0
Total Number	129	100.0	18	100.0	55	100.0	202	100.0	129	100.0	25	100.0

Table T-20   SOCIAL SERVICE ACTIVITIES OF COUNCILS OF CHURCH WOMEN BY SIZE OF POPULATION

Social Service Activities	Total	Number of Local Councils Serving in Places with Populations of							
		State councils	Less than 2,500	2,500-9,999	10,000-24,999	25,000-99,999	100,000-499,999	500,000 or more	Not given
Councils of church women									
Returning questionnaires	698	31	78	181	142	152	47	14	53
With social concerns	516	31	47	113	109	115	46	13	42
Reporting social service activities	300	24	16	43	55	88	41	12	21
Visits to or entertainment of institutionalized persons	99	9	3	7	18	28	24	7	3
Direct relief as emergency measure	136	10	9	24	24	36	20	6	6
Volunteers for health or welfare agencies	37	4	3	3	—	8	9	8	1
Assistance to community financial drives	101	10	3	9	19	29	17	9	5
Discussion, co-operative planning for social welfare	46	5	—	3	7	16	9	4	1
Representation in community groups	95	8	1	8	17	28	22	6	4
Welfare Council	56	—	—	—	—	—	—	—	—
Community chest	28	—	—	—	—	—	—	—	—
Counsel to church women on health and welfare	33	5	—	3	6	5	8	4	2
Other regular, organized, direct service	69	7	—	7	12	22	15	2	4
Others	90	6	3	16	18	25	8	6	8

Table T-5

TITLES OF SOCIAL SERVICE STAFF
POSITIONS MENTIONED

	Full-time	Half-time or more	Less than half-time
I. SOCIAL SERVICE EXECUTIVES			
a. Assistant General Secretary (primarily social welfare)	—	1	—
Executive Secretary (primarily social welfare)	—	2	—
Minister-co-ordinator (primarily social welfare) ..'	—	1	—
b. Director Christian Social Relations	1	—	—
Director Department of Social Service	5	—	—
Executive Secretary Department Christian Social Relations	—	3	4
Assistant Executive Secretary Department Christian Social Relations	—	1	—
Executive Secretary Community Services Department	1	—	—
Director Council of Church Women and Social Service Department	—	—	—
Director, Department of Social Education and Action	—	—	1
Director, Department of Church and Community	1	—	1
Director, Public Affairs	—	—	1
Director, Family Life Education	1	—	—
Director, Church Youth Service	1	—	—
Secretaries	2	—	—
II. INSTITUTIONAL CHAPLAINS			
Chaplains (no specific designation)	32	1	—
Hospital chaplains	6	1	15
Prison chaplains	3	—	1
Marriage Counsellor in Court	1	—	—
Juvenile Court Chaplain	—	—	2
Protestant Consultant in Children's Court	1	—	—
Old Age Chaplain	—	1	—
Scout Chaplain	—	—	2
Youth House Chaplain	—	—	1
Youth Service Chaplain	1	—	—
III. YOUTH AND DAY CARE CENTER, ETC.			
Supervisor Youth Center	1	—	1
Youth Leaders in Youth Center	8	—	—
Fieldworker	—	—	1
Religious Instructor in Special Institution (Deaf, Blind, etc.)	—	—	—
Staff Day-care and Community Center	10	3	15
Director Friendship House	1	—	—
Caseworkers Youth Service	5	—	—
IV. MIGRANTS AND REFUGEES			
Manager Refugee Office	—	1	—
Director Department of Ministry to Migrants	1	—	—
Executive Migrant Commission	2	—	—
Migrant Supervisor	1	—	—

100

Table T-5 (continued)

	Full-time	Half-time or more	Less than half-time
V. RURAL CHURCH			
Director Rural Church Institute	1	—	—
Director Town and Country	1	—	—
Rural Church Co-ordinator	1	—	—

In answer to the question: "Does your council or any department or committee of your council participate as a member agency of your community's health and welfare council?" There were 67 affirmative answers as compared with 22 "no's" and 9 "no answers"

Table T-6

PARTICIPATION OF CHURCH COUNCILS IN LOCAL
HEALTH AND WELFARE COUNCILS

	Number	Per cent
Councils Participating	67	68
Councils Not Participating	22	23
No Answer	9	9
Total	98	100

In other words, two-thirds of the councils dealing with social concern work as member agencies in the local health and welfare council, by whatever name it may be called. This pattern of relationship must be qualified by stating that in a number of cases the negative responses came from state councils of churches. Thus an even higher per cent of local councils than shown above would be related to their community health and welfare organizations.

Very few of the councils replying to the questionnaire receive financial help from either community or public (tax-supported) funds and only a few receive other-than-financial help from public sources, (Table T-7). Seventy-six of the councils reported no

Table T-7

COUNCILS RECEIVING FINANCIAL AID FROM COMMUNITY
CHESTS AND PUBLIC FUNDS IN TERMS OF SIZE
OF COMMUNITY

	State Councils	Local Councils				
		25,000	25,000-100,000	100,000-500,000	500,000 or more	Total
Receive Financial Aid from Chest Only	1	—	—	1	3	5
Receive Financial Aid from Public Sources Only ..	—	1	—	2	1	4
Both	—	—	—	—	2	2
Total	1	1	0	3	6	11

101

help of any type from these sources. Those receiving help were mostly located in the large communities with population above 700,-000. Six councils did not answer the question.

These figures must be compared with a 1953 survey of Income and Financial Data compiled by Central Department of Field Administration of the National Council of Churches.[6]

In this summary, it appears that 8.2 per cent of the income of 201 local councils came from community chests. Fifteen councils received financial income from these sources while two councils also received city, county, or municipal funds. The summary by the Central Department of Field Administration also showed, by analyzing the data by population of the area that the councils in larger communities were more apt to receive community chest funds.

The broad range of council concerns in the social service field is shown by the listing of departments, committees, and subcommittees of the councils working in the field of social education and action and social welfare. The names of these units and the num-

Table T-8

DEPARTMENTS AND COMMITTEES DEALING WITH
SOCIAL CONCERNS

	Names	Number of times mentioned	Totals
General	Social Education	1	
	Social Action	15	
	Social Education and Action	17	
	Christian Social Relations	14	
	Public Education and Religion	2	
	Christian Life and Work	3	
	Community ministry	1	
	Community co-operation	1	
	Community relations	16	
	Community service	1	
			70
Social Service	Social Service	16	
	Social Welfare	13	
	Social Welfare and Relief	1	
	Social Agencies	1	
	Church/Social Agencies Relations	1	
	Ministers/Social Workers Relations	2	
	Christian Outreach	1	
			35
Civic Affairs	Civic Affairs and/or Public Morals	14	
	Public Relations	4	
	Citizenship	2	
	Civic Projects	1	
	Political Education and Action	1	
	Social Betterment	1	
	Social Issues	1	
			24

Table T-8 (continued)

Names		Number of times mentioned	Totals
Legislative	Legislative	10	
	Legislation and Public Morals	1	
	Legislation and Religious Freedom	1	
	Civic Welfare and Legislation	1	
	Legislative Seminar	1	
	Religious Liberty	1	
			15
Interfaith Relations		3	
			3
Racial and Cultural Relations	Race Relations	10	
	Discrimination	1	
	Brotherhood	1	
	Human Relations	6	
	Intergroup (racial) Relations	1	
			19
Religion and Labor	Industrial Relations	5	
	Labor, Religion and Management	3	
			8
International Relations	International Relations	14	
	World Peace	1	
	Human Rights	1	
	World Friendship (or Fellowship)	4	
	Church World Service	4	
			24
Refugee Resttlement		5	
			5
Migrants		11	
			11
Indian Work		1	
			1
Economic Justice		5	
			5
Housing		1	
			1
Gambling		1	
			1
Alcoholism		3	
			3
Tornado Relief		1	
			1
Service to Men in Service		1	
			1
Institutions Chaplaincy	Hospitals	31	
	Chaplaincy	4	
	Religion and Health	4	
	Pastoral Services	1	
			40

Table T-8 (cont'd.)

Names		Number of times mentioned	Totals
Counseling	Counseling	2	
	Counseling Seminars	1	
	Family Life	3	
	Child Welfare	1	
	Marriage Round Table	1	
			8
Scouting		12	
			12
Courts	Juvenile Courts	4	
	Juvenile delinquency	3	
	Crime and delinquency	1	
			8
Youth Center Program		3	
			3
Other		5	5
Total number of committees, departments, etc. mentioned			307

ber of times each was mentioned are given in Table T-8. In all, 307 different units and committees were mentioned covering many areas of concern and representing both social education and action and social welfare interests.

In addition to these departments and committees, it was indicated that many councils carry on social service activities through regular council units not specifically labeled as social service units. The list of these regular organized units through which service activities are carried on together with the number of councils indicating their type of activity appears in Table T-9.

The second half of the schedule was completed by staff members responsible for social welfare or social education and action committees and departments or by chairman of such units. The questionnaire allowed each individual to check the types of activity in which his unit participated and for each type of activity so checked to indicate the subjects of social concern with which the activities dealt and the types of people for whom the activity was conducted, in other words "the target group." The types of activity reported in relationship to the subject dealt with and the people at whom the activity was aimed are summarized in Table T-10. The most common activities are the distribution of literature and the conduct of study groups and conferences. Racial and cultural relations and social welfare were the most frequent subjects involved and the church people themselves were, in the main, the target group.

The social education and action and social welfare units work through the local churches as a channel of outreach as would be

104

Table T-9

REGULAR COUNCIL UNITS DEALING WITH SOCIAL CONCERN

Name of Unit	Number of times mentioned
Council itself	39
Church Women	12
Men	1
Youth Council	19
Young Adult	
Christian Education	30
Radio and/or T.V.	18
Other	29
C.I.C.E. Newsletter	1
Evangelism	2
Evangelism and devotional services	1
Public relations	1
Press	1
Publications	3
Downtown Interchurch	1
Town and Country Church	5
Urban Church	1
Church Extension and Comity	1
Planning and Adjustment	1
United Church Canvass	2
Overseas Service	1
Christian Rural Overseas Program	1
Community Ministry	1
Indian Work	1
Missions	2
Music	1
Puerto Rican Ministry	2
Number of Units mentioned	148

expected but also rely heavily upon other religious organizations. While many secular noncurch organizations were mentioned, they covered a wide range of types and indicated no pattern of use of such groups as channels of outreach.

Since these channels of outreach were listed in order of importance, it was possible to arrive at a score which indicates roughly the rank order of importance as means of implementing the program. The local church ranked highest and the National Council of Churches and national denominational agencies lowest (Table T-11). It would be assumed that this would be the way in which local councils would operate in putting their program to work at the local level.

Likewise, as would be expected, the councils turn to the National Council most frequently for materials to assist them in carrying out their programs (Table T-12). Thus, there appears a definite communication pattern in which the local or state council acts as intermediary between the national organization and the local churches

Table T-10 SOCIAL EDUCATION AND ACTION ACTIVITIES OF COUNCILS OF CHURCHES BY SUBJECTS TREATED AND TYPES OF PERSONS REACHED

ACTIVITIES	Subjects						Types of People									
	Racial and Cultural Relations	International Affairs	Religious and Civil Liberties	Church and Economic Life	Social Welfare	Not Classifiable	Public in General	Church Members	Local Church Pastors	Laywomen	Laymen	Youth	Youth Leaders	Children	Religious Education Leaders	Community Leaders and Professional Groupings
Prepared or published literature ..	32	20	15	16	33	7	24	35	34	13	8	4	5	1	8	7
Distributed literature	45	37	28	26	45	5	28	52	50	21	15	10	9	2	17	8
Conducted conferences, study groups, etc.	36	35	20	30	46	5	24	47	41	31	24	10	8	1	15	10
Provided speakers	32	26	18	14	36	3	18	38	22	21	12	8	3	3	12	5
Passed resolutions	32	25	22	12	27	3	28	26	18	5	4	—	—	—	4	10
Wrote letters to public officials	26	26	28	11	48	8	14	12	13	8	6	4	4	2	5	28
Made representations to public officials	24	12	19	7	38	5	8	11	11	6	4	—	—	2	2	22
Used mass media	4	4	3	1	6	—	3	3	3	2	2	2	2	—	3	—
Arranged exhibits, dinners, open house, etc.	1	2	—	—	—	—	2	1	1	1	1	2	1	—	—	—
	232	187	153	117	279	36	149	225	193	108	76	40	32	11	66	90

Table T-11

CHANNELS OF OUTREACH THROUGH WHICH THE UNITS
REACHED THE PEOPLE IN THE ABOVE ACTIVITIES

Channels of Outreach	Number of times "channel" was checked or mentioned	Average score
Local churches	96	1.81
Local church societies	61	2.69
Local council of churches	54	2.44
State or regional denominational agencies	34	3.91
State councils of churches	33	3.52
Local denominational agencies	25	3.60
Secular welfare councils or social agencies	16	4.69
National Council of the Churches of Christ in the U.S.A.	15	4.93
National denominational agencies	9	6.56
OTHER. 50 different organizations, associations, councils, mainly secular	71	4.75

and local church organizations, making use of materials prepared by national leaders in their work at the local level.

The councils also report a wide range of *social service* activities as compared with the previous analysis of *social education* and *action* activities. Table T-13 presents a listing of these social service activities with the number of councils or council units participating in such activities. It appears that the councils are not only prepar-

Table T-12

SOURCES OF INFORMATION AND GUIDANCE WHICH THE
UNITS USED IN PLANNING AND CONDUCTING SOCIAL
EDUCATION AND ACTION ACTIVITIES

Sources of Information and Guidance	Number of times "channel" was checked or mentioned	Average score
National Council of the Churches of Christ in the U.S.A.	70	1.77
State councils of churches	44	2.79
Local councils of churches	38	2.71
Local churches	30	3.17
National denominational agencies	27	3.59
State or regional denominational agencies	25	3.64
Secular welfare councils or social agencies	24	2.92
Local denominational agencies	14	3.64
Local church societies	13	5.31
OTHER. 57 different organizations, associations, councils, etc., mainly secular	81	4.30

Table T-13

NUMBER OF COUNCILS OR UNITS OF COUNCILS ENGAGED IN DIFFERENT KINDS OF SOCIAL SERVICE ACTIVITY IN THE PAST TWO YEARS

44 Conducted or arranged for visiting or entertaining *by laymen* of institutionalized persons (in homes, hospitals, prisons, etc.)

36 Gave direct aid (food, clothing, furnishings, money, etc.) to persons or groups in need as an *emergency measure.*

38 Recruited, trained, or referred volunteers for health or welfare agencies.

46 Gave organized assistance to community fund-raising drives. Of those:
    42 assisted community chest or fund
    23 assisted Red Cross
     5 assisted polio campaign
    13 assisted cancer campaign
     9 assisted tuberculosis campaign
     9 assisted crippled children campaign
     9 assisted heart campaign
    14 assisted other drives

52 Organized a channel for discussion and co-operative planning of church and social welfare interests.

75 Represented church social welfare interests in co-ordinated community planning and financing groups.
    63 Welfare council, council of social agencies, etc.
    37 Community fund or chest
    47 Other groups

37 Counseled local church groups on health and welfare matters.

83 Provided ministerial or chaplaincy services in institutions:
    63 in hospitals   40 in homes
    28 in prisons   21 Other: e.g. camps, courts, etc.

---

ing materials and holding discussion groups and so on but are also actively at work in social service. This list further indicates the involvement of the councils in community social service activities.

Regular, organized, direct social service programs of the councils are designed to serve the special needs of people through the program of the councils. This means direct work with and for people with social welfare needs. Such direct services are summarized in Table T-14.

While replies to this question came from only about two-thirds of the council units reporting, these replies show the councils to be participating actively in these direct social service activities.

In this pattern one sees the important role played by the church councils in the whole field of social education and action and social welfare. It appears that national leaders either in interdenominational or denominational work can look to the councils of churches for help and find there, in most cases, a ready made channel for bringing social welfare concerns to the attention of local churches.

Table T-14

REGULAR ORGANIZED DIRECT HEALTH OR WELFARE SERVICES OF 59 COUNCILS OR UNITS OF COUNCILS

21	have referral services
14	offer court services
18	serve migrants, trailer-residents and sharecroppers
6	serve racial or nationality groups
10	provide counseling
3	maintain camp service
8	sponsor homes, day care centers, community centers, etc.
3	render other direct services

When this aspect of the social welfare role of the councils is coupled with the many and varied council activities which provide local churches with an opportunity for the expression of social concerns, the place of the church councils assumes real importance in the over-all Protestant social welfare picture, even though much Protestant welfare activity is still denominationally oriented.

In an effort to discover the proportion of the total program given to the subject of social concern, the respondents to Part 2 of the questionnaire were asked to estimate the per cent of the units' total program given to subjects of social concern. Nearly one-third of the units reported that they devote all of their program to social education and action and social welfare. Table T-15 shows a summary

Table T-15

PER CENT OF PROGRAM GIVEN TO SUBJECTS OF SOCIAL CONCERN BY UNITS OF COUNCILS

	Responsive number	Per cent
100 per cent	37	31.6
75-99 per cent	18	15.4
50-74 per cent	12	10.3
25-49 per cent	17	14.5
Under 25 per cent	33	28.2
	117	100.0
No answers	38	
	155	

of these responses. It is undoubtedly true that these figures reflect the fact that some of the units reporting have primary social service responsibilities while others are regularly organized units of the councils which have social service as one responsibility among many. Even recognizing this difference in the type of unit it can be said that the average unit reporting gives more than half its time to social concerns.

The researchers were requested to seek an estimate of the number of people who participated in or used the materials produced in the social service programs. Obviously, in most cases, the units could only estimate since the very nature of some of the activities precluded the keeping of detailed records. Replies were received from 102 departments or committees in 47 councils. The total estimate of these units was 6,297,659. This is a large number for less than one-fourth of the councils to reach and may reflect the optimism that so often appears in estimates of this kind. However, allowing for some considerable reduction in the estimate, in the interests of conservatism, it is still apparent that the councils of churches are working with and through a large number of people in their programs of social concern.

Further evidence of the scope of the council's participation in social welfare activities is found in the fact that 76 council units representing about 50 councils reported that 9,879 volunteer workers were used in rendering the regular organized *direct* social service program of the councils. The importance of the volunteer is recognized by the councils, and the participation of the councils in social welfare is increased by the use of volunteers.

It is not possible to analyze the use of these volunteers by type of activity but reference to Table T-12 will show the range of types listed by the council units.

Several broad generalizations can be drawn from this analysis—

1. It would appear that the councils of churches are playing an important role in the total Protestant program of social service and social education and action. Both the nature and scope of their activities would seem to point to the councils as a significant factor in the field of church-related social welfare.

2. The councils seem to be involved directly in a number of ways with secular social agencies and may be in an excellent place to represent the churches in the planning and co-ordination of community social service programs.

3. The church councils may well be the channel through which the local church and the local community can best be reached in areas of social concern by leaders in the field. This may apply not only to the implementation of program but also to helping with the development of local policy and structure in the social welfare field.

4. There seems to be no observable tendency for the councils to swing toward a secularly (nonchurch) oriented social service program or to retreat from direct social service leaving the field to professional social welfare agencies. In other words much of the program seems to represent an effort to maintain certain aspects of traditional church-related social service while at the same time working constructively in co-operation with the professional agencies.

FOOTNOTES FOR CHAPTER 8

1 H. Paul Douglass, *Protestant Co-operation in American Cities* (New York: Institute of Social and Religious Research, 1930), p. 47.

2 "The Social Welfare Department in a Local Council of Churches" (New York: Intercouncil Field Department, 1950), p. 2.

3 *Ibid.*, p. 3.

4 *Ibid.*, pp. 4–5.

5 See p. 112 for brief methodological statement under "Councils of Church Women."

6 W. P. Buckwalter, Jr., "Survey of Income and Financial Data" (New York: National Council of the Churches of Christ in the U. S. A., 1953).

9

If it be true that most of the contribution of protestantism in social work is indirect and informal and that the churches' influence on the climate of public thinking toward social welfare is possibly a more significant role of the churches than the direct sponsorship of welfare enterprises—we need somewhere to examine the extent and nature of the operation of protestantism in social welfare in the activities that are not usually taken into account in the consideration of more institutionalized social work.

Some of the social welfare activities of the churches of the less formal kind have been described in other sections of the book. These are integrated within home mission endeavors, the usual responsibilities of the pastor to his church families, and the local church's interdependence as an institution in the community in which it is situated. None of these, however, demonstrates the functioning of lay persons, consciously acting with Christian motivation in social service and social education and action activities to improve the conditions of society.

It is fortunate, therefore, that we have the preliminary findings[1] of a study of the social service and social education and action activities of councils of church women, initiated in May, 1955.

By means of a mailed questionnaire, all of the 1,974 state and local councils of church women were requested to provide information for the study. More than 35 per cent responded promptly enough to be included in the preliminary analysis, and although New England was somewhat over-represented and the West South Central under-represented, the proportions of response from the seven other geographic census divisions were less than 4 per cent removed from the per cent of response for the total. Thirty-one of the fifty state councils and about 35 per cent of the local councils returned questionnaires. More detailed documentation of the geographic representativeness of the study is presented in Table T-19, which may also be of incidental interest in showing where councils of church women are located.

One further note on whether the findings from a study of a little over a third of the councils can be generalized for all councils of church women—generally, questionnaires directed to getting information on particular subjects get disproportionately heavy returns from respondents who are interested in these things. In order to counteract this tendency, we used a device whereby those councils which did not engage in social service or social education and activities could quickly indicate that fact on the first page of the questionnaire and simply mail without having to finish the remaining more than three pages.

A brief historical description of the national organization for interdenominational women's work may help to give the long perspective in our view of today's councils of church women at work in the fields of social service and social education and action:

It is a far cry from the Female Society for Missionary Purposes organized by the Congregational and Baptist women of Boston in 1800, to the 1954 streamlined General Department of United Church Women of the National Council of the Churches of Christ in the United States of America, with 2,000 local councils, and a total budget of $700,000.

In those early days women thought in terms of pennies rather than dollars. They had a long row to hoe before they won the right to speak in a meeting or to vote, but their thoughts and prayers circled the globe then as they do now, and they gave their egg money and their sons and daughters to the mission fields. As they met with women of other communions to study the mission books their sisters had prepared and published, their eyes were opened to needs in their own communities, and they began to think in terms of child welfare, law enforcement, and race relations.

As their interests grew, their numbers grew also, until all over the country there were local interdenominational organizations of church women meeting together for worship, study, and action. Their representatives came together in Boston in 1929 to form the National Council of Federated Church Women. They set up a joint committee to work with the national denominational women's boards through the Council of Women for Home Missions and the Federation of Women's Boards of Foreign Missions and assigned responsibility for their various activities. In 1941 the three bodies came together in one organization, thus joining the two national mission groups with the great local council movement across the country. Out of this union was born the United Council of Church Women, which in 1950 became the General Department of United Church Women of the National Council of the Churches of Christ in the U.S.A., composed of:

Church Women who, with courage and consecration, declare their purpose to be:

"To unite church women in their allegiance to their Lord and Savior, Jesus Christ, through a program looking to their integration in the total life and work of the church and to the building of a world Christian community."

Church Women—Protestant, Evangelical, Orthodox—in local communities, who work together through their denominations, through local councils of church women, and with like-minded groups in the community on problems and issues of mutual concern.

113

Church Women who work together through state councils of church women.

Church Women who work together through the National Council of Churches, and its General Department of United Church Women.[2]

It is within this context of avowedly Christian purpose that the work of councils of church women is undertaken in the areas of concern to this study, which fall primarily within the activities of the Christian Social Relations Committee of the General Department.

This committee, established in 1941 with a grant from the Julius Rosenwald Fund for work in the field of race relations, now encompasses a broad range of social interests. A recent report states:

> We seek to understand and accept our responsibilities as Christian citizens, to *study* the social and economic causes of human need and to *act* to alleviate the causes of misery and injustice in contemporary American life.
>
> The Christian Social Relations Committee concerns itself with human relationships and social problems and their causes as they affect local communities and national life. The committee works in the following areas:
>
> > Children and Youth: Christian Family Life
> > Economic and Industrial Relations
> > Race Relations and Civil Liberties
>
> A scrutiny of current national legislation is maintained in order that church women may be informed on all pertinent legislation. Recommendations are made to state and local councils when local action is needed to influence public opinion.[3]

The 1,924 local councils of church women in the United States and Hawaii today probably represent an organized channel of potential contact with millions of women members of thousands of local churches. The possibilities of systematic and continued communication with the grass-roots female membership of the churches are of rather extensive dimensions.

What is remarkable about the character of the organization of United Church Women is that it provides a structure of communication between local councils of church women and the active national leadership constantly in touch with the moving events of society in which public expression of opinion counts heavily. Thus, local councils of church women often have a spokesman for them at governmental hearings regarding such matters as child welfare, housing, and fair employment practices, and in national voluntary groups working together on social problems. In consultation with these groups and with a national Committee on Christian Social Relations, policy and program are determined on the national level for the stimulation of education and action among the nearly 2,000 local councils. These communications are generally addressed through the state chairmen of Christian Social Relations of the state councils of church women, who, in turn, are in frequent touch with the leaders of local councils of church women. In addition, the staff spends much time in the field to encourage active participation in these programs. The local councils are constituted of representatives of local churches co-operating on the interdenominational level.

Here is a communication set-up which starts on the national level as *mass* communication, that is, the ultimate consumer is largely unknown and cannot be presumed to have amenable interests in the social realm. The women in local churches are, however, likely to be in the same circle of concerns, frequently in intimate contact with one another in a relatively homogeneous socio-economic setting. Their representatives in the local council of church women stand in an enviable position of influence among their fellow women. The collective action of these local church leaders in interdenominational councils, in frequent touch with national headquarters, mounts to a picture of phenomenal potential for the social welfare.

Now, returning to the study findings, we shall examine the extent to which these possibilities of contact are being used in the interests of social service and social education and action. In the analysis, an attempt is made to point out any significant differences among geographic regions and among population sizes of places in which councils serve.

Just under three-fourths of the councils that answered the questionnaire said they, in some way, deal "with subjects of social concern such as health and welfare, family life, racial and cultural relations, church and economic life, international affairs, religious and civil liberties, legislation, etc."[4]

All of the state councils responded affirmatively. There seems to be definite indication the larger the population of the place the councils serve, the more likely they are to show social concerns through their activities. Table T-16 indicates that three-fifths of the councils in places less than 2,500 population had activities dealing with social problems, and there is a consistent increase in the proportion to almost 100 per cent for councils serving in places with populations of 100,000 or more. Although only a little more than a fourth of the local councils answering the questionnaire reported how many individuals participated in their organizations, the councils with social-concern activities have a larger average participation by about 80 per cent (see Table T-17).

Another indication that the larger local councils are more active in social concerns is that those reporting councils with such activities have an average membership of thirty-two local church women's

115

Table T-16
COUNCILS OF CHURCH WOMEN DEALING WITH SOCIAL CONCERNS BY STATE COUNCILS AND POPULATION SIZE OF PLACE OF LOCAL COUNCILS

State councils and population size of place of local councils	Total responding	Dealing with social concerns	
		Number	Per cent
United States	698*	516	74
State Councils	31	31	100
Local Councils	667	485	73
Less Than 2,500	78	47	60
2,500-9,999	181	113	62
10,000-24,999	142	109	77
25,000-99,999	152	115	76
100,000-499,999	47	46	98
500,000 or More	14	13	93
Not Given	53	42	79

* Includes Hawaii.

Table T-17
INDIVIDUALS PARTICIPATING IN LOCAL COUNCILS OF CHURCH WOMEN BY WHETHER OR NOT COUNCILS DEAL WITH SOCIAL CONCERNS

Councils of Church Women	Councils reporting	Individuals	
		Total	Average*
All reporting	180	72,049	400
Dealing with social concerns	120	56,526	471
Not dealing with social concerns	60	15,523	259

* Mean.

groups as contrasted with thirteen for councils that do not. This is based on a response from more than half of the local councils returning questionnaires and, though the relative differences vary somewhat from region to region, and from small to large populations of places, the councils that have some activities in social matters uniformly have more local church groups represented (see Table T-18).

Preliminary analysis seems to suggest that the average amount of annual expenditures for all reporting local councils was $291. Those with social-concern activities spent $408 on the average, and those without, $239. Here again is evidence that the more active the councils are the more likely they are to have activities related to social interests.

To summarize the differences between councils that do and do not engage in activities in social matters, we may state that councils

Table T-18

GROUP PARTICIPATION IN COUNCILS OF CHURCH WOMEN BY WHETHER OR NOT THEY DEAL WITH SOCIAL CONCERNS

Councils of Church Women	Councils reporting	Groups Participating	
		Total	Average
All Councils	368	10,345	28
Dealing with social concerns	273	9,070	33
Not dealing with social concerns	95	1,275	13
State Councils	24	1,020*	42
Dealing with social concerns	24	1,020	42
Not dealing with social concerns	—	—	—
Local Councils	344	9,325†	27
Dealing with social concerns	250	8,074	32
Not dealing with social concerns	95	1,275	13

* Local councils of church women.
† Local church groups.

Table T-19

COUNCILS OF CHURCH WOMEN DEALING WITH SOCIAL CONCERNS BY GEOGRAPHIC DIVISION

Geographic division	Total responding	Dealing with social concerns	
		Number	Per cent
United States	698	516	74
New England	68	56	82
Middle Atlantic	117	89	76
East North Central	151	112	74
West North Central	103	66	64
South Atlantic	74	54	73
East South Central	29	25	86
West South Central	44	33	75
Mountain	42	35	83
Pacific*	70	46	66

* Includes Hawaii.

that deal with social affairs: 1) are more likely to be found serving in larger places, 2) have more individuals and local church groups participating, and 3) spend more money. The geographic divisional differences reported are slight, ranging from 64 per cent in one division to 83 per cent in another of the total reporting councils showing some involvement in the social sphere.

What do councils of church women do in relation to social concerns? Three-fifths of the councils reporting social-concern activities are engaged in some sort of social service, and about half showed some social education or action activity.

Generally speaking, the most frequent kind of social service rendered by the interdenominational organizations of women is giving "direct aid (food, clothing, furnishings, money, etc.) to persons or groups in need as an emergency measure," and the second is giving "organized assistance to community fund-raising drives," such as Red Cross, community chest or fund, cancer, polio, tuberculosis, crippled children, and heart, financial campaigns in that order of importance. Here, juxtaposed, are the most *informal* and *direct* type of social service in the checklist and probably the most *indirect* type of contribution to the most highly *formalized* and organized aspect of health and welfare activities today. And the third most often reported social service activity is to "conduct or arrange for visiting or entertaining by lay persons of the institutionalized (in homes, hospitals, prisons, etc.)." Here is *direct* service, that is, face-to-face contact with the ultimate recipients of service, within a highly *organized*, institutional framework.

These elements, the *informal* nature of service of church women and assistance of a voluntary nature to be organized, *formalized* social work, are the crucial points to be understood in this analysis of the activities of state and local councils of church women.

The activities of councils compared by geographical divisions do not show any significant differences, the three activities mentioned being almost without exception the major activities in all divisions. There is some transposition of these three kinds of activities among the divisions but the pattern is quite consistent.

A more fruitful kind of analysis, it was believed, would be by the size of population of the places in which local councils of women serve. This disclosed that in the smaller or more rural places, it is far more likely that councils give larger emphasis to direct aid of an emergency nature to persons or groups in need. In cities of 100,000 or more, however, this activity ranks third in importance, and in the very large cities of 500,000 or more, this direct aid ranks fourth in importance. More important in the larger size cities is the rendering of volunteer services that have direct contact with the people that the agencies and institutions serve, but the volunteer efforts of women are given within the framework of formally organized social work institutions. In the largest cities of 500,000 or more, the most important type of service is giving organized assistance to community fund-raising drives in which there is no contact with the persons served and frequently not even with the agencies through which the social service is ultimately given. The training, recruitment, and referral of volunteers is of second major emphasis in the large cities, whereas in the smaller cities and rural towns this is found to be of least importance.

The rendering of direct *and* organized health and welfare services by the councils seems to occur more often in cities and towns that are not in the largest metropolitan areas. It is found more frequently to be important in places that are smaller, which could possibly be an indication that they are less adequately equipped with community-organized services (see Table T-20). This table gives some indication that the character of services to social welfare rendered by councils of church women changes as the size of place changes. That is, the smaller the community in which the women serve, the more direct and informal are the activities; and the larger the place, the more likely it is that services are provided indirectly to aid formal, organized community-wide types of agencies and institutions.

A further bit of documentation of this finding is the nature of services specified that were outside the categories of the checklist. In the largest cities of 500,000 or more, one council provides a Protestant consultant to the children's court, another finances a juvenile court worker, and in another, camp placements are made for "hard to place children." One council reported a community self-survey and another a survey of social service needs. These were in addition to a number of councils which reported acting as hostesses for the U.S.O. and rendering other volunteer services in welfare programs.

Comparing this with the places of less than 10,000, we find that there is some interest in religious education and other religious services for institutionalized persons such as by the distribution of literature and the conducting of religious education classes. This type of activity was not reported in the larger cities. But more frequently reported is the giving of holiday baskets and gifts of money, of the sponsoring of play lots and other informal group work services.

It is in the medium-size places that the sponsoring of golden age clubs and the giving of supplies for welfare agencies and for migrants, sponsoring a school for retarded children, a kindergarten for non-English-speaking children, a children's guidance clinic, a Negro child care center, health care of two women migrants, etc., were reported. Here we see the provision of welfare activities of a probably less professional nature by the women themselves. It may be assumed that these represent needs for services in the community that are not presently being met by existing agencies.

There were some reports of efforts to represent the social welfare interests of church women in co-ordinated community planning and financial groups. This activity seems to assume more importance in the larger towns between 25,000 and 500,000 and being less significant an effort in small towns and the very largest cities.

Here is some beginning evidence that tends to reinforce the notion that the role of volunteer efforts in social service has a changing character with urbanization.

If it can be thought that the rural areas represent a more informal face-to-face community, which was more typical of earlier life in

America, some trend generalizations might be made of these findings. Today, America is characterized by the elements associated with urbanization, and what we found in the smaller communities might be considered more typical of the past in America and what we found in the largest cities the more modern role of volunteer efforts.

The almost completely voluntary character of these extensive social services of councils of church women is apparent in that 40 per cent of the local councils reporting had no operating expenses and the great majority of those with expenses used less than $100 in 1954.

Only a very small number of the 698 councils who returned questionnaires had any paid staff. There were reported seven full-time directors; two, half-time; and one, employed less than half-time. All of these were in the employ of state councils or in large urban centers. Other nonclerical employees were: one "children's worker" and one "social worker at children's court."

One hundred thirty-two of the 300 councils that engaged in social service activities reported having a total of nearly eleven thousand different volunteer workers last year, an average of about 130 per council.

Social service is a major emphasis in local councils, occupying about a third of their total activities. In state councils there seems generally to be less of the program given to social service. This may be reflective of the different function of state councils, which act primarily to stimulate local council activities and generally serve in liaison between the national office of United Church Women and the local groups. Size of place seemed to have no bearing on the proportion of council activity given to social service.

Here, then, is part of the picture of Protestant effort in social welfare—fitting the pattern of need and generally supportive of whatever the structure of welfare might be in the various local situations, with services rendered on an almost entirely voluntary basis as an expression of avowedly Christian concern.

In addition to these social services, the interdenominational efforts of church women to learn about and influence social conditions is important to this description of the nature of their involvement in social welfare interests.

The range of activities for social education and action purposes is great, and we present only a brief and cursory analysis of the most general of these.

Table T-21 shows the order of frequency with which various types of social education and action activities were reported in the study.

It can be seen here that although nearly three-fifths of the councils reporting social education and action activities distribute literature, only roughly half as many pass resolutions or make representa-

Table T-21

SOCIAL EDUCATION AND ACTION ACTIVITIES OF COUNCILS
OF CHURCH WOMEN

Type of Activity	Number of councils	Per cent of all councils reporting
Total	261	100
Distributed literature	155	59
Provided speakers	145	56
Heard lecture, book review, etc.	120	46
Conducted conferences, study groups, etc.	102	39
Made representations to public officials	90	35
Passed resolutions	78	30
Included articles in regular council publications	61	23
Prepared original literature	34	13

tions to public officials regarding social issues. As might have been anticipated, more councils engage in efforts for *learning* about social concerns than in social *action* to improve conditions. Nonetheless, that 35 per cent of the councils do actively attempt to influence public officials is not an insignificant finding in terms of the importance of the segment of the public they represent. It has been said that organized church women are not an easy constituency to disregard.

Race relations, international affairs, social welfare, church and economic life, and religious and civil liberties—is the general order of frequency with which subjects were treated in social education and action activities. In all types of activities race relations is either the first or second most important subject dealt with.

Although social welfare is the third most important concern in terms of most types of activities, it assumes first importance as the subject matter of representations to public officials, and second importance as the content of resolutions. This seems to suggest that social welfare, contrasted with the other concerns, is more the kind of subject in which church women find they can effectively engage in direct political action. It may also be more a fruitful area for local action than the other subjects, since it is likely that social welfare matters are more local in concern than, for example, international affairs, economic life, or religious and civil liberties. On the other hand, that race relations takes a secondary position in this kind of activity, is perhaps suggestive of its more controversial nature, for surely problems of race relations on the local scene must be prominent.

The most frequently studied subjects were found to be race relations and international affairs. This probably reflects two of the major general educational emphases of the national program of United Church Women conducted through the committees on Christian Social Relations and Christian World Relations. The other major educational emphasis, the Christian World Missions program, was not included in the study.

Although only 128 councils reported the proportion of their total activities that were given to social education and action, it seems that this is a major emphasis of these councils—an estimated average of 40 per cent of their entire program.

The 143 councils that gave estimates of the number of persons who participated in their social education and action programs in 1954 reported a total of 47,562 different persons, an average of more than 300 per council. Although nearly half of the councils indicating social education and action activities could give no estimate, we may assume that their participants would add a considerable number to the total.

In any case, the potential for continuous and organized social education and action outreach among church women is enormous and there is every indication that United Church Women will continue to gain from cumulative experience with methods and materials in a more effective use of this vast resource of Christian laywomen in the interests of the social welfare.

FOOTNOTES FOR CHAPTER 9

1 Actually, the study encompassed far more than is pertinent here; an exploratory evaluation of methods and materials of the Christian Social Relations national office of the General Department of United Church Women in its outreach to councils of church women.

2 "Report of the General Department of United Church Women," *Workbook for the Third General Assembly; National Council of the Churches of Christ in the U. S. A.* (New York, 1954), p. 107.

3 *Ibid.*, p. 110.

4 See Appendix B, Questionnaire for Councils of Church Women.

CHURCH-RELATED AGENCIES AND INSTITUTIONS: A Statistical Description

10

Comprehensive data on the extent of church-related health and welfare agencies and institutions have never been compiled, except by a few commissions with highly organized welfare operations.

This report[1] represents the most summary findings of what was hoped would be a national inventory of agencies and institutions related to the Protestant, Anglican, and Eastern Orthodox[2] communions in the United States.[3] However, roughly only a third of the agencies known to be related to these bodies participated in the questionnaire study.

Number and Location

Known to be related to 37 Protestant bodies in the country are 2,783 health and welfare agencies and institutions. The total number of Protestant bodies for which information was made available was 50 (14 of which were reported to have no agencies), with a combined membership covering more than 70 per cent of the total Protestant church membership in the country and more than 40 per cent of the total membership of all faiths.

Eighteen per cent or 494 of these agencies were homes for the aged; 15 per cent or 424, hospitals; 14 per cent or 377, neighborhood houses or settlements; 10 per cent or 269, institutions for the care of children.[4] These were the major types of agencies that responded to the questionnaire study and in almost the same proportion (within 3 per cent).

The 493 homes for the aged constitute about 16 per cent of the latest total estimate of 3,000 nonprofit private and governmental homes for the aged in the United States in 1952,[5] 271 of these being Catholic[6] and 80, Jewish.[7]

The 1952 Census of Hospitals conducted by the American Medical Association disclosed a total of 6,665 hospitals, 2,078 of which were under governmental auspices, 1,113 church-controlled and 2,146 other nonprofit. Catholic hospitals in that year were reported to number 858;[8] Jewish hospitals, 63.[9] That there were 395 church-related Protestant hospitals discovered in this incomplete study is probably indicative of the difference in definition of "church-control" as conceived in the American Medical Association census, but these figures are given in order to give some idea of the relative extent of Protestant church-related hospitals.

Of the total number of known church-related agencies, 20 per cent are in the Middle Atlantic; 19 per cent, East North Central; 16

per cent, West North Central; 12 per cent, South Atlantic; 10 per cent, Pacific; 6 per cent, East South Central; 6 per cent, West South Central; 5 per cent, Mountain; 4 per cent, New England. Agencies participating in the study showed almost the same proportionate distribution by geographic divisions, with the largest difference being only 2 per cent.

The distribution of agencies compared to the distribution of the United States population, showed some differences, the largest being in the West North Central, where 9 per cent of the population resides but where 16 per cent of the agencies were located. The correspondence in the other divisions were within 1 or 2 per cent.

Homes for the aged, institutions for the care of children, and hospitals were as frequently found in places with populations of less than 2,500 as in the largest cities of 500,000 or more, and in places of other population sizes roughly proportionate to the distribution of the United States population. However, neighborhood houses, residences, and child placement and adoption agencies tended to be more numerous as the population of places increased.

Of the 986 denominationally related agencies participating in the study more than one-fifth had been established prior to 1900 and nearly half, before 1920. Close to half of the institutions for the care of children originated before the turn of the century, and those established within the last twenty-five years consituted less than a tenth. Whereas, in the other major types of agencies about the same

CHART 2

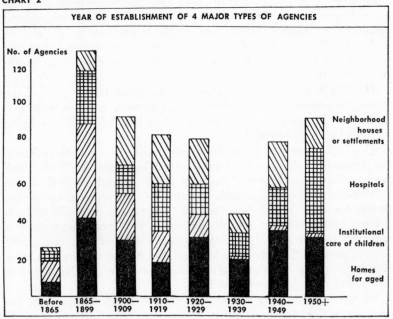

number were established in the last twenty-five to thirty years as they were in the years preceding. More than a fourth of the hospitals were founded within the last five years. (See Chart 2)

In the New England, Middle Atlantic, East North Central, and West North Central geographic divisions, the median year of establishment was 1905; the West North Central, South Atlantic, East South Central, and Pacific, 1925; in the West South Central, 1935; and the Mountain division, 1945.

Services

Of the 986 denominationally related agencies that returned questionnaires sufficiently complete in time for inclusion in the study,

Table T-22

MAJOR AND OTHER SERVICES OFFERED BY REPORTING AGENCIES

Type of Service	Number of Agencies Offering	
	Major service	One of its services
Home for aged	215	254
Other services to aged	12	121
Institutional care of children	126	165
Child placement and adoption	30	75
Day nursery	22	90
Other services to children	24	164
Hospital	166	194
Clinic or dispensary	12	136
Health education	1	81
Convalescent care	7	54
Other health services	8	40
Temporary shelter	13	63
Residence	40	119
Other residential services	2	26
Neighborhood house or settlement	139	191
Camp or vacation	16	173
Other group work	22	150
Other recreational services	15	136
Maternity home	1	16
Protective services	4	18
Family welfare	11	128
Employment and vocation	1	62
Rehabilitation	5	67
Sheltered workshop	2	28
Social education and action	10	99
Chaplaincy: in prisons	2	41
Chaplaincy: in hospitals	19	101
Other chaplaincy services	4	71
Other major services	42	218

211 or 21 per cent were homes for the aged, 166 or 17 per cent were hospitals, 139 or 14 per cent were neighborhood houses or settlements, and 118 or 12 per cent were institutions for the care of children. Church-related agencies are apparently heavily concentrated in institutional care.

But a number of other agencies rendered these services, even though they were not the major service on which basis the classification of "Types of Agencies" was made. Column B of Table T-22 indicates the number of agencies that offered the services listed.

Persons Served

963 agencies reported the total unduplicated number of persons served in 1954—a grand total of over four million persons. 863 agencies reported serving an estimated total of about 1,300,000 persons who were not of the Protestant, Anglican, or Eastern Orthodox religious traditions. This was on the average about 35 per cent of the total number of persons served.

Personnel

A total of 55,045 full-time employees and 12,830 part-time employees were reported by 1,103 agencies. Of full-time employees, 1,255 of these were social workers, 4,015 were medical doctors, 8,193 registered nurses, 5,860 other professionals, and 34,960 nonprofessional personnel. Of the part-time employees 406 were social workers, 3,247 medical doctors, 2,206 registered nurses, 1,092 other professionals, and 5,887 nonprofessional employes.

Eight hundred seventy-four ordained persons were reported employed by agencies, 71 of whom had degrees from schools of social work accredited by the Council on Social Work Education or its predecessor agency.

Of the 1,641 social workers reported employed by 451 agencies, 675 or 41 per cent had accredited degrees.

Social workers in the employ of church-related agencies were largely on the staff of neighborhood houses and settlements (27 per cent), child placement and adoption agencies (13 per cent), hospitals (12 per cent), and institutions for children (12 per cent).

Nine hundred seventy-four agencies reported a total of 37,993 volunteers in 1954 and 17,079 persons serving on their governing boards.

Finance

The total amount of operating expense reported by 978 agencies participating in the study was $256,506,000. Two-thirds of this total expenditure was by 176 hospitals, which spent a little over $173,000,-000 in the last complete fiscal year. The next largest expenditures were reported by sheltered workshops, spending more than $23,-000,000 last year; this figure includes the Goodwill Industries of America, Inc., which has 110 autonomous local units. One hundred ninety-seven homes for the aged reported spending more than $15,000,000; and 128 institutions for the care of children had a total expenditure of nearly $13,000,000.

Total operating income roughly paralleled the above, but our interest in income here is in its sources. Of a total operating income of $262,782,000 indicated by 1,011 agencies, contributions from religious organizations reported by 748 agencies amounted to $15,-234,000 or 5.4 per cent of the total. Of this contributed income from religious sources, $8,049,000 came from local churches, to 583 agencies, $796,000 from other local religious organizations to 147 agencies, $2,390,000 from state or regional organizations to 240 agencies, and $2,801,000 from national religious organizations to 300 agencies. Contributions from individuals was roughly $1,025,000 more than from religious sources. Community chest contributions were reported received by 251 agencies in the total amount of $5,140,000; and contributions (not including service fees) from public, tax-supported funds amounted to $1,217,000 for 69 agencies. Only a fifth of the total operating income was contributed income.

Approximately four-fifths of operating income was earned income; and by far the most important source of earned monies was service fees from individuals, amounting to more than $174,000,000 or more than three-fourths of the total income from all sources. Service fees from public funds, reported received by 132 agencies, amounted to about $6,000,000; more than $11,500,000 was income from invest-

CHART 3

SOURCES OF INCOME OF TOTAL REPORTING AGENCIES: 1954

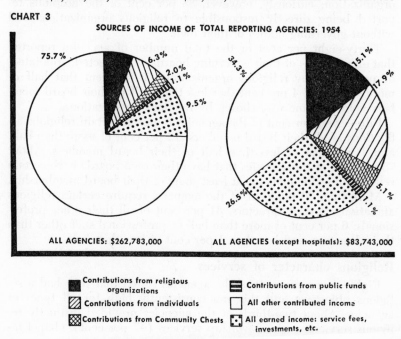

ALL AGENCIES: $262,783,000   ALL AGENCIES (except hospitals): $83,743,000

■ Contributions from religious organizations

▨ Contributions from individuals

▩ Contributions from Community Chests

▤ Contributions from public funds

☐ All other contributed income

⊡ All earned income: service fees, investments, etc.

127

ments for 421 agencies; and a little under $11,500,000 was other kinds of earned income for 389 agencies. (See Chart 3)

Variations in sources of support for major kinds of agencies can be seen in the accompanying graph. (See Chart 4)

Eight hundred and thirty-two agencies provided figures on their capital assets, which amounted to $701,000,000. Of this, $377,000,000 was in buildings, land, and equipment; and $265,000,000 was valued in endowments and investments.

Plans for major expansion in the next five years were reported by 362 agencies amounting in estimated dollar value to $162,000,000; $134,000,000 of this was reported by 279 agencies for buildings and land, $45,000,000 for equipment in 193 agencies; and $5,500,000 for staff and program expansion in 181 agencies.

Retraction plans were reported by only four agencies.

Religious Involvement

Religious control

Of the total of 986 denominationally known agencies and institutions 87 per cent reported official recognition by religious organizations as related to them and 78 per cent reported having an officially stated relationship to religious organizations.

Eight per cent of all agencies indicated that they had no governing boards of their own and were directly responsible to a religious organization; curiously, however, 85 per cent of the hospitals reported being directly responsible to religious organizations and without governing bodies of their own.

Thirty-eight per cent of the total number of agencies reported that all members of their governing boards were elected, appointed, or nominated by religious organizations; 6 per cent that half or more were; and 4 per cent that less than half of their board members were in some way chosen by religious organizations.

Fifty-seven per cent of the agencies required certain religious affiliations of all their board members; 12 per cent of more than half, and 1 per cent of less than half of their board members. About 75 per cent of the agencies that have their own boards have certain religious requirements for at least some of their board membership.

More than 80 per cent of the agencies require certain religious affiliations of their directors; 31 per cent of all their other professionals; 6 per cent of more than half of professional staff other than their directors; and less than 1 per cent of less than half.

Religious character of services

Eighty-seven per cent of the agencies stated that they had a religious objective; and this ran consistently high for all types of agencies. About two-thirds of the agencies provided distinctly religious services, such as worship services (47 per cent), chapel fa-

CHART 4

SOURCES OF INCOME OF FIVE MAJOR TYPES OF AGENCIES: 1954

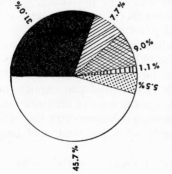

Child Placement and Adoption: $3,647,000

31.0%
7.7%
9.0%
1.1%
5.5%
45.7%

Contributions from religious organizations

Contributions from individuals

Contributions from Community Chests

Contributions from public funds

All other types of contributed income

All earned income: service fees, investments, etc.

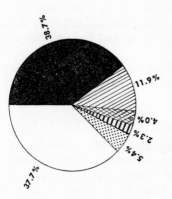

38.7%
11.9%
4.0%
2.3%
5.4%
37.7%

Institutions for Care of Children: $11,887,000

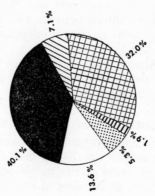

7.1%
32.0%
1.9%
5.3%
13.6%
40.1%

Neighborhood Houses or Settlements: $3,342,000

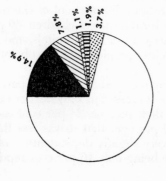

14.9%
7.8%
1.1%
1.9%
3.7%

Homes for Aged: $16,699,000

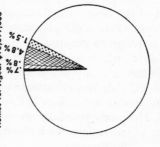

.7%
4.8%
1.5%

Hospitals: $179,039,000

cilities (8 per cent), religious instruction (5 per cent), chaplaincy services (2 per cent), pastoral services (1 per cent), and evangelistic programs (less than ½ of 1 per cent).

Official requirements for the limitation of service to persons of certain religious affiliations was indicated by 17 per cent of the agencies studied. However, 39 per cent of the homes for the aged, 28 per cent of the residences, 27 per cent of the child placement agencies, and 16 per cent of the institutions for the care of children reported having such requirements. Neighborhood houses with this religious limitation on persons served were only 4 per cent, and hospitals less than 1 per cent.

The practice of serving primarily persons of certain religious affiliations was reported by 28 per cent of all agencies; 67 per cent of child placement agencies, 57 per cent of the homes for aged, 36 per cent of the institutions for the care of children, and 30 per cent of the residences. Neighborhood houses and settlements with this practice were 6 per cent and hospitals, less than 1 per cent.

The contrast between official requirement of limitation of services to persons of certain religious affiliations and the practice can here be noted.

Almost all of the agencies (96 per cent) checked that they considered themselves Christian agencies in tradition, spirit, motivation of personnel, etc.

Assistance from religious sources

Religious organizations were reported to have been the originating auspices of 78 per cent of the agencies included in the study; 94 per cent of the neighborhood houses, 85 per cent of the residences, 85 per cent of the institutions for children, 80 per cent of the child-placement agencies, 71 per cent of the homes for the aged, and 53 per cent of the hospitals.

Fifty-one per cent of the agencies used buildings owned by religious organizations, and 42 per cent of these were provided rent-free. Eighty-four per cent of the neighborhood houses and settlements, nearly three-fourths of which were provided rent-free, used buildings owned by religious organizations; 80 per cent of the residences, 49 per cent of the institutions for the care of children, 40 per cent of the homes for the aged, 25 per cent of the hospitals, and 23 per cent of the child placement agencies occupied buildings belonging to religious groups.

Two-thirds of the agencies said they received a significant part of their financial support from religious sources, but only 22 per cent reported that this constituted all of their income, 24 per cent indicated it was more than half, and 19 per cent that it was less than half. Hospitals generally were only very slightly dependent on religious organizations for income, there being only 16 per cent reporting that this support was significant; less than ½ of 1 per cent reported that all their income came from religious sources; 3 per cent, more than half; and 13 per cent, less than half. For the other types of agencies related to the churches more than three-fourths reported significant income from religious sources, but most of these reported less than half of the total income from this kind of organization. This should be contrasted with the actual proportionate amounts reported for the agencies (see above).

Sixty-two per cent of church related agencies in the study sample indicated receiving assistance other than financial from religious sources. Forty-nine per cent said they received gifts in kind such as food, clothing, etc.; 34 per cent, promotion or fund-raising; 31 per cent, ministerial or pastoral services; 26 per cent, consultation services; and 20 per cent, recruitment, training or referral of volunteers. Only 38 per cent of the hospitals indicated that they received these services; whereas 86 per cent of the institutions for the care of children received this nonfinancial help.

These highlights serve to give some indication of the extent and nature of religious involvement in health and welfare agencies. Source tables in Appendix D are available for the more detailed interest of denominations, social work fields of specialty, and geographic regions.

A note is added regarding two nondenominational Protestant efforts in the welfare field, the Young Men's Christian Association and the Young Women's Christian Association—and the Salvation Army. These were not included in the questionnaire study.

Young Men's Christian Associations in the United States are organized in 1,804 places, with members totaling 2,128,689.[10] Much of the work of the Associations is done through groups and clubs having a total enrollment of 3,983,437 in 1954. Full-time secretaries of the Y.M.C.A.'s number 3,768 certified by the Y.M.C.A. as having fulfilled certain qualifications of professional Y.M.C.A. training; in addition there are 904 other persons employed full-time, and 6,058 on part-time assignments, not including clerical and other nonprofessional personnel. One hundred and sixty-six thousand different persons served on boards, committees, and councils of the Y's and 118,341 served as volunteer leaders of groups and activities.

Residences, camps, group work and recreational activities, employment services, social and citizenship education, and counseling are the major activities of the Y's.

Most local Y.M.C.A.'s are affiliated with interdenominational councils of churches, and the National Council of Y.M.C.A.'s is a related agency in the National Council of the Churches of Christ in the U. S. A. Approximately two-thirds of the membership in the United States is Protestant, and a little less than one-third, Roman Catholic. The Y.M.C.A. is a lay Christian organization without ecclesiastical control. In this country, board members are predominantly Protestant.

The total current income of the United States Y's during 1954 was $119,985,200. Investments amounted to $365,339,300.

The Young Women's Christian Association is at work in 438 communities throughout the country[12] and on 641 college campuses. In addition, the Y.W.C.A. provides services for military personnel and defense workers and their families. The community Y.W.C.A.'s had a membership of more than 3,000,000 in 1954.

More than 3,000 professional employees and 100,000 volunteer leaders were reported serving in the Y.W.C.A.'s of the country in 1954.

Among the major services of the Y.W.C.A. are group work with young adults and teen-agers, informal educational programs, residences, camps, health education and recreation.

The Y.W.C.A. as a Christian movement is described in the Work Book prepared for the twentieth national convention, April 21-27, 1955:

> "The Y.W.C.A. must continue to provide opportunities for the kinds of experiences for members which will deepen their understanding of the meaning of the Christian faith and lead them to responsible action in their daily lives. It creates a setting where members can know themselves and develop their potentialities, one which encourages in individuals a sense of belonging and kinship to others of different race, religion, nationality, background, occupation, and age.
>
> "Several characteristics distinguish the Y.W.C.A. as a religious movement. While its leadership and electoral membership continue to be predominantly Christian, it is free of organizational ties to the church. It is an ecumenical movement, seeking to increase understanding and respect for all branches of the Christian Church. The Y.W.C.A. has always encouraged responsible church membership in the church of the member's choice. At the same time, it has carried a special concern for reaching and including those young women and girls who are not church members, who are unorthodox, sceptical, or agnostic."[13]

The Y.W.C.A., like the Y.M.C.A., is a related agency of the National Council of Churches. The community Y.W.C.A.'s throughout the country spent in excess of $33,000,000 in 1952. In aggregate, the 366 community Associations reporting in 1952 were 68 per cent self-supporting and received 32 per cent from community chests and united funds.

The Salvation Army's 1,893 "centers of operation"[14] in the United States are engaged in many types of informal and professionalized social welfare services. Structurally, however, services are divided into the welfare activities of the Army Corps and social welfare projects conducted by the Army's Department of Social Service. Assistance given individuals or families on a temporary basis and emergency in character is generally under the direct supervision of The Salvation Army Corps. The other services—hospitals, child-care, and other services of a more permanent nature—are the responsibility of the social service departments.

The Army's three general hospitals and 34 maternity homes provided care for 20,526 patients. Another 8,370 patients were treated in the Army's two clinics. More than 200,000 children were served in the seven children's homes and foster care services and more than 150,000 were served in settlements and nurseries. On hundred homes, shelters, etc., provided 711,218 lodgings and 66,614 meals. "Social service centers" operated on a bigger scale in the same category as shelters, etc., and offered 2,033,284 lodgings and 5,286,088 meals. Additional services such as summer camps and youth community centers provided for hundreds of thousands. Employment placement services secured more than 45,000 jobs. Extensive work is carried on in prisons, aiding parolees, assisting homeless individuals, and a host of other social welfare services.

Almost all of the Salvation Army units throughout the country conduct various forms of social service, ranging from minimum emergency services when required in fires, floods, local disasters, etc., to direct assistance to individuals to full-fledged programs of casework and welfare assistance.

Something of the religious involvement in the Army's welfare activities was given in an interview with Lieutenant Colonel Chester R. Brown, National Social Welfare Consultant of the Salvation Army:

> The Salvation Army's service to people's needs is motivated by the illustration of the compassionate Christ to Jews and non-Jews and to any human in need. . . . We never attempt to use the service we render as a means of religious pressure, because we realize that the choice must be their own and their decision arrived at without pressure. This is not to say, however, that we are not a religious group. . . . The Army is an independent religious body with a set of its own religious principles.[15]

Although financial data were not available, Lieutenant Colonel Brown estimated that in 85 per cent of the communities where both Salvation Army units and community chests exist, the Army receives community chest funds.

FOOTNOTES FOR CHAPTER 10

[1] Some data are referred to in other sections of the book. Source tables appear in Appendix C. Further analyses will be found in a thesis now in process, a pilot study of Protestant church-related social welfare in the U.S.A. by Ruth

Laverty at the New York University Center for Human Relations.

2 Hereafter, for the sake of brevity and with sacrifice of accuracy, the term "Protestant" will be used to refer generally to Protestant, Anglican, and Eastern Orthodox communions.

3 See Appendix A for the method and procedures of the study.

4 Agencies were classified according to the one most important type of service rendered.

5 Clark Tibbitts, "The Aging," *Social Work Year Book, 1954* (New York: American Association of Social Workers, 1954), p. 38.

6 Thomas Gill, "Catholic Social Work," *Social Work Year Book, 1954* (New York: American Association of Social Workers, 1954), p. 78.

7 Martin M. Cohn, "Jewish Social Work," *Social Work Year Book, 1954* (New York: American Association of Social Workers, 1954), p. 289.

8 Gill, *op. cit.*, p. 77.

9 Cohn, *op. cit.*, p. 289.

10 Data from the 1955 Year Book, National Council of the Young Men's Christian Associations, National Council of the Y.M.C.A.'s.

11 Data on the Young Women's Christian Association provided by Mrs. Savilla Simons, general secretary of the Young Women's Christian Association of the United States of America.

12 Data on the Young Women's Christian Association provided by Mrs. Savilla Millis Simons, general secretary of the Young Women's Christian Association of the United States of America.

13 *Our Task Today and Tomorrow*, Work Book, Twentieth Convention, Young Women's Christian Association in the United States of America, New York, April 21-27, 1955, p. 12.

14 Data on the Salvation Army were provided by Lieutenant Colonel Chester R. Brown, Social Welfare Consultant of The Salvation Army.

15 Interview with Lieutenant Colonel Chester R. Brown, National Welfare Consultant of The Salvation Army, June 23, 1955.

PART IV

THE CHURCHES AND THE SOCIAL WELFARE STRUCTURE

Social work in the United States has undergone great change in the past fifty years. Its philosophy has become secular. The workers have become professionalized. The field has grown and become specialized, and community-wide federating organizations have developed. To a large extent the churches were outside this new social work structure both organizationally and philosophically. To it the churches and church-related agencies have had to adjust. This section will discuss the problems and form of that adjustment.

The church-related agencies standing between the churches and the social work organizations often found themselves in a difficult position. The demands and expectations of the churches tended to be religious and frequently called for the inclusion of some forms of religious observances. On the other hand the demands of the community agencies—the council of social agencies and the community chest—usually condemned or forbade religious services. The question of church or community identification presented problems which were present in the control, financing, staffing, and programs of these agencies.

To meet the problems which arose through the secularization of social work the churches developed a program of co-operation. An expression of this is the Church Council of Social Work.

Other conferences, workshops, and local and national meetings work to bring about a greater understanding and a closer co-operation between the churches' activities and those of the formally organized social work groups.

However, there remains a difference in role and goal between the churches' activities in social welfare and those of the professional social work organizations. The different philosophies describe different goals. The goals of the churches are personal salvation and the reconstruction of society. Those of the professional social workers are adjustment of the individual to society and social changes which will allow the individual to find more complete expression. A greater understanding of each group by the other would lead to more co-operation and mutual understanding. This would not, necessarily, resolve the difference in approach, philosophy, or objective of either. It would, however, tend to define the areas of co-operation and conflict.

PROBLEMS OF THE CHURCH-RELATED AGENCY

11

We turn now to a discussion of the problems of church-related welfare agencies and programs. Such programs can, of course, have many kinds of problems, and many of these problems they would share with agencies that are not church-related: problems of increasing costs, of obsolescence of facilities, and numerous others. But our concern here centers in the problems that are connected with their "church-relatedness." We are concerned to define, in the mid-twentieth century America, the perplexities and ambiguities and obstacles that are peculiar to the agency that attempts to meet a recognized social welfare need, but wishes to be understood also as a legitimate expression of Christian faith and Christian fellowship.

The Change in Status of the Church-related Agency

The first problem for the church-related agency is basic to many others, and is essentially a problem of orientation. The problem is the tremendous change in status that has come within the past few decades, a change not so much in the church-related agencies themselves as in the environment in which they have operated. Where they had considered themselves pace-setters in both the religious and the welfare fields, church agencies now find themselves often to be marginal enterprises, uneasily rooted in two different traditions and two different kinds of philosophy, and sometimes even suspect in each tradition because of their alliance with the other. Organized religion and organized social welfare have both been in the midst of a tremendous expansion since the 1930's, but their respective directions of development have diverged sharply—each finding its independent rationale and support and control—and church-related social welfare, which had thought itself central to both developments, now finds itself increasingly peripheral to both, often with no clear comprehension of what has happened.

The ideals of the pioneers of church social work, which were built firmly into the philosophy of so many church-related agencies, have simply not become dominant in either religion or social work. Unlike the earlier conception that social service was religious work and that religious service was social work, today, the individual makes a choice between the two distinct vocations, or adds one on top of the other, and finds that his status in one vocation is largely independent of his status in the other. And similarly the church-related agencies are in an ambiguous situation, where status in one field not only has little to do with their standing in the other, but may even create barriers to their full acceptance either as professional social work agencies or as full members of a community of Christian institutions.

The Place of Religion in a Church-related Welfare Program

The developing conflict of philosophies indicated above often becomes most evident at the points where some form of overt religious activity is a part of the social work program religious education, evangelism, pastoral counseling, worship services, and so on. In the early days of religious social work, there was seldom any question but that the church-sponsored worker who dealt with human need also ministered to souls. The visiting nurse closed her visits with prayer. The boys' club reader urged youngsters to come to Sunday school. The church visitor dispensing relief also attempted to convert unbelievers—and what was "worse" (by contemporary social work standards) argued the merits of the Protestant faith as against Roman Catholic or Jewish beliefs. One may turn to the records of such an agency as the New York City Mission Society, one of the oldest of Protestant welfare agencies in this country, and pick almost at random from the annual reports to illustrate the complete integration of the evangelical and welfare motivations, as in this passage taken from the annual report of a century ago:

> The degraded and ignorant, who care not for their own souls,
> are sought out, and instructed and urged to come to Jesus;
> Sabbath schools, congregations, and churches are enlarged;
> the sick are visited in their affliction, and the poor in their
> poverty; many dejected ones are cheered and assisted to rise
> above their difficulties; many a fatherless one has found a
> friend; and many a widow's heart has leaped for joy. . . .
> Jesus Christ is our Captain.[1]

The Society's workers warred with equal zeal on alcohol and Romanism, prostitution and profanity, ignorance and atheism, poverty and Sabbath revelry. But it was also from this undifferentiated concern for body, character, and soul that much of modern social work arose; in these same New York City Mission Society records we observe the emergence of the visiting nurse, charity organization, the free library, "Americanization" classes, the "fresh-air" camp, and much else that is basic to the professionalized welfare program of today.

Today, as professional standards have developed, religion in any form except the most generalized of naturalistic and humanistic tenets has tended to be excluded from the church-related agencies that seek to maintain professional status in the social work world. In the study of church-related agencies referred to in the preceding chapter, only 3 out of a total of 986 denominationally known agencies reported having evangelistic programs and 53 or 5 per cent providing religious instruction, 16 of these being institutions for children and 15, neighborhood houses (See Table S-34). This was so, despite the fact that 17 per cent or 164 of the total number of agencies in the study officially required the limitation of their services primarily or entirely to persons of a certain religious affiliation and 28 per cent or 280 agencies served such persons.

Along with the disappearance of overt religious content has gone much of the moral exhortation that characterized earlier welfare work under religious auspices (which may, incidentally, have something to do with the bafflement of the modern group worker facing a problem such as delinquency). Social service programs in general and group work programs in particular are expected to be innocent of any formal religious content, such as evangelism or religious education. If a boys' worker wishes to invite a child to Sunday school, such invitation must be personal and even surreptitious; it must not be public in a group of mixed religious composition; and above all it must not be mentioned in the annual request for support from the community chest.

On the other hand, any successful religious activity is reported and even played up in annual reports to a sponsoring religious body:

> While our work is primarily community service rather than evangelism, it is interesting to note that thirty-nine youngsters from the community program came into the Sunday school last year, and eleven persons were received into church membership.[2]

Formal religion is permitted a place in the social work program, but this place has been increasingly isolated and segregated. For example, only half of all agencies in the study referred to above reported providing worship services, almost two-thirds of the homes for the aged, three-fifths of the institutions for children, one-third of the neighborhood houses and residences, about one-fourth of the hospitals and child placement agencies, and half of all other types of agencies. Eighty or 8 per cent of the agencies, 63 of these being hospitals and 9 homes for the aged, had chapel facilities; and 24 agencies provided chaplaincy services, 11 of these being hospitals.

The neighborhood house may have a minister, a Sunday school, and a church service, but it is explicitly understood that the social work program is not the context in which the minister recruits his constituency. Rather the religious program is in the nature of a specialized service (equated to a dental clinic, for example) for a group whose needs for this service have developed outside the house. Or a church-related hospital maintains a chaplain, but the chaplain is expected to confine his religious services to those of his faith (plus backsliders) and others who specifically request it.

The social agency, in other words, understands that nowhere in its program shall a religious faith be *urged* on people as, for example, mental health education or participation in civic and political life or the achievement of an advanced education are urged as opportunities and responsibilities. Religious activity is not frowned on, by any means, but neither is it actively and systematically promoted (or supported) in the church-related agencies whose service is nonsectarian and whose aspirations are for full acceptance in the social work profession.

If the receiving of community chest money can be assumed to be indicative of a desire or necessity for "acceptance by the social work profession," the findings from the study of its effect on the agencies' religious services is of pertinence here and is presented in the accompanying table.

Table T-23

RELIGIOUS SERVICES OF AGENCIES BY WHETHER OR NOT THEY RECEIVE COMMUNITY CHEST FUNDS

	Per Cent of Agencies	
Religious Services	Receiving Community Chest Funds	Not Receiving Community Chest Funds
Total	100.0	100.0
	(251 agencies)	(866 agencies)
Evangelistic programs	.9	14.0
Religious instruction	27.9	33.6
Pastoral services	25.1	41.7
Worship services	35.9	48.6
Chapel facilities	27.5	36.5
Chaplaincy services	25.1	41.7

The generalization is evident that acceptability to the profession (almost always a requirement of receiving community chest funds) tends to reduce the number of agencies providing religious services.

This problem is considerably less critical, of course, in agencies that confine their work to a particular sectarian group (about a fourth of the agencies in the study sample), or even those who secure their support predominantly from particular religious constituencies (about half of the agencies in the study), which are presumably sympathetic to a frankly religious program. The following thoughtful comment is pertinent to this general problem:

> One of the primary problems of mixing protestantism with a religious content into a program of social service is that we often have in mind getting more Protestants. We have not been forthright and honest as to our aims and goals some of the time. Jews and Catholics are more honest. They will say we are a Jewish or Catholic organization and we intend to advance our religion. When you go to those organizations you

know that. Protestant organizations and agencies have retreated in a number of ways, retreated from their religion.
One way is not to say anything about it. On the other hand
sometimes Protestant organizations have been so democratic
that they have lost their religious importance. Religion did
not dictate or control their work; any nonreligious group could
often be doing the same thing that a Protestant agency might
be doing. The church will have to decide what it is, what
these organizations are and what they should do. This is one
issue we have to face: What is peculiar about a Protestant
agency?[3]

The Place of Social Welfare in a Religious Program

We have given less attention to the place of welfare work in the
regular parish program, but there is no doubt that it presents a critical problem in many situations, and has indeed been the stimulus
for much of the organized welfare work that has developed under
church auspices. In a study made a quarter-century ago, which has
not so far as we know been adequately duplicated since, two pioneer
church sociologists reported the following:

> While only a small fraction of churches are so characterized
> by social welfare activities as to be labeled "institutional"
> churches, "community serving" churches, "Christian social
> centers" and the like, most of the departmental specialists who
> make up 15 per cent of the subordinate workers in city
> churches, many of the age and sex group specialists who con-
> stitute 8 per cent of this total, and many of the pastoral work-
> ers, such as deaconnesses and visitors who make up 14 per
> cent of the total, are in fact engaged primarily in welfare
> work, and their positions to the needs of church constituencies
> whose living standards are below normal or whose racial or
> other handicaps are extreme. A very considerable amount,
> also, of the demands put upon the secretarial workers in church
> offices arise out of the pressure of such social needs. Conse-
> quently, though ordained ministers as a whole give relatively
> little time to social work, and although the information avail-
> able does not fall strictly into the categories now being em-
> ployed, it seems reasonable to guess that approximately one-
> third of the paid professional service of the staffed church in
> the city falls into this field. This is in addition to the primary
> social values of wholesome group fellowship furnished by the
> total life of the church.[4]

We turn now to some of the more specific problems of the church-
related agency that derive particularly from its church relationship.

The Problem of Religious Identification

The matter of the identification of an agency, in name (incidentally, there were 691 in the total study sample of 1,117 agencies

that were so identifiable) or otherwise, with a particular religious group seems to be the source of a number of problems, except for those agencies which either confine their services to one religious group or secure all their support from it. Interviews revealed numerous experiences such as that of the agency director who was told by a foundation he approached: "You're the sixth Protestant agency today. Why don't your people support you like the Catholics and Jews support their agencies?"[5]

Identification with a religious group also can produce problems in regard to the participation of people of other faiths or other denominations, even when services are avowedly nonsectarian. And more than a third of all persons served by agencies in the study were not Protestant, and about three-fourths of the agencies do not confine their services to Protestants. The director of a neighborhood house attached to a church said: "I think if our Center was across the street or down the block from the church, there would be a different attitude towards us."[6] (Eighty-five per cent of the neighborhood houses in the study used buildings owned by religious organizations).

There is a lot of testimony to the effect that Roman Catholic parishioners avail themselves of nonsectarian services under auspices identified as Protestant, however, of which the following excerpt from an interview record is typical: "Rev. M. smiled and said: 'A lot of the kids have told us that the priests tell them not to come here, but they come nonetheless.' "[7]

But one cannot doubt that to whatever extent this is true, it is damaging to interfaith relations, and equally one cannot doubt that there is a marked coolness on the part of the Roman Catholic hierarchy and priesthood toward Protestant welfare enterprises, however noble in aim and nonevangelistic in character, when these offer their services to Roman Catholics. The pressure on Protestant agencies is to minimize their identification with any Protestant faith. Interestingly, although 97 per cent of the denominationally recognized agencies, said they considered themselves Christian agencies in tradition, spirit, or motivation of personnel and 87 per cent had religious objectives, less than two-thirds had any kind of identifiable religious service, however neutral in character. Another part of the study, in which an attempt was made to identify church-related agencies in ten states,[8] 27 per cent of a total of 481 agencies participating indicated that they considered themselves Christian agencies although they had no religious connection or services except, in some cases, in their origin or purpose. This poses a curious dilemma, in that so often Protestants justify their support of nonsectarian social service by describing it as a public witness to the nature of their Christian faith and its concern for human welfare. If the service cannot be identified as an expression of specifically

142

Christian concern without restricting its usefulness, then what happens to the witness?

The Problem of Support

There seems little doubt that the problems of church-relatedness become most acute at the point of financial support. The problems here are probably not the most fundamental, but undoubtedly they are the symptoms which come most frequently to the surface and are in the forefront of the awareness of the men and women involved professionally in church social work, as well as the executives to whom they are responsible.

There is a recurrent theme of complaint, even bitterness, running through the interviews with executives of church-related agencies. The complaint is that the churches which are so ready to claim credit for sponsoring and initiating welfare programs are notably reluctant to enlarge their direct financial support, or even to solicit such support energetically from lay church people. It has been noted already that the past two or three decades have been ones of tremendous expansion of social work under nonchurch auspices, both public and private, and in this setting many church-related agencies feel themselves often to be standing still or even going backward so far as their support from the churches is concerned. This period has also, of course, been one of rapidly rising costs, not only because of the rising cost of living, but also because of the increased costs involved in professionalizing social work and raising standards. Often, these executives feel, it is their very church-relatedness that cuts them off from public funds or community chest support, while the churches themselves seem year by year more reluctant to stand behind their own enterprises financially. It is particularly galling to the church social worker when a wealthy church member makes a nominal contribution to the agencies of his own church, then makes a large and well publicized contribution to a nonsectarian agency. To the church social worker, this not infrequent experience is a demonstration of the failure of pastors to interpret to their constituents the welfare work of their own denomination.

There are church-related agencies which are exempt from these financial pressures, some through large endowments, some through well developed financial campaigns, some by careful adherence to the standards of community chests and similar nonchurch sources— but few, apparently, through the voluntary assumption of financial responsibility by the churches to which they are related. The study of church-related agencies indicated that less than 5.5 per cent of their total operating income came from religious organizations, mostly from local churches. Excluding hospitals, which receive 89 per cent of their income from service fees, the agencies received 15 per cent from religious organizations, 9 per cent being from local churches (See chart No. 4 on page 129 for variations in this pattern for certain major types of agencies). In terms of number of agencies, rather than dollars, however, religious organizations appear to take more financial responsibility, two-thirds of them reported receiving significant financial support from religious sources—22 per cent, all their income; 24 per cent, more than half; and 19 per cent, less than half.

The interviews give frequent testimony to the feelings of church social workers on this score:

> The director was outspoken and highly critical of the denomination and what he termed its "small efforts in helping finance this great work that is being done here." Dr. B., the interviewer gathered, seemed quite resentful of the fact that each year the agency ended up with a deficit that eventually became his responsibility to meet through personal appeals and other means of fund-raising.

> This is where Protestants miss the boat. You know the story. The Jews have a big campaign, the Catholics do the same, but there is no correlated Protestant group that does this. (He indicated that, if you want to maintain agencies, you have to give them money).

> If we could say to our children and parents that we have the Protestant churches of New York standing behind us and helping us, it would mean a great deal. Large organizations don't contribute.

> 75 per cent of our budget now comes from the community. If an agency is a church agency the church should support it. This is the pattern of Jews and Catholics. It isn't the Protestant pattern. [Protestant denominations] should work out a philosophy for their interest in social work and should then support their stand. Generally they beg the question. If the [local denominational organization] wants to keep its agencies it ought to give real financial and moral support. It ought to have strong convictions about its relationship to social welfare. Agencies shouldn't be a part of the [denomination] because of historical circumstances or as a practical measure to enhance its own status.[9]

The Problem of Standards

This volume has already documented the rapid rise of professional standards in social work in the past few decades. The enforcement of standards has been closely related to centralization of funds for social work. Protestant agencies, pressed for funds and seeking aid from community chests and foundations, have found more and more vigorous conditions placed upon the disbursement of such funds. The following excerpt from an interview with a representative of the Community Chests and Councils of America is an excellent illustration:

> I would expect you to find that most chests require their member agencies to comply with the following general principles:
> The agency should be representative of the community; that is, the policy-making body should have a broad base and should attempt to include the major elements of the community which it serves.
> The agency should serve the total community; that is, it should not restrict its intake in terms of serving only one segment of the people needing its service.
> The agency should provide a service which is needed by the community in which it is located.
> The agency should not provide a service which is strongly controversial.

The interviews pointed to the first and the fourth criteria as most frequently presenting a problem for church-related agencies. The criterion of representativeness obviously calls for Catholic and Jewish representation in communities where these groups are present, and this is difficult to reconcile with "church-relatedness." The fourth criterion, that services be noncontroversial, comes into prominence when religious services are provided, because religion seems by definition in social work circles to be a "controversial" matter. (Detailed indication from the study of agencies of the relation of community chest contributions to the nature of religious involvement is given in the accompanying table.)

Table T-24

RELIGIOUS INVOLVEMENT OF AGENCIES BY WHETHER OR NOT THEY RECEIVE COMMUNITY CHEST FUNDS

	Per Cent of Agencies	
	Receiving community chest funds	Not receiving community chest funds
Total	100.0	100.0
	(251 agencies)	(866 agencies)
I. Recognition of Relationship		
a. Officially recognized by a religious organization as related	78.0	82.3
b. With *officially stated* relationship	67.3	74.5
II. Nature of Religious Control		
a. Directly responsible to a religious organization with *no* board of its own	.2	9.1
b. Have own board where		
1. *All* members are chosen by religious organization	27.1	37.4

145

Table T-24 (continued)

	Per Cent of Agencies	
	Receiving community chest funds	Not receiving community chest funds
2. *One-half or more* are chosen by religious organization	8.0	4.6
3. *Less than one-half* are chosen by religious ganization	5.6	2.8
c. Have own board which requires certain religious affiliation of members		
1. *All* board members *must* be of a certain affiliation	33.1	59.0
2. *One-half or more* of its members must be of a certain affiliation	21.1	8.2
3. *Less than one-half,* but some of its members must be of a certain offiliation	.02	.08
d. Make official reports to religious organization	60.1	77.8
1. Number where religious organization has final authority	33.1	51.2
III. Control and Character of Services		
In practice, require certain religious affiliation of		
1. Director	62.9	79.0
2. All other professional staff members	25.9	31.6
3. One-half or more of other professional staff members	9.2	4.4
4. Less than half of other professional staff members	.03	.8
IV. Religious Character of Service		
a. With religious objective, whether or not services are secular	76.5	85.6
b. Provides distinctly religious services	54.2	65.9
1. Worship services	35.9	48.6
2. Religious instruction	27.9	33.6
3. Evangelistic programs	.9	14.0
4. Chapel facilities	27.5	36.5
5. Chaplaincy services	26.6	27.9
6. Pastoral services	25.1	41.7
7. Others	.8	.9
c. Officially limiting services to persons of certain religious affiliation	10.0	17.2
d. In practice, serves persons of a certain affiliation	21.5	27.9
e. Consider themselves Christian agencies in tradition and spirit	96.4	95.5
f. In practice require certain religious affiliation of		
1. Director	62.9	79.0
2. All other professional staff members	25.8	31.6
3. One-half or more of other professional staff members	.9	.4
4. Less than one-half of other professional staff members	.02	—

Table T-24 (continued)

	Per Cent of Agencies	
	Receiving community chest funds	Not receiving community chest funds
V. Nature of Assistance		
a. Originated under auspices of a religious organization	23.1	20.2
b. Uses building owned by religious organization which is	41.4	48.7
1. Provided rent free	34.2	39.6
2. Provided below market rental	.02	—
3. Provided at full market rental	—	—
c. Receives significant financial support from religious sources	55.4	62.7
1. All of income	—	26.1
2. More than one-half of income	27.5	20.9
3. Less than one-half of income	26.6	15.0
d. Receives assistance (other than financial) from religious organization	62.5	57.9
1. Volunteer training or recruitment	23.1	18.0
2. Promotion or fund-raising	33.9	30.9
3. Consultation services	27.1	22.4
4. Ministerial or pastoral services	26.7	29.9
5. Gifts in kind (food, clothes, etc.)	47.0	44.9
6. Others	.09	.9

Standards are not confined to such general matters, however, nor are they applied only in relation to financial support. Each branch and specialization of social work has proliferated in statements of standards as it has become established as a profession, and these standards have not only been written into the policies of community chests, but also into those of the public agencies which license and inspect such programs.

The rigid standards for control set up by governmental agencies and less rigidly by community councils and community funds creates problems for an agency which wants to maintain some relationship between the common practices of a religious tradition and the standards of the social work profession and public health requirements. For example, New York city assigns to its Department of Public Health the enforcement of a section of the sanitary code relating to day-care centers. Detailed regulations exist for the admission of children, their separation by age groupings, numerous requirements regarding the type of structure and its permitted usage, staff, intake policies, and the like.

These policies, which must be met before a license is issued, applies, for example, to vacation church schools. They give an extreme illustration of the kind of problems faced by some church-

147

related agencies. The following are some of the areas in which problems occur.

A. *Intake and admission.* It is deep in the church tradition that no applications are turned away from a welfare program if they can be accepted, even where crowding and inefficiency result. Social work and public health standards tend to put upper limits on case loads, use of space, size of groups, etc. They also define the criteria for selection of clients or members, thus removing from the agency any autonomy of decision in selection.

B. *Personnel.* Protestant agencies have traditionally relied heavily on volunteers, especially in educational and group work programs. Standards of the social work profession tend to exclude volunteers except in circumscribed roles. Social work standards further tend to require professional training in schools of social work, few of which are church oriented, and to frown on the employment of personnel who do not have this training. Protestant churches and Catholic alike have been guilty of placing their social work under the direction of persons who had little understanding of its professional aspects, whatever their qalifications in the religious field may have been. There has been a serious attempt in recent years in many quarters to remedy this situation, and in a number of places well trained workers have been secured.

But taken as a whole, the social work of the churches is probably still more inadequately staffed than is considered desirable by professional standards. So long as this situation continues, it will be difficult for the church agency to take its proper place in a general community program.

Our study has revealed some interesting findings in regard to the employment of trained social workers in church-related agencies:

451 of the 1,117 agencies in the entire study sample employed social workers

34 of the 211 homes for the aged employed 68 social workers, 19 with accredited degrees

39 of the 166 hospitals employed 173 social workers, 116 with accredited degrees

109 of the 139 neighborhood houses employed 538 social workers, 97 with accredited degrees

72 of the 118 institutions for children employed 170 social workers, 104 with accredited degrees

9 of the 40 residences employed 12 social workers, 4 with accredited degrees

29 of the 30 child placement agencies employed 176 social workers, 101 with accredited degrees

In a number of interviews, these findings consistently astound experts on professional standards in general and in various specialized fields, not only regarding the number of social workers employed

148

and the proportion of these with degrees from accredited schools of social work, but also regarding the number of various types of agencies that employ social workers at all.

And an important note of caution should be interjected. It is hard to believe that the reputation of church-related agencies as having low professional standards could have been so widespread among professional as well as church people without some confirmation in fact. Such questionnaires as the one used in the study, without exception, draw disproportionately heavy participation from better staffed, financed, and generally equipped respondents. But there was no way, in the time available, to check on the characteristics of the nonresponding agencies, and we simply do not know how general these indications of the employment of social workers in church-related agencies might be.

However, a more reliable aspect of the study analysis was a comparison among the participating agencies themselves. Here we compared the proportion of social workers with accredited degrees with degrees of religious control of the employing agencies. (See Appendix A, for method). The analysis revealed a decrease in the proportion of social workers with accredited degrees as the degree of religious control increased, and this is evident in the table below.

Table T-25

EMPLOYMENT OF SOCIAL WORKERS AND THOSE WITH
ACCREDITED DEGREES
By Degrees of Religious Control

Degrees of control	Employing agencies	Social Workers		
		Total	With degrees	Per cent
All degrees	451	1,641	675	41
0	49	245	154	63
1	32	136	83	61
2	46	196	81	41
3	51	204	88	43
4	56	236	92	39
5	61	185	45	24
6	69	218	65	30
7	60	141	54	38
8	14	42	6	14
9	13	38	7	18

A further bit of pertinent evidence of the influence of professional standard-enforcing agencies, by the proportion of social workers with accredited degrees employed, is given in a comparison of employing agencies receiving and not receiving community chest funds. Although 49 per cent of the social workers employed by agencies receiving community chest funds had accredited degrees, only 31 per cent employed by agencies not receiving community chest contributions had such professional degrees.

C. *Working Conditions.* Church-related agencies have gloried in the "dedicated" worker who placed no limit on hours or the kinds of service he might be called on to perform. Professional social work sets standards which protect the worker from exploitation. There was frequent comment in the interviews as to the tension and misunderstanding between those whose motives are in terms of "dedication" and those whose motives are "professional."

The Diffusion of Protestant Support

It has been the viewpoint of leading Protestant groups, rooted deep in the Calvinist tradition in particular, that social welfare programs even when initiated by the churches may move out from under church control and sponsorship to that of the general community, as either public or private nonsectarian welfare. Church groups may spark welfare programs, churches may even sponsor and finance new types of social work, but in the long run social service should be available to all on the basis of need rather than faith, and the burden of support and administration should be on the community at large. The role of the church member here is to be generous in support of all such welfare enterprises, but the budget he supports is not administered through ecclesiastical channels.

There have been many rumblings of dissatisfaction with this traditional Protestant philosophy in recent years, paralleling similar expressions of discontent with the comparable philosophy of protestantism in regard to education. These fall into three categories.

First, the inevitable result of such a philosophy is to produce a sense of insecurity on the part of agencies that are, and intend to continue to be, "church-related." This has been adequately documented in section 5 above.

Second, while this philosophy was perhaps entirely workable in Calvinist New England, it runs into serious difficulties when the religious environment is a composite of Roman Catholic, Jewish, Protestant, and secular. Roman Catholics and Jews are well organized for welfare work among their own groups, both in the definition of their clientele and the soliciting of support. Protestantism, in contrast, seems to be in a state of utter confusion. The logic of community-wide support of an agency in any way identified as "Protestant" becomes suspect when "Catholics" and "Jews" are already supporting "their own" welfare efforts. The reactions of Protestant welfare agencies to this ambiguous situation are too varied to list; they range from complete retreat into the ecclesiastical structure (sectarian services, sectarian support) to an almost frantic rejection of any hint of connection with the organized church.

150

And thirdly, there is a growing suspicion that large blocks of Protestants may be losing their habits of stewardship in relation to private philanthropy. No matter what the clergyman may say from his pulpit about the obligation of the Christian to support worthy welfare enterprises (and even this note seems less frequently sounded in sermons), if there is little visible connection between the church and private welfare efforts, then the sanctions of the religious community do not seem to apply very effectively to the giving habits of the church member. Where Jews and Catholics alike use the voluntary organizations of their faith as part of the machinery for the support of their welfare programs, the efforts of the Protestant churches in this direction seem increasingly to be hortatory only. Adequate evidence is not available, but many persons today —including income tax consultants—are prepared to say privately that benevolent giving of the Protestant church member is not on a par with that of Catholics and Jews, particularly Jews—even in relation to causes that are nonsectarian.

The responsibility for social welfare in some cities seems to be carried by Jews, more so than is proportionate to their numbers in the population. Catholics are trying to take care of their own. Jews are consistently interested and active in all fields—housing, race relations, FEPC, etc.

It may well be time to re-examine honestly a philosophy which, however noble in purpose, seems to provide an excuse for the evasion of responsibility. The truth seems to be that no one really knows where the benevolent efforts of concerned Protestants are chiefly directed today, nor even whether those efforts are of the magnitude the churches have complacently claimed. In some cities the weakness of organized Protestant work has become glaringly evident as large numbers of Negroes, overwhelmingly Protestant, have moved into the disorganized inner-city areas and the absence of social work resources to meet their needs has become all too apparent.

<h2 style="text-align:center">FOOTNOTES FOR CHAPTER 11</h2>

[1] New York City Mission Society, *Annual Report* (New York: New York City Mission Society, 1856), p. 15.

[2] Interview Record No. 36.

[3] Interview Record No. 11.

[4] H. Paul Douglass and Edmund de S. Brunner, *The Protestant Church as a Social Institution* (New York: Harper and Brothers, 1935).

[5] Interview Record No. 26.

[6] Interview Record No. 3.

[7] Interview Record No. 14.

[8] See Appendix A.

[9] Interview Records Nos. 21, 3, 29, 18.

For many years church leaders have felt the urgent need of correlation, more efficient organization, and of standards among church
social workers.[1] Worth M. Tippy, executive secretary of the Department of Social Service of the Federal Council of Churches conceived the idea of organizing and improving church social work.
It was planned that this Church Conference on Social Work was to
meet in connection with the National Conference of Social Work.

The Church Conference met for the first time in Boston in 1930.
There a committee was appointed, consisting of representatives of
denominational and interdenominational executives, educators, city
federation executives, social workers, pastors, editors, and other
leaders, to consider the situation and make recommendations.

It is clear from the statement of objectives prepared by the committee that the Church Conference had as its primary goals a more
complete understanding of the techniques, concepts and theory of
social work and the encouragement of a closer co-operative working relationship with social work groups. The purposes of the conference were set out as follows:

> To contribute to the development of scientific methods in the
> social work of the Protestant churches and councils of churches
> of the United States;
> To bring church social workers together for acquaintance and
> discussion of common problems;
> To bring to church social workers the value of discussions and
> associations of the National Conference of Social Work;
> To develop understanding and co-operation between churches
> and social agencies in communities;
> To make religion a greater redemptive force in all social work.

Following the conference in December of 1930, the Federal Council's Executive Committee approved the organization and purposes
of the Church Conference and recommended to its own constituent
bodies their hearty co-operation in the enterprise. The conference
asked that each denomination make a fresh study of its relation to
the whole program of social work in communities, and that church
social work leaders enter into close relations with both the Church
Conference and the National Conference of Social Work. Programs
were planned to serve the interests of the Church Conference, such
as: the National Council of Federated Church Women, the Association of Executive Secretaries of Councils of Churches, the National
Conference of Jews and Christians, the Child Welfare League of

America, the American Social Hygiene Association, the Goodwill Industries, and other groups. The Conference also worked closely with the Episcopal Social Work Conference, which pioneered in the field of Protestant social work.

The development of the Church Conference of Social Work received the interest of church leaders and the co-operation of leaders in the National Conference of Social Work. It had as its speakers not only leaders in church life, but presidents of the National Conference and other individuals ranking high in professional social work. It served as a study and fellowship group in the field of the spiritual and religious forces in social work.

The Church Conference of Social Work has always been concerned over the problem of education and standards in church social service. As early as 1933, it appointed a study committee on curriculum which interested itself in the development of courses of study for the preparation not only of professional but also volunteer workers. This committee was interested in having the International Council of Religious Education include courses on the Church and Social Work in its New Leadership Curriculum issued in 1935.

In 1933, the Church Conference of Social Work also set up a Permanent Committee on Standards. Its general purpose was the elevation of standards in church social work with respect to administration and leadership training. This involved continued study of current problems in the field and the discovery of constructive methods for their solution. The committee was also to serve as a center of information regarding standards in church social work. It was composed of officially delegated representatives of the following groups: The Department of Social Service of the Federal Council of Churches, the International Council of Religious Education, the Association of Church Social Workers. Section I of the Church Conference of Social Work, the Association of Church Executives, the National Council of Federated Church Women, the Association of Theological Seminaries, the group of professional schools serving employed social workers, the Home Missions Council, and the Council of Women for Home Missions.

When the Committee on Standards met in Detroit it organized Section I of the Church Conference of Social Work, a section for employed church social workers. During the ensuing year investigations were continued and in 1934 at the conference in Kansas City a report was submitted suggesting a definite standard for training and a somewhat detailed proposal for a professional organization of church workers together with recommendations for further study.

The Committee on Standards had not expected that any further organization would take place at that time, but the section insisted that a professional association be set up before the close of the conference. Committees then worked on the proposal and finally, the section organized "The Association of Church Social Workers" with a constitution, bylaws, and an executive committee. On June 13, 1935, the first annual meeting of the Association was held in Montreal, Canada. On May 27, 1936, the second annual meeting was held in Atlantic City.

The Association of Church Social Workers continued until 1953 when under the sponsorship of the Department of Social Welfare of the National Council of Churches it merged with the Church Conference of Social Workers to form the Christian Social Welfare Associates. The Associates is a membership organization for professional and lay persons interested in the program of the churches for social welfare. The conference continues as the forum of the Associates. Members of the Associates support and share in the program of the Department of Social Welfare of the National Council of Churches. They co-operate with the department in the publication of *Christian Social Welfare,* a periodical devoted to the interests of Christian social work.

The Church Conference of Social Work, as an associate group of the National Conference of Social Work, is held annually and is sponsored by the Department of Social Welfare of the National Council of Churches with the co-operation of the Christian Social Welfare Associates.

From its beginning it was apparent that the Church Conference on Social Work did not consider itself a competitive but a co-operative and supplementary body to the National Conference of Social Work, expressing the peculiar concern of the churches in the field. It was stated in the proceedings at the Boston meeting in 1930 that:

> It should be said emphatically that the Federal Council is sympathetic to the community organization of social work, and that the church conference has no idea of trying to recover it for the Protestant churches. But the churches have great institutions of mercy and relief-hospitals, orphanages and homes of various kinds. Local councils of churches in cities have important contacts with juvenile and family welfare courts and other public institutions, which are developing rapidly and on a professional basis. Many strong churches have a social worker or workers on their staff and a considerable amount of social casework will always be done by local churches. Spiritual casework must also learn to follow scientific methods. . . . The great work of churches in the fields of social work in the future, however, will be in forms of collaboration with community agencies, with especial emphasis on the spiritual factors in personal and family adjustment.[2]

When the Constitution of the Conference was officially adopted in 1934, the objectives were set forth outlining the purpose for which the conference was organized. The original objectives were amended at the Seventh Annual Meeting of the Conference held at Grand Rapids, Michigan, May 30, 1940. These objectives were:

1. To bring church social workers together for acquaintance and discussion of common problems.

2. To bring to church social workers the value of the discussion and associations of the National Conference of Social Work.

3. To develop interest in the whole field of co-operation between churches and social agencies.

4. To study current problems within the scope of church social work and to make constructive recommendations looking toward their solution.

5. To gain wider recognition of the indispensible resources of religion in the rehabilitation of individuals and groups.

6. To further the use of approved methods in the social work field and to give leadership in the development of a strategy in church social work for the Protestant constituency.[3]

The objectives of the conference were again amended to relate the conference more directly to a fuller form of co-operation between Protestant social workers and the social service structure and the National Conference of Social Work. In addition, these amendments set forth a more complete program with much more attention to the program of church-related agencies and the expansion of the activities of the conference.

Structural avenues of co-operation between the churches and church-related agencies exist on every level of the social structure. The church-related agencies have representation on the local councils of social agencies as members and serve on the various committees of the councils. Ministers and lay members of churches, and board members and staffs of church-related agencies serve on the board of directors of the councils of social agencies. The same is true of the local community funds.

The local councils of churches, too, play an important role in bringing about co-operation between organized social work and the churches. This matter has been dealt with at some length in a previous section of the study.

However, in the literature there is evidence of more attempts of co-operation both from the professional social worker and from the churches and church social workers than there is of criticism of the latter. An example of an attempt on the part of those interested in church social welfare is that of the Protestant Welfare Agencies of New York in September, 1952, which has been referred to before.[5] At this conference, titled "Co-operation Between Churches and Welfare Agencies," twenty-one leaders and laymen in both fields gathered for the purpose of trying to find a common ground of understanding of the following questions:

1. Should churches and welfare agencies be "natural partners"?
2. Do social workers and ministers understand each other?
3. Can the person in need be helped more by co-operation between ministers and social workers?
4. Do laymen have a special role in fostering this co-operation?

This small but significant gathering came to several basic conclusions. Among them were:[5]

Descriptions of courses from the school bulletins illustrate that the schools of social work give less attention to the subject of religion than theological seminaries give to social problems.

The minister should refer a case to a social agency where the need is mainly for the kind of community help the agency gives. . . .

The training schools for both professions (the ministry and social workers) require much the same personal qualifications for admission, such as emotional maturity, leadership qualities, sound motivation for graduate study, and evidence of a concern for social problems and human needs. In addition, recognized schools of social work and theological seminaries both require for admission a regular course of academic study and a degree from an accredited college. . . .

The common interests of the two professions of social work and the ministry suggest further practical co-operation. This trend should be reflected in the schools where social workers and ministers are so trained that each will appreciate and depend upon the other.[6]

Earlier a most important meeting called the Great Lakes Institute was sponsored by the Community Chests and Councils of America to deal with the subject, "Social Services under Catholic, Jewish and Protestant Auspices in the Total Welfare System." The Institute was attended by leading social workers, religious leaders, and lay persons. In his opening remarks Robert H. MacRae, of the Community Chest of Detroit, stated:

I believe that social work needs the church just as the church needs social work. They need to understand each other. They are partners in a common enterprise of serving people. If organized religion were to disappear much of the social work would disappear in time, because it would have lost its roots.[7]

The findings of the conference in regard to Protestant social work were as follows:

1. The Protestant churches' concern in the field of social work is deeply embedded in a religious motive which is perhaps best summarized in the words of its founder, "Inasmuch as ye have done it unto one of the least of these my brethren, ye have done it unto me."

2. Beginning in the middle of the nineteenth century with the opening of the era which we commonly speak of as the era of the social gospel, the churches began to show an increasing concern with their responsibility for the community as a whole. This meant the evolving of new techniques, new methods, new approaches and in some instances an almost complete "about face" from traditionally held positions. This deep concern is a continuing interest today. While recognizing the tremendous contribution that modern secular social work has made to community well-being, the churches still are jealous to preserve their heritage and feel that they can preserve that heritage and at the same time make a valid contribution to community well-being.

3. We believe we can say fairly that the churches feel that this contribution can best be made; first, through co-operation on the denominational level; second, through co-operation on the interdenominational level; third, through co-operation on the intercultural level; and fourth, on the community level.

The above are the reasons for the organization of departments of social service in our local and state councils of churches on the denominational level and on the state and local level, as well as the national level.

In conclusion, while recognizing that there are, and will continue to be areas of misunderstanding, we believe sincerely that through such conferences as this Great Lakes Institute between the representatives of religion and representative leadership in the field of social work much will be accomplished toward bringing about a better understanding between the two groups. We may be using different nomenclatures and different techniques, but our objective is the same—a ministry or a service to people, regardless of race, color, or creed.[8]

There have been many other meetings, too many to enumerate, between the churches and community social welfare organizations, between groups of church-related agencies and community welfare organizations, and between the churches and community welfare action on a local, regional, state, and national level. Institutes, seminars and conferences have been held not only between those active in the field but between students in seminaries and those training for social work activities. The following is just an indication of a few of the types of meetings which have taken place in recent years:

A secular-church gathering called by the Council on Clinical Training, Inc. held at the Chicago Theological Seminary, October, 1950.

The Norfolk Institute on Church and Social Work, sponsored by the Co-operating Council of the Methodist Churches of Norfolk, Va.

Three Family Education Projects, called by the Family Life Education Committee, Social Service Department of the Detroit Council of Churches in 1950.

A Metropolitan Detroit District gathering of church representatives in co-operation with Wayne University, psychiatric, casework and educational groups in 1950.

The Church and Social Welfare Institute, held February 9, 1955, by the Rhode Island Council of Churches in Providence, R. I.

Institutes for Clergymen and Social Workers, sponsored jointly by the Massachusetts Council of Churches and the Federation of Social Workers of Greater Boston.

Virginia Conference on Social Work, April, 1954, where a panel was held on "The Church's Role in Community Teamwork."

The work of the councils of churches, local, regional, and state, are particularly important in bringing about co-operation between organized social work and the churches and church organizations.[9] These 900 councils, over 200 of which have paid workers, and a good number of which have departments of social welfare, have as part of their functions to provide professional social work assistance to denominational and Protestant agencies in matters of welfare policy and planning, to provide a liaison service between Protestant churches and the public and private social agencies of the community, to help the churches and social agencies make use of one another's services in assisting families and individuals with their problems and to interpret social agencies, public and private, the resources of the churches and the reconstructive values in the Christian religion for personal growth and development. This is accomplished through formal committees, meetings, representation on boards, committees, and groups. Informal conferences and consultations are also important in bringing about understanding and co-operation. On the state and local level, the councils of churches have acted both as a channel of communication between social work and the churches and have acted creatively to work out and instrument new relationships to meet new situations. They are the grass-root organizations through which practice is developed and from which policy is formed.

A review of the evidence clearly indicates that there is a developing effort on the part of the churches and of the social work groups toward co-operation. Structurally every avenue has been opened to bring about such co-operation. The church-related agencies have representation on the local councils of social agencies as members and serve on the various committees of the councils. Ministers and lay members of churches, and board members and staffs of church-related agencies serve on the boards of directors of the councils of social agencies. The same is true of the local community funds. The same would hold true of state and national bodies.

The attitudes of both the churches and the social work leaders and organizations are in the direction of co-operation. Social work groups are anxious in their hope for the avoidance of fragmentation of social work and desirous of further integration of efforts. The churches, too, even though there is a resurgence of concern for Protestant representation, are still in general "sympathetic to the community organization of social work, [and do not wish to] recover it for the Protestant churches."

FOOTNOTES FOR CHAPTER 12

[1] Material on the formation of the Church Conference of Social Work was taken from the March 28, 1936 (Volume XV, No. 13) and January 22, 1938 (Volume XVII, No. 4) issues of *Information Service,* Department of Research and Education, Federal Council of the Churches of Christ in America, New York.

[2] Proceedings of the Church Conference of Social Work, Boston, 1930 (New York: Federal Council of Churches of Christ in America, 1930), pp. 4–5.

[3] *The Church Conference of Social Work* (New York: Federal Council of the Churches of Christ in America, undated).

[4] See Chapter 8, "State and Local Councils of Churches."

[5] *Co-operation Between Churches and Welfare Agencies* (New York: Federation of Protestant Welfare Agencies, 1952), p. 18.

[6] *Ibid.*

[7] *Social Services Under Catholic, Jewish, and Protestant Auspices in the Total Welfare System.* Great Lakes Institute. (New York: Community Chests and Councils of America, Incorporated, 1948), p. 1.

[8] *Ibid.,* p. 30.

[9] See Chapter 8 for a fuller discussion.

THE QUESTION OF ROLES AND GOALS

13

Many of the questions and problems with which social work deals have at one time fallen within the province of the churches. For many years the minister and the church worker helped families in economic distress or at the time of family crises such as illness, death, or divorce. With the growth and extension of social work more and more of these problems have been handled by the professional social worker who was armed with a number of tools derived from the scientific study of social life and individual personality. There developed, then, the situation where the churches felt themselves infringed upon by a new "scientific" approach to human relations and the social agencies, with their scientific facts, felt convinced of their competence to deal more adequately with many problems hitherto dealt with by the churches. It was inevitable that confusion and conflict would develop in working out a proper relationship between the two.

There is the assumption on the part of many in the field that the churches and the social workers have the same goals and need only an understanding to bring about good working relations. One writer, for example, comes to the conclusion that the ministry and the social work profession are two aspects of the same thing.

> When a young man, as now frequently happens, deliberates whether he shall enter the ministry or enlist in the calling of social service, he is in fact choosing, not between two vocations, but between two departments of one calling. Social service should be recognized as a religious work, precisely as religious service is recognized as a social work, and to draw a line between the two is to rob religion of its reality and social service of its sacredness.[1]

But in spite of the assumption of a common interest and goals, and of the insistence on the necessity for co-operation, there continues to exist an area of conflict between the churches and professional social work. "There is much," states Frank Bruno, "that the church can contribute in method to social work out of its age-long experience in human relations, but yet the way to its utilization has not been found." Mr. Bruno continues to say:

> . . . The one social institution with which the objective of social work is in closest agreement is the church, and yet the give and take between the two has been less significant than between the other professions and social work.[2]

160

Another writer states:

> With many notable exceptions, especially among the great leaders of our faiths, there is a serious lack of understanding between the clergy and the churches on the one hand and our professional social workers and agencies on the other hand.[3]

One of the difficulties between religious workers and social workers is that of philosophy.

> At one extreme there may be a projection of the old conflict between science and religion—many churchmen view the modern professionally trained social worker in the secular agency as a devotee of everything that today's psychological and social sciences have to offer and contrariwise, indifferent or antagonistic to religious concepts and spiritual forces.[4]

The difference in philosophy really describes a difference in goals, which is not often admitted. The goal of the churches is, primarily, to bring the individual to a knowledge of God; that of the social worker is to help the individual make an adjustment to society. One writer describes this difference in the following terms:

> For example, social work's judgment about behavior is determined more by whether or not it produces conflict within the individual, interferes with his contribution to the group, or has a destructive or harmful effect upon society itself, than by abstract concepts of right or wrong . . . the caseworker would call a symptom what some ministers might name a "sin." . . .
>
> In addition, casework does not, in any formal sense admit God's presence into the relationship between the worker and a person in difficulty. This does not mean that casework is anti-religious as it is often believed by ministers to be, but rather that it operates outside religion and is neither anti- nor pro-religious in its approach. . . . As in other areas of life, the individual's religious adjustment may be either mature and healthy or immature and neurotic. When the caseworker observes religion being used neurotically by the client, she would believe, in many instances, that it should be examined critically in terms of its meaning to the person concerned.[5]

The above approach has led many religious leaders to consider the professional social worker as "nonreligious as well as nonsectarian in her work and quite unappreciative of the spiritual in the sense of religious values."[6]

The charge of ungodliness causes a prominent social worker to write defensively:

> In facing these difficulties, I should like to say first, after more than thirty years in social work with a wide acquaintance among social workers, that social workers are certainly not ir-

religious, godless souls without a sense of spiritual values. For the most part, as I have known them, social workers have active church connections. As to those who make no explicit religious profession, I have known them as being quite generally highly dedicated people, believing in and practicing ideals in harmony with those of organized religion. . . .[7]

It is assumed and stated, by both churches and social workers, that the churches have a specific and unique service to perform in addition to the alleviation of distress. This contribution lies in the field of spiritual values.

> There is a distinct contribution needed by multitudes of erring and troubled souls which can hardly be expected of mere social agencies. That contribution is in the way of a spiritual dynamic for the attainment of a better life, and just such a spiritual dynamic we assume religion to be. The church worker then "is not only skilled in the techniques of the social work profession . . . [but] . . . is rooted and grounded in the faith by which the churches live.[8]

> We could illustrate and amplify this point in a number of ways but it all comes to focus in this: we are concerned primarily with persons who are made, we believe, in the image of God. Social workers who have this conviction recognize techniques for what they are—tools to be used to help people. But the worker will understand quite clearly that techniques and tests and the art of counseling were made for man and not man for the social worker's skill. That is not always understood by social workers. There are some who are so engrossed in their methods and so captivated by the jargon . . . that they lose sight of the fact that they are working with persons.

> There again is an underlying religious conviction which is essential for the church social worker. It is the awareness that the worker is not the source of the healing power of life, but the channel, the agent. The personal relationship which finds its meaning in God, must be achieved and maintained.[9]

The professional social worker, on the other hand, has reservations about the churches' activities in social work. Often there is the feeling that the churches' primary interest and chief motive is to evangelize.

> But there can be no doubt that many lodging houses and ophanages and much family relief has been provided by the church when the chief motive has been to secure a favorable opportunity for bringing religious influences to bear upon the client. Medical and social work as instruments for opening up the heathen's heart to Christian doctrine were frankly used in the earlier days of foreign missions, and the earlier arguments for establishing the physical department of the Young Men's Christian Association were that it would provide an attraction

for young men to bring them under the religious influence of the association. Baseball leagues in Sunday schools have not infrequently been promoted, not with the primary motive of providing wholesome recreation but as an inducement to boys to attend Sunday school.

It is probably inevitable that an institution whose central purpose and reason for existence is the promotion of religious faith should subordinate to this central purpose all other activities in which it engages.[10]

In an attempt to find a comparable relationship some persons have turned to that which exists between the social workers and the medical profession.

There is a curious contrast between the caseworker's contact with the medical profession and her contact with the church. In the first instance she gives what aid she can to the physician without presuming on his professional prerogatives, but as she goes back again and again, not only depending upon the medical profession to carry its responsibility but insisting that it do so. . . . [11]

This type of relationship is not carried out, however, between the social worker and the church.

Admitted that the spiritual problems in any given family are not as apparent as are health or environmental difficulties, the symptoms, such as laxness in church attendance, indifference to the religious training of children and the like certainly are observable. There would seem to be no excuse for not insisting in a perfectly courteous yet firm manner, that the church carry its responsibility in exactly the same manner as is taken for granted in our contact with the medical profession.[12]

The comparison of the relationship of the social worker to the physician and of the social worker to the minister, illustrates the different goals which are held by the social worker and by the churches. The social worker can accept completely the goal of the physician. Physical health is within the social worker's professional frame of reference. It is a goal which is given value by his training and is prescribed as a necessary step in the adjustment of the individual to society. The social worker, on the other hand, as a social worker, does not have as a goal the relating of the individual to God. An adequate adjustment on the part of a client, from his point of view, might or might not include any religious conviction or church activity. Insistence on religious behavior, in most instances, would be thought by professional social workers to be an infringement on the personal liberties of an individual. An adequate spiritual adjustment might be the adoption of a working philosophy which would allow the individual to relate himself to the social order in a way which would not be destructive to him-

163

self or society. Any suggestion, then, that the social worker pay attention to laxness in church attendance or indifference to the religious training of children would not be accepted by them except as a method of treatment if suggested by the client-family. Both social workers and the churches accept the goals of the physician. Social workers and the churches may have some goals in common but they do not share all goals.

The question of the role of the pastor toward his relationship to his parishioners and to the social agencies is difficult. The pastor is deeply and inevitably involved in problems of human welfare. Not only does his work take him intimately into the life situation of many families, but it is deep in the tradition of religious institutions that people should bring their problems to the pastor, and he is expected to help resolve them. The pastor then decides upon the question of what type of problems he will refer to social work agencies, his feeling toward them and his conception of the role they should play in relationship to the church.

One study is indicative of the kinds of problems on which a pastor typically seeks help from agencies outside the church. A statistical analysis of problems referred by pastors in New York city to the central Protestant welfare agency showed the following:

> 50 per cent were requests for financial help and employment
> 15 per cent involved the need for some adjustment with a public welfare agency (delayed relief checks, etc.)
> 35 per cent were a miscellaneous category including problems related to the institutional care of the aged, placement of children at a time of crisis, marital disturbances requiring drastic court action, and so on.[13]

In all but a very few of the referrals, the immediacy and acuteness of the need were striking; where difficulties in family relationships were involved, an almost negligible group of families were discussed before rather marked emotional or psychological breakdown had occurred. We may conclude, then, that the ministry in general conceives of social casework only as the administration of tangible resources.

In other words, pastors apparently tend to turn to outside agencies when (1) there is need for financial help, (2) a problem has been clearly defined as requiring specialized professional or institutional services (legal, psychiatric, child placement, custodial, etc.) Social workers do not appreciate this attitude of pastors. On the other side, a booklet by a leading clergyman on pastoral counseling may be all too typical of an erroneous view which still prevails. This booklet, while assuming that counseling on some of the most involved forms of personal and family problems will naturally be undertaken by the minister, states that it is the cases with an economic angle which normally belong to the social agencies.

But it also seems clear that pastors tend to be reluctant to seek outside help where the intimate problems of parishioners are concerned. Pastoral counseling is "trained listening" whose aim is to discover the internal tensions and external pressures with which the parishioner is struggling, to evaluate his capacity for dealing with these tensions and pressures; then without removing the parishioner's personal responsibility, to let him marshall his capacities and resources (social, personal, and religious) so he may relieve these pressures at the point where with an understanding of his situation, he is able to deal with them creatively.

It is, nevertheless, small wonder that often ministers are unable to relate to social agencies except as a court of last resort when all else has failed, or as a mother of necessity when social work seems to control the administration or specific functions such as public relief, admission to institutions, etc. In other words, the individual ministers' reluctance to use the social agency may not always be due to his lack of knowledge of its functions, but rather may have more to do with his conception of his own work.

And the evangelical motivation of the church is not without influence in discouraging the use of welfare resources.

Difficulties arise out of the conflicting philosophies of the two types of agencies and the disparity of their technical standards. Social work agencies commonly hold that the churches should refer to them exclusively all cases of people not definitely connected with the church in some way. They are sure that the church should report its cases to the central welfare registry, so that there may be no duplication of aid or difference in counsel. Church social workers on the contrary sometimes want to get their hands on new cases in order to bring them under church influence and are gravely disinclined to expose the needs of the "church's own" to the unsympathetic secular agency.

It seems safe to say, on the basis of numerous case histories of individual churches, that the parish church is less directly involved in welfare work today than at the time Douglass and Brunner made their study. Deaconnesses who used to visit the poor now have become instead directors of religious education. The movement in the 1920's to make city churches community recreation centers, with boys' clubs and bowling alleys and swimming pools, has largely disappeared, and in place of general community programs, churches now tend to have the content of all programs "church-related," or oriented specifically to some aspect of church life.[14] Churches have tended to reduce the staff working with welfare needs and increase the staff responsible for education, evangelism, organization, fellowship, and worship.

They have done so on the apparent assumption that public and private welfare agencies now exist to take over the welfare work.

Yet the churches have been obviously ill at ease about this transfer of responsibility, and they are not at all sure that the professional of today is doing what the pastor and the church worker in more amateur fashion, used to do. The specialty of the church was described as follows in the *Social Work Year Book, 1935:*

> The social work which is most distinctive of the church and probably most productive of results is not its relief or other organized activities, but the informal casework carried on from day to day in which the end sought is the rehabilitation of individuals and families within a framework of social and spiritual relationships which the church regards as its function to create and maintain.[15]

The following quotation from a professional social work source summarizes succinctly the nature of the uneasiness of the church when it considers the professionalization of this field:

> Another question raised by the church, is as to whether the claim of the family social work agency to being truly community wide is justified. Is it really comprehensive in its practice and at the service of the church? Can the church safely entrust to the civic agency the social problems of the families for whose spiritual welfare it is responsible? The church is clearly in doubt as to the method in social casework, not only as to value but as to its outlines and processes as well.[16]

The formula which has evolved for bridging the gap between the churches and its ministry and the professional nonsectarian social worker is that of co-operation. The Federation of Protestant Welfare Agencies in a workshop on the question formulated this idea in the following fashion: "An essential of good relations is through co-operation. A state of full confidence between church and agency should be sought and is necessary for greatest effectiveness."[17]

This workshop, however, like many others, failed to develop any clear-cut principles of co-operation. The common goal of the churches and the professional social worker the workshop decided was "the integration of the individual and the realization of his greatest contribution to society." The area of concern of both the churches and the professional workers was then outlined.

The churches:

> The church's contribution is highly personal and interpretative from the point of view of religious tradition. It is moral and helps man to religious conviction through an awareness of his value as a child of God and thus to find peace and security. Its standards of reference are to God who desires the eternal salvation of each individual soul and the radical reconstruction of society into the likeness of his everlasting kingdom. The church knows that no individual can go it alone.

166

The social agency:

The agency's contribution is primarily psychological and environmental. It is ethical and helps the indivdual to a satisfactory adjustment within himself and in relation to his community. The social agency aims to aid the client to maintain himself without the help of the agency.[18]

Thus are stated, to explain the common interest of the churches and social workers, two different frames of reference and two different sets of objectives. For the churches and the ministry the "standard of reference is God;" for the social worker the frame of reference "is primarily psychological and environmental." The goals of the churches are personal salvation and the reconstruction of society; for the social workers they are the adjustment of the individual within himself and to society. It is obvious, then, that the ministry might achieve its primary goal of salvation without necessarily approaching that of the social worker, which is the adjustment of the individual to society. Similarly the social worker might adjust the individual to society, and thus achieve his goal, without either relating the individual to God or remaking society into the kingdom of God. Similarly the frame of reference of the social worker does not, necessarily, include God, nor does that of the ministry, necessarily, include the psychological and environmental analysis of the social worker. Injunctions for co-operation, then, should be instrumented by some principle on which co-operation could be based. But the assumption that the goals are identical and that the frames of reference are the same, without a critical analysis of the differences, leads to confusion. That there must be co-operation between the two approaches to human behavior is obvious. It is doubtful, however, that they will be arrived at until a clearer analysis of the points of difference, and sometimes conflict, in approach and goals is clearly stated.

A greater understanding of each profession by the other—its language, aims, goals, and methods—would lead to more co-operation and mutual understanding. This would not, necessarily, resolve the differences in approach, philosophy, or objectives of either. It would, however, tend to define the areas of co-operation and conflict.

FOOTNOTES FOR CHAPTER 13

[1] Francis G. Peabody, "The Socialization of Religion," *Papers and Proceedings of the American Sociological Society,* Vol. VII, December 1912 (Chicago: University of Chicago Press, 1913), p. 199.

[2] Frank J. Bruno, *Trends in Social Work as Reflected in the Proceedings of the National Conference of Social Work 1874–1946* (New York: Columbia University Press, 1948), pp. 181–182.

[3] Stanley P. Davies, "The Churches and the Nonsectarian Agencies," *Better Times,* January 22, 1954 (New York: Welfare and Health Council, 1954), p. 1.

4 *Ibid.*, p. 1.

5 Alice R. McCabe, "Pastoral Counseling and Casework," *The Family*, Vol. XXIV, No. 7, November, 1943, pp. 260–261.

6 American Association for Organizing Family Social Work, "Report of the Committee on Relations with Casework Organizations Operating Under Religious Auspices," 1926 (New York: *Family Welfare Association of America*, X), p. 3.

7 Davies, *op. cit.*, p. 6.

8 Charles R. Zahnizer, "Casework Evangelism," *Revell*, 1929, p. 10.

9 Arthur C. Lichtenberger, "A Social Agency of the Church," *The Witness* (New York: Episcopal Service for Youth, Inc., 1948).

10 Cecil Clare North, *The Community and Social Welfare* (New York: Mc-Graw-Hill Publications in Sociology, 1931), pp. 86–7.

11 American Association for Organizing Family Social Work, *op. cit.*, p. 4.

12 *Ibid.*, pp. 4–5.

13 Alice R. McCabe, *op. cit.*

14 It might be noted that this is less true of many new suburban churches, where the philosophy of making the church the "community center" bears a marked resemblance to the concept of the inner-city "institutional church" of two or three decades ago, with the difference that the suburban group is dealing with people at a considerably higher economic level and, usually, predominantly Protestant.

15 F. Ernest Johnson, "Protestant Social Work," *Social Work Year Book, 1935* (New York: Russell Sage Foundation, 1935), p. 346.

16 American Association for Organizing Family Social Work, *op. cit.*, p. 68.

17 *Co-operation Between Churches and Welfare Agencies* (New York: Federation of Protestant Welfare Agencies, 1952), p. 11.

18 *Ibid.*, p. 11.

APPENDICES

A Note on the Method and Procedures for the Extent and Nature of Involvement of Protestant, Anglican, and Eastern Orthodox Religious Interests in the Various Types of Health and Welfare Agencies and Institutions in the United States[1]

I. PURPOSE

The purpose of this study was to provide information regarding the extent and nature of involvement of Protestant, Anglican, and Eastern Orthodox religious interests in the various types of health and welfare agencies and institutions in the United States as part of the basis for discussion at a National Conference on the Churches and Social Welfare to be held in Cleveland, Ohio, in November, 1955.[2]

Thus, this study began essentially as an inventory of religiously related (to the member denominations of the National Council) health and welfare agencies and institutions to discover how many, where, rendering what types of service, to how many people, with how much and what kind of personnel and financial support, there are in the United States.

In addition, the study proposed to explore the following problems: 1. To what extent and in what manner is religious control from religious sources and the religious character of the services interrelated in the agencies. 2. It was hoped, furthermore, that some of the data might be analyzed for indications of trends and of relationships to the issues of the larger field of social work.

II. SCOPE

The scope of the study was defined as follows:

A. *Health and Welfare Agencies and Institutions*

Only those agencies and institutions whose major function is health or welfare service were included. This meant the exclusion of health and welfare activities and programs that are incidental to many agencies whose primary function is distinctly religious service. For example, a local church that has a recreation program, though rendering a group work service, was not included as a welfare agency. However, if that church sponsors an organizationally distinct recreational program, such as through a neighborhood house with group work as its major function, that organizational unit was included.

It is recognized that in some cases, such as many mission agencies and institutions where religious service may be expressed primarily in health or welfare activities, the distinction is not very clear. For the thirty member denominations of the National Council of Churches the study relied upon the judgment of the denominational offices regarding whether an agency or institution's major function is health or welfare service. In addition, for the ten selected states, listing in a health or welfare directory was the criterion for inclusion.

B. *Protestant, Anglican, and Eastern Orthodox*

Of primary concern to the study were the health and welfare agencies and institutions known to the denominational offices of the thirty member communions of the National Council of Churches as related to them. In addition, the study included the Salvation Army, the Volunteers of America, and the Southern Baptists.

In the exploratory study of ten selected states, all health and welfare agencies and institutions that were identified as religiously related to any Protestant, Anglican, or Eastern Orthodox denominational, interdenominational, or nondenominational interests were included.

C. *Extent and nature of involvement of . . . religious interests*

The study attempted an inventory of the extent and nature of the operation of church-related health and welfare agencies as well as the extent and nature of involvement of religious interests in these agencies. The presentation itself indicates the analyses made in these two dimensions.

D. *In the United States*

All health and welfare agencies and institutions anywhere in the forty-eight states, Alaska, Hawaii, Puerto Rico and the Virgin Islands, known to the offices of the thirty member denominations of the National Council were included.

Ten states were selected for an exploratory study of all health and welfare agencies and institutions with any Protestant, Anglican, or Eastern Orthodox religious involvement. These states were selected on the basis of representativeness (in the judgment of the directors of the Central Department, now the Bureau of Research and Survey, the Department of Social Welfare and the National Conference on the Churches and Social Welfare, and the Research Unit in Christian Life and Work) in member denominational interest and in rural-urban distribution of the geographic area and for the existence of religious research resources for possible co-ordination in other aspects of research for the conference. They are as follows:

1. California
2. Colorado
3. Kansas
4. Illinois
5. Indiana
6. Maryland
7. Massachusetts
8. South Carolina
9. Pennsylvania
10. Tennessee

Note: The study did not expect to make generalizations about the total United States except as they relate to the agencies and institutions known to the offices of the thirty member denominations of the National Council and certain other organizations noted in II, B, above. For certain findings, if there were extraordinary consistency in the ten selected states, it was thought possible to make precisely qualified generalizations.

III. PROCEDURE

A. The study design was developed with necessary adjustments and compromises in co-operation among:

1. Mrs. Ruth Laverty representing her thesis interests in consultation

171

with her thesis committee at New York University, Center for Human Relations.

2. Director of the National Council's Department of Social Welfare and the National Conference on the Churches and Social Welfare representing the conference's program research needs in consultation with the executive and research committees of the conference.

3. The former director of the Central Department of Research and Survey, who was at that time representing the total general research program in preparation for the conference in consultation with the General Committee of the Central Department.

4. Staff of the Research Unit in Christian Life and Work representing its concern for a methodologically sound research project in consultation with the chairman of the Advisory Committee on Research in Christian Life and Work and the staff of the Bureau of Applied Social Research, Columbia University.

B. A check-list of criteria of religious relationship or involvement was developed for identification of religiously related health and welfare agencies and institutions listed in directories (from welfare councils, community chests and councils, state departments of welfare, and specialized health and welfare state and national organizations) in the ten selected states. All those agencies and institutions which were listed as church-related or which, by an identification questionnaire, were found to have some religious relationship, were included in the study.

A note should be added here about the problem of agencies and institutions not responding to the identification questionnaire. A systematic sample of fifty agencies and institutions that did not respond was approached by repeated mailings and direct personal contact in order to assess in what manner, if any, there was any significant difference between the responding and nonresponding agencies and institutions. It may be assumed that those that did respond to the initial mailing covered fairly comprehensively the church-related agencies.

C. A questionnaire instrument was developed and, following a pre-test, adjustments were made.

Wherever possible, the offices of the thirty member denominations of the National Council sent the questionnaire with a letter requesting participation directly to the health and welfare agencies and institutions known to be related to them. Those denominations that were unable to do this provided a list of their agencies and institutions for mailing by Mrs. Ruth Laverty.

In the ten selected states, the questionnaire and a letter from the Department of Social Welfare were mailed by Mrs. Ruth Laverty, as part of her thesis interest, to religiously-related agencies and institutions that were not included in the mailings of the denominations.

Two follow-up mailings were done through the same offices that sent the initial mailings.

D. Results were coded and mechanically tabulated by IBM by contract with the Bureau of Applied Social Research, Columbia University.

E. Analysis of religious involvement: A somewhat more detailed description of the analysis of the extent and nature of religious involvement is

172

here presented. Certain quantitative values were assigned to the selected indices of religious control, assistance, and character of services in order to ascertain the degree of correlation that exists among these dimensions of religious involvement. This was in addition to a more simple frequency tabulation: i.e., how many agencies, rendering what types of service, etc., have what kind of religious involvement.

These indices, plus a formal recognition by a religious organization or by the agency or institution of relationship to a religious organization were the criteria of religious involvement.

The indices and weighting system were as follows:

IF AN AGENCY OR INSTITUTION:

Control	*Numerical Value*
1. Has no governing body of its own and is governed by or is directly responsible to (a) religious organization(s)	6
2. Has its governing board members elected, appointed, or delegated by (a) religious organization(s)—All, half or more, less than half	(5, 3, or 1)
3. Has its own provisions for electing or appointing its governing board, but requires the members to have certain religious affiliations*—All, half or more, less than half	$\left(\begin{array}{c} 4, 2, \text{or } 1 \\ X \\ 1, \frac{1}{2}, \text{or } \frac{1}{4} \end{array} \right)$
4. Reports to (a) religious organization(s) which has (have) ultimate or final responsibility	4
5. Requires its director to have certain religious affiliations*	$\left(\begin{array}{c} 4 \text{ or } 2 \\ X \ 1, \frac{1}{2} \end{array} \right)$
6. Requires by policy or practice its professional staff (other than the director) to have certain religious affiliations*—All or some	$\left(\begin{array}{c} 4 \ X \\ 1, \frac{1}{2}, \text{or } \frac{1}{4} \end{array} \right)$
Maximum total for "control"	*18*

Assistance	
1. Receives a significant part of its financial support from religious sources—All, half or more, less than half	(10, 5, or 2½)
2. Was originated under auspices of (a) religious organization(s)	2
3. Uses a building owned by a religious organization—Rent free, below market rental, or at full rental value	(2, 1, or 0)
4. Receives assistance (other than financial) from religious organizations—volunteers, promotion or fund-raising, consultation services, other	1 each
Maximum total for "assistance"	*18*

Character   *Numerical Value*

1. (Same as item 5 under Control above).. $\quad$ (2 X 1, ½, or ¼)
2. (Same as item 6 under Control above).. $\quad$ (2 or 1 X 1, ½, or ¼)
3. Has an explicit or implied statement of religious objective or purpose, whether or not its services may be secular in nature .... $\qquad$ 1
4. Provides distinctly religious services or activities

Worship	1½
Religious instruction	2
Evangelistic program	2½
Chapel facilities	½
Chaplaincy services	1
Pastoral counseling	1

5. Requires its services to be limited entirely or primarily to persons with certain religious affiliations* .... $\quad$ (2 X 1, ½ or ¼)
6. Actually serves primarily or entirely persons with certain religious affiliations* ... $\quad$ (1 X 1, ½ or ¼)
7. Has a religious identification in its name. $\qquad$ ½
8. Considers itself a Christian agency in tradition, character, spirit, motivation of personnel, etc., regardless of other answers .... $\qquad$ 1

$\qquad\qquad$ *Maximum total for Character* .... $\qquad$ 18

FOOTNOTES FOR APPENDIX A

[1] This represents the point of view of the Research Unit in Christian Life and Work, which has had consultative responsibility in a thesis project of a graduate student at New York University, Mrs. Ruth Laverty, in the interests of research in preparation for the National Conference on the Churches and Social Welfare. Consult her thesis statement, available from the Department of Social Welfare, National Council of Churches, for details of her conception of the project.

[2] See conference statement for the purpose, scope, participation, and sponsorship of the conference.

* Types of religious affiliation were weighted throughout as, 1, ½, or ¼ multiplied by the value of the indices. They are:

$\quad$ 1—Affiliation with the religious organization (s) to which the agency has some relationship

$\quad$ ½—Affiliation with the denomination (s) to which the agency has some relationship

$\quad$ ¼—Affiliation with any Protestant, Anglican, or Eastern Orthodox denomination

These indices of religious relationship and the weighting system were submitted to the judgment of a select number of experts in the field of Protestant social welfare for their criticism.

174

APPENDIX B

NATIONAL COUNCIL OF THE CHURCHES OF CHRIST
in the United States of America
New York 10, N. Y.

A National Inventory of Health and Welfare Agencies and Institutions Related to the Protestant, Anglican, and Eastern Orthodox Churches and Their Organizations

IDENTIFICATION
5,6

1. Name of Agency in full..

2. Address...
          (Number and Street)   *(City or Town)*   *(County)*   *(State)*   7,8

3. What is the population of the city or town in which your agency is located?   *(Check one)*

         Less than 2,500 population .... □ 9-1
         2,500 to but not including 10,000 .... □ -2
         10,000 to but not including 25,000 .... □ -3
         25,000 to but not including 100,000 .... □ -4
         100,000 to but not including 500,000 .... □ -5
         500,000 or more .... □ -6

4. What is the year in which your present agency was established? 10

5. Is your agency a branch or subsidiary of another health or welfare agency?   □ Yes   □ No
    IF "YES": What is that agency's name and address?

        (Name in full)   *(Number and Street)*   *(City or Town)*   *(County)*   *(State)*

6. Does your agency have branches or subsidiaries?   □ Yes   □ No
    IF "YES": Please give the name and address of each branch or subsidiary.

        (Name in full)   *(Number and Street)*   *(City or Town)*   *(County)*   *(State)*

(If more space is needed, please report the additional information on a separate sheet of paper, which can be inserted in the questionnaire when you mail it.)

PERSONNEL

7. How many persons does your agency have on its regular staff? *(Please fill in the number in each category.)*

	FULL-TIME	PART-TIME	TOTAL
Social workers			
Medical doctors			
Registered nurses			
All other professionals			
All non-professional workers			
Total..............			

II/8-25

8. Of all your social workers, how many have degrees from schools of social work accredited by the Council on Social Work Education or its predecessor agency? ....

9. a. How many ordained persons does your agency have on its regular staff?...
    b. How many of these ordained persons have degrees from schools of social work accredited by the Council on Social Work Education or its predecessor agency? ....

10. Approximately how many different volunteer workers did your agency have last year?.................................

11. How many persons are members of your agency's governing board?...
II/26-30

SERVICES

12. IN COLUMN I BELOW, please check the type(s) of service(s) performed by your agency *today*. *(If there is no listing for a service your agency performs, write it in the space provided, and then check it in column I.)*

13. IN COLUMN II, check the *one* most important type of service by which your agency should be classified *today*.

14. Does your agency have any service for which it is operating at capacity *and* has a waiting list? □ Yes   □ No.
    IF "YES": Please put a check in COLUMN III opposite that service.

15. IN COLUMN IV, please indicate the number of different persons (unduplicated count) served in 1954 by each of the services you have checked in column I.

16. Did your agency *in the past* offer any types of services which are now discontinued? □ Yes   □ No. IF "YES": Please check these discontinued services IN COLUMN V.

175

17. Was the most important service rendered by your agency in the past *different* from the service which is most important today?
☐ Yes   ☐ No. IF "YES": Please check that service IN COLUMN VI, whether or not you have checked it as a discontinued service.

Type of service	I Services offered today 1	II Most important service (Check one) 2	III Operating at capacity with waiting list 3	IV Number served in 1954 (unduplicated count)	V Discontinued services 4	VI Previous most important service (Check one) 5	VII Do not write in this column
Home for the aged (12)	☐	☐	☐	_____	☐	☐	_____
Other service to the aged (*Specify*) (13)	☐	☐	☐	_____	☐	☐	_____
Institutional care of children (14)	☐	☐	☐	_____	☐	☐	_____
Child placement and adoption (15)	☐	☐	☐	_____	☐	☐	_____
Day nursery (16)	☐	☐	☐	_____	☐	☐	_____
Other services to children (*Specify*) (17)	☐	☐	☐	_____	☐	☐	_____
Hospital (18)	☐	☐	☐	_____	☐	☐	_____
Clinic or dispensary (19)	☐	☐	☐	_____	☐	☐	_____
Health education (20)	☐	☐	☐	_____	☐	☐	_____
Convalescent care (21)	☐	☐	☐	_____	☐	☐	_____
Other health services (*Specify*) (22)	☐	☐	☐	_____	☐	☐	_____
Temporary shelter (*Specify for whom*) (23)	☐	☐	☐	_____	☐	☐	_____
Residence (*Specify for whom*) (24)	☐	☐	☐	_____	☐	☐	_____
Other residential services (*Specify*) (25)	☐	☐	☐	_____	☐	☐	_____
Neighborhood house or settlement (26)	☐	☐	☐	_____	☐	☐	_____
Camp or vacation (27)	☐	☐	☐	_____	☐	☐	_____
Other group work (*Specify*) (28)	☐	☐	☐	_____	☐	☐	_____
Other recreational services (*Specify*) (29)	☐	☐	☐	_____	☐	☐	_____
Maternity home (30)	☐	☐	☐	_____	☐	☐	_____
Protective services (*Specify*) (31)	☐	☐	☐	_____	☐	☐	_____
Family welfare (32)	☐	☐	☐	_____	☐	☐	_____
Employment and vocational (33)	☐	☐	☐	_____	☐	☐	_____
Rehabilitation (34)	☐	☐	☐	_____	☐	☐	_____
Sheltered workshop (35)	☐	☐	☐	_____	☐	☐	_____
Social education and action (36)	☐	☐	☐	_____	☐	☐	_____
Chaplaincy: in prisons (37)	☐	☐	☐	_____	☐	☐	_____
Chaplaincy: in hospitals (38)	☐	☐	☐	_____	☐	☐	_____
Other chaplaincy service (*Specify*) (39)	☐	☐	☐	_____	☐	☐	_____
Other major service (*Specify*) (40)	☐	☐	☐	_____	☐	☐	_____
Other major service (*Specify*) (41)	☐	☐	☐	_____	☐	☐	_____

18. What is the total number of different persons (unduplicated count) served by your agency in 1954? (Approximate, if necessary) _____42

19. Approximately, what is the number of these persons served by your agency last year who were *not* Protestant, Anglican, or Eastern Orthodox in religious affiliation? _____43

RELATIONSHIPS TO RELIGIOUS ORGANIZATIONS

20. Please check "Yes" or "No" for each of the following numbered statements and answer each of the questions that applies. (*In the following statements, when we use the term "religious," we are referring to the Protestant, Anglican, or Eastern Orthodox communions.*)

YOUR AGENCY OR INSTITUTION:	Yes	No
1. Is Officially recognized by a religious organization(s) as related to it (them)	☐ 44-1	☐ 2
2. Has an officially stated relationship to a religious organization(s)	☐ 45-1	☐ 2
3. Has a separate governing body of its own	☐ 46-1	☐ 2
a. IF "YES": Are the members of the governing body elected, appointed, delegated, or nominated by any religious organization(s)?	☐ 47-1	☐ 2
What proportion of the members of the governing body? (*Check one*) All	☐ 48-1	
Half or more	☐ -2	
Less than half	☐ -3	
b. IF "NO": Is your agency governed by or directly responsible to a religious organization?	☐ 49-1	☐ 2
4. Is required to make official reports to a religious organization(s)	☐ 50-1	☐ 2
a. IF "YES": Does this religious organization have final or ultimate authority over your agency?	☐ 51-2	☐ 2
5. Was originated under the auspices of a religious organization(s)	☐ 52-1	☐ 2

176

6. Uses a building(s) owned by a religious organization(s) .... □ 53-1   □ 2

   a. IF "YES": On what basis is this provided? (*Check one*)

            Rent free .... □ 54-1

            Below market rental .... □   -2

            At full rental value .... □   -3

7. Receives assistance (other than financial) from a religious organization(s)........ □ 55-1   □ 2

   a. IF "YES": Check the kinds of assistance received:

       Referral, recruitment or training of volunteers .... □ 56-1

       Promotion or fund-raising .... □   -2

       Consultation services .... □   -3

       Ministerial or pastoral services .... □   -4

       Gifts in kind (food, clothes, etc.) .... □   -5

       Others (*Specify*) .... □   -6

21. For *each* different religious organization to which you have referred by checking "Yes" to an item in question 20, please provide the following information. (*Please use a separate line for each religious organization, and be sure to account, in Column V, for the number of each item in question 20 for which you checked "Yes."*)

Name of religious organization	Type* of organization (Use code below)	Address (City, State)	Full name of the denomination to which the religious organization is related. If inter- or non-denominational, so state.	Items in Q. 20 in which this religious organization is referred to. (Write in item numbers.)

II/31-45

*For TYPE of religious organizations, please use the following code letters:
  A. Local Churches or their Societies (Women's Society, men's group, missionary group, etc.)
  B. Local Organizations (Presbytery, association, district, city or county council or federation of churches or church women, etc.)
  C. State or Regional Organizations (Synod, state convention, diocese, state or regional council or federation of churches or church women, etc.)
  D. National Organizations (National boards of missions, welfare or charities, homes or hospitals, evangelism, etc.)

22. Please check "Yes" or "No" for each of the following statements and answer each of the questions that applies. (*Remember that we refer only to the Protestant, Anglican, or Eastern Orthodox communions when we use the term "religious" in the following statements.*)

YOUR AGENCY OR INSTITUTION:	Yes	No
1. Has a separate governing body of its own *and* requires the members thereof to have certain religious affiliations	□ 58-1	□ 2
a. IF "YES": To what proportion of the governing body members does this requirement apply? (*Check one*)		
All .... □ 59-1		
Half or more .... □ -2		
Less than half .... □ -3		
2. In practice, requires its director to have certain religious affiliations	□ 60-1	□ 2
3. In practice, requires its professional staff members (other than the director) to have certain religious affiliations	□ 61-1	□ 2
a. IF "YES": To what proportion of the professional staff does this requirement apply? (*Check one*)		
All .... □ 62-1		
Half or more .... □ -2		
Less than half .... □ -3		
4. Officially requires its services to be limited entirely or primarily to persons with certain religious affiliations	□ 64-1	□ 2
5. Actually serves primarily or entirely persons with certain religious affiliations	□ 65-1	□ 2

23. For each different *type** of religious affiliation to which you have referred by checking "Yes" to an item in question 22, please provide the following information. (*Please use a separate line for each type, and be sure to account for every item number in question 22 for which you checked "Yes."*)

Type* of Affiliation (Use code below)	For type E: give full names of organization and denomination (if inter- or non-denominational, so state.) For type F: give full name of denomination.	For type E only, give type of organization (A, B, C or D) from code for Q. 21.	Items in Q. 22 in which this type of affiliation is referred to. (Write in the item number(s)).

II 46-54

*For TYPE of religious affiliation, please use the following code letters:
  E. Affiliation with the particular churches or religious organization(s) to which your agency is related.
  F. Affiliation with the denomination(s) to which your agency is related.
  G. Affiliation with *any* of the Protestant, Anglican or Eastern Orthodox denominations.

24. Please check "Yes" or "No" for each of the following statements and answer each of the questions that applies. (*When we use the terms "religious" or "Christian" we are, again, referring only to the Protestant, Anglican or Eastern Orthodox communions.*)

YOUR AGENCY OR INSTITUTION:	Yes	No
1. Has a religious identification in its name	☐ 66-1	☐ 2
2. Has a religious objective or purpose, explicitly or implicitly whether or not its services are secular in nature	☐ 67-1	☐ 2
3. Provides distinctly religious services or activities	☐ 68-1	☐ 2

a. IF "YES": Check those services offered:

Worship services .... ☐ 69-1   Chapel facilities ....☐ -4

Religious instruction .... ☐ -2   Chaplaincy services ....☐ -5

Evangelistic programs .... ☐ -3   Pastoral services ....☐ -6

Other (*Specify*) ....☐ -7

	Yes	No
4. Considers itself a Christian agency in tradition, character, spirit, motivation of personnel, etc., regardless of other answers	☐ 70-1	☐ 2
5. Receives a significant part of its financial support from religious sources	☐ 71-1	☐ 2

a. IF "YES": What proportion of the total income is this? (*Check one*)

All ....☐ 72-1

Half or more ....☐ -2

Less than half ....☐ -3

FINANCES
(*Please give the amounts for the last fiscal year for which figures are available. Fill in each category. If the answer is "None," please write "None."*)

25. OPERATING INCOME

A. Contributed Income

1. Religious organizations* (Protestant, Anglican and/or Eastern Orthodox)
   (For definitions of the following, see note at end of question 21.)
   a. Local churches and their societies ....$____III-8
   b. Local organizations ....$____III-9
   c. State and regional organizations ....$____III-10
   d. National organizations ....$____III-11

   Total, all religious organizations ....$____III-12

2. Community chest or fund ....$____III-13
3. Public (tax-supported) funds ....$____III-14
4. Individuals ....$____III-15
5. All other contributed income ....$____III-16

   Total, all contributed income ....$____III-17

B. Earned Income

1. Service fees from individuals ....$____III-18
   (Hospitals: Include income from insurance plans.)
2. Service fees from public (tax-supported) funds ....$____III-19
3. Income from investments ....$____III-20
4. All other earned income ....$____III-21

   Total, all earned income ....$____III-22

Grand total operating income ....$____III-23

* For every category of contributions from *religious* organizations, please provide the following information.

Type of religious organization	Name of organization	Address (City and State)	Full name of denomination to which organization is related. (If inter- or non-denominational, so state.)
a. Local churches and their societies			
b. Other local organizations			
c. State and regional organizations			
d. National organizations			

178

26. **TOTAL OPERATING EXPENSES**
(Give amount for the last fiscal year) .... $_____III-25

27. **CAPITAL ASSETS** (Give amounts at end of last fiscal year. Fill in each category. If *none*, so state.)

   A. Endowments and investments .... $_____III-26

   B. Buildings, land and equipment .... $_____III-27

   C. All other capital assets .... $_____III-28

          Total, all capital assets .... $_____III-29

28. Is your agency planning any major expansion or retraction in the next five years?   ☐ Yes   ☐ No
   a. IF "YES": Indicate amounts, where expansion or retraction will take place, in each of the following categories. Show retraction by placing figures in parentheses. If none, so state.

   A. Buildings and land .... $_____III-30

   B. Equipment .... $_____III-31

   C. Staff and program .... $_____III-32

   D. Other (Specify) _____ $_____III-33

              Total expansion .... $_____III-34

              Total retraction .... $ (_____)III-35

      Total, net expansion or (retraction) .... $_____III-36

29. a. Date_____ b. Name of director of agency _____
                                                         (please print)

30. a. Name of respondent_____b. Position in agency_____

Thank You Very Much

Please fold and seal with the attached gummed tab and mail as soon as possible.

APPENDIX C

Table S-1 Reported Total (T) and Responding Number[1] (R) of Agencies — By Denominational Relationship and Type of Agency

Denominational relationship	All types T	All types R	Home for aged T	Home for aged R	Other serv. to aged T	Other serv. to aged R	Inst. care child. T	Inst. care child. R	Child place. & adopt. T	Child place. & adopt. R	Day Nursery T	Day Nursery R	Other serv. child. T	Other serv. child. R
All denominations	2783	986[5]	494	211	11	20	269	126	30	30	49	22	165	24
A.M.E.	11		2		1	1	15	9			3			
American Baptist[2]	84	67	37	16										4
A.M.E. Zion	3		3	1			2	2						
Assemblies of God	6	3					2	2	2	1	2			
Church of the Brethren	23	17	4	1			1	1						
Cong. Christian	39	7	13	9			8	6						1
Disciples of Christ	22	19	8	9	1	8	10	1		1				
Evang. & Reformed	42	32	8	4			2				2		17	
Evang. Free Church	1	1	18	10										
Evang. United Brethren	9	4	5	3			2	1						
Lutheran Bodies														
American Evangelical	6	1	3	1			2				1	1	1	1
American	16	12	7	6			5	3	3		1	1	1	1
Augustana Evangelical	53	40	21	14	1	1	8	5						
Evangelical	64	24	22	12			9	5						
Missouri Synod	84	30	18	6			20	4		5			2	2
Lutheran Brethren	4	2	3											
Lutheran Free	1													
Inter-Lutheran[3]	187	113	30	17	1	3	8	1	14	12	11	1		1
United	51	27	24	9	1	1	13	5	1	1				
United Evangelical	5	5	4	3										
Methodist	498	292	74	31		1	57	29		4	11	10	2	6
Moravian	6	4	4	2										
Presbyterian Bodies														
Assoc. Reformed	2				1		1							
Cumberland	2				1									
Presbyterian, U. S.	36	12	12	2	1	2	16	8	2	2	1	5		
Presbyterian, U. S. A.	156	120	41	29			10	12						3
United	6	6	4	3				1						
Other Presbyterian	4		3		1									
Protestant Episcopal	269	99	63	20	1	1	44	23	3	3	3	2	17	2
Reformed in Amer.	3	2	1	1	5		1	1						
Friends, Phila. and Vic.	14	9	12	5										
Russian Orthodox	1							*						
Seventh Day Adventist	78	14					8							
Salvation Army	569	1	6	4	1	1	22		5		13	3	133	4
Southern Baptist	57						3							
Volunteers of America	372	23	43	1						3	14	3	13	3

Table S-1—(Continued)

Denominational relationship	Hospital		Clinic or disp.		Health ed.		Convales. care		Other health services		Temporary shelter		Residence		Other res. serv.	
	T	R	T	R	T	R	T	R	T	R	T	R	T	R	T	R
All denominations	424	166	23	12	1	1	11	7	11	8	92	13	132	40	110	2
A.M.E.	7	2	1					1					1	1		
American Baptist[2]																
A.M.E. Zion																
Assemblies of God			2													
Church of the Brethren	2	1			1											
Cong. Christian	3	1											1			
Disciples of Christ														3		
Evang. & Reformed	10	6		1					2	1						
Evang. Free Church																
Evang. United Brethren	2															
Lutheran Bodies																
Amer. Evangelical	1										1					
American	11	7							3	2	1	1	7	5		
Augustana Evangelical	3	1						1		1	1		1	1		
Evangelical																
Missouri Synod	26[4]	5														
Lutheran Brethren	1	1														
Lutheran Free																
Inter-Lutheran[3]	86	59						1	4	1	1	1	3			
United																
United Evangelical										1		3		1		
Methodist	84	44	5	6		1				1		3	41	26		
Moravian																
Presbyterian Bodies																
Assoc. Reformed																
Cumberland			1	1												
Presbyterian, U. S.	2	1	7	2					1							
Presbyterian, U. S. A.	16	16	1											1		
United	2	1														
Other Presbyterian																
Protestant Episcopal	54	17					11	2		1	3	1	11	2		
Reformed in Amer.	2	1	1													
Friends, Phila. and Vic.																
Russian Orthodox								2								
Seventh Day Adventist	74[4]	4	4	2												
Salvation Army	11		2								85		13		110	
Southern Baptist	29								1	1			53[6]			
Volunteers of America												5		1		1

1. Responding in the questionnaire study. N.B.: The reported total number and responding number by type of agency are not necessarily comparable because of lack of information for or discrepancies in classification.
2. Includes also North American Baptist Conference, Baptist General Conference of America, Danish Baptist Conference, and National Baptist Conference.
3. Several Lutheran bodies co-operatively sponsoring.

Table S-1—(Continued)

Denominational relationship	Neigh. hse. settle.		Camp or vacation		Other grp. wk.		Other rec. srv.		Matern. home		Protective srvcs.		Family welfare		Employ. & vocat.	
	T	R	T	R	T	R	T	R	T	R	T	R	T	R	T	R
All denominations	377	139	118	14	93	22	1	15	41		10	4	84	11		1
A.M.E.		22	1	1		4		2						1		
American Baptist[2]																
A.M.E. Zion																
Assemblies of God																
Church of the Brethren	1		12		1			1								
Cong. Christian	2	1					1									
Disciples of Christ	2	2														
Evang. & Reformed																
Evang. Free Church																
Evang. United Brethren																
Lutheran Bodies																
Amer. Evangelical																
American	1	1	1													
Augustana Evangelical			2	1												
Evangelical									1		6		6	1		
Missouri Synod																
Lutheran Brethren																
Lutheran Free	4	2	2	1		1			3				9	3		
Inter-Lutheran[3]	1	1	1										1	1		
United																
United Evangelical																
Methodist	108	69	12	5	92	12		8	2		4	1	1	1		1
Moravian			2	2												
Presbyterian Bodies																
Assoc. Reformed																
Cumberland	5	1														
Presbyterian, U. S.																
Presbyterian, U. S. A.	76	33	1	3		3		3								
United																
Other Presbyterian	12	5	1	2					2			3		3		
Protestant Episcopal																
Reformed in Amer.																
Friends, Phila. and Vic.																
Russian Orthodox																
Seventh Day Adventist																
Salvation Army	112		56	1					26							
Southern Baptist													67			
Volunteers of America	42	2	27		1	1		1	7	1				1		

182

Table S-1—(Continued)

Denominational relationship	Rehabilitation		Shltrd. workshop		Social ed. and Act.		Chaplain. prisons		Chaplain. hosp.		Other chap. srv.		Other major serv.		Not ascertainable	
	T	R	T	R	T	R	T	R	T	R	T	R	T[8]	R	T	R
All denominations	98	5		2	2	10	12	6	13	19	36	4	70	42	6	19
A.M.E.									1							
American Baptist[5]							12		12					2		
A.M.E. Zion																
Assemblies of God														2		2
Church of the Brethren					2											
Cong. Christian													9	2		
Disciples of Christ	1					1							3	3		
Evang. & Reformed														3		
Evang. Free Church																
Evang. United Brethren																2
Lutheran Bodies																
Amer. Evangelical																
American																
Augustana Evangelical										2	20	1		1		
Evangelical	3	2		1												
Missouri Synod										3			8	2		
Lutheran Brethren																
Lutheran Free	5															
Inter-Lutheran[6]								1		7	13	1	10	1		2
United										1	3	4	1	4		1
United Evangelical	1			1		6										
Methodist														13	4	12
Moravian																
Presbyterian Bodies																
Assoc. Reformed																
Cumberland																
Presbyterian, U. S.						1				1		1		3		
Presbyterian, U. S. A.																
United																
Other Presbyterian						1		1								
Protestant Episcopal	2									5		2	28	6		
Reformed in Amer.																
Friends, Phila. and Vic.																1
Russian Orthodox																1
Seventh Day Adventist																
Salvation Army																
Southern Baptist	86[7]	3														
Volunteers of America		3											11			

4. Includes sanatoria.
5. Not including ten-states and New York city samples.
6. Includes temporary shelter.
7. Includes sheltered workshops.
8. City mission societies, welfare federations, co-ordinating councils, services to seamen, etc.

Table S-2 Reported Total (T) and Responding Number[1] (R) of Agencies — By Denominational Relationship and Geographic Division[2]

Denominational relationship	All divisions T	All divisions R	New England T	New England R	Middle Atlantic T	Middle Atlantic R	East North Central T	East North Central R	West North Central T	West North Central R	South Atlantic T	South Atlantic R
All denominations	2783	986[4]	94	27	421	184	406	200	332	180	250	113
A.M.E.	11				4		2				5	
American Baptist	84	67	6	3	16	14	14	18	10	9	3	
A.M.E. Zion	3											2
Assemblies of God	6											
Church of the Brethren	23	17			2	5	1		1	1	1	1
Cong. Christian	39	7	14	2	6	1	8	6	2	2	2	2
Disciples of Christ	22	19			2	1	5	3	4	4	5	1
Evang. & Reformed	42	32			9	5	20	17	10	7	2	2
Evang. Free Church	1	1										
Evang. United Brethren	9	4			3	2	3	3	1	1		1
Lutheran Bodies												
Amer. Evangelical	6	1			1	1	1		2			
American	16	12			1	3	7	5	7	5	2	
Augustana Evangelical	53	40	3	4	5		14	11	24	18	7	5
Evangelical	64	24			5		17	9	30	10		
Missouri Synod	84	30	1	1	14	2	25	12	29	12	4	
Lutheran Brethren	1								1			
Lutheran Free	4	2							2	2		
Inter-Lutheran[3]	187	113	1	2	18	13	37	14	82	47	7	2
United Lutheran in Amer.	51	27	1		31	19	8	2	3	2	6	5
United Evangelical	5	5					1					
Methodist	498	292	14	8	58	29	85	51	55	36	94	59
Moravian	6	4			4	2			1	1		
Presbyterian Bodies												
Assoc. Reformed	2										1	
Cumberland	2											
Presbyterian, U. S.	36	12							1	1	22	4
Presbyterian, U. S. A.	156	120	25	6	46	32	32	24	8		18	13
United	6	6			1	3	1		1	1	1	
Other Presbyterian	2				2							
Protestant Episcopal	269	99			88	35	30	17	15	5	38	14
Reformed in Amer.	3	2			1	1			1	1		
Friends, Phila. and Vic.	14	9			14	9	11	3				
Russian Orthodox	1				1			1				
Seventh Day Adventist	78	14	8	1					2		17	3
Salvation Army	569	1										
Southern Baptist	57						11	3	2	1		
Volunteers of America	372	23	21		86	7	81	4	36	2	23	2

Table S-2—(Continued)

Denominational relationship	East South Central		West South Central		Mountain		Pacific		Outside Cont. U.S.		Not Given	
	T	R	T	R	T	R	T	R	T	R	T	R
All denominations	128	58	119	59	106	62	219	86	39	17	669	
A.M.E.												0
American Baptist	1	1	1	2	1	6	6	10	2	3	25	2
A.M.E. Zion											2	
Assemblies of God			1	1	1		1	2				
Church of the Brethren			1				4	2	4	2		
Cong. Christian	6	3	4	3	1	1	1		2	2		
Disciples of Christ	3	1	1	1	1	1	4	1				
Evang. & Reformed							1					
Evang. Free Church							1					
Evang. United Brethren							2					
Lutheran Bodies												
Amer. Evangelical			1				1					
American			1	1	1							
Augustana Evangelical					3	1	4	4				
Evangelical			1	1	1	1	10	2				
Missouri Synod			1		5	1	5	1				
Lutheran Brethren												
Lutheran Free							2					
Inter-Lutheran[3]	2		2	1	26	26	14	8				
United Lutheran in Amer.							1	1				
United Evangelical			1	1			1					
Methodist	59	36	61	37	15	6	33	23	8	7	16	
Moravian							1		1	1		
Presbyterian Bodies												
Assoc. Reformed	1											
Cumberland												
Presbyterian, U. S.	10	5	3	2	18	13	20	14				
Presbyterian, U.S.A.	4	4	4	5			1	1	6	4		
United	1	1					1	1				
Other Presbyterian					15	7	19	7				
Protestant Episcopal	10	6	14	2					15			
Reformed in Amer.	1											
Friends, Phila. and Vic.												
Russian Orthodox												
Seventh Day Adventist	15	1	1		5							
Salvation Army							18	5	1		569	
Southern Baptist				2	15	1	75	5			57	
Volunteers of America	14		21	2								

1. Responding in the questionnaire study, N.B.: The reported total number and responding number by geographic division are not necessarily comparable in some instances because of lack of information.
2. Standard geographic divisions of the U.S. Census.
3. Several Lutheran bodies co-operatively sponsoring.
4. Not including ten-states and New York city samples.

185

Table S-3   Population Size of Place in Which Agencies Serve — By Type of Agency

Type of agency	All sizes	Number of agencies serving in places of						Not given
		Less than 2,500	2,500-9,999	10,000-24,999	25,000-99,999	100,000-499,999	500,000 or more	
All types	986¹	171	124	79	118	206	247	41
Home for the aged	211	41	38	23	30	31	41	7
Other service to aged	12	1	5		2		3	1
Inst. care of children	126	28	21	13	13	22	23	6
Child placement and adopt.	30	3	1	3	5	4	13	1
Day nursery	22		1	2	4	7	8	
Other services to children	24	8	3		3	6	2	2
Hospital	166	40	29	16	18	25	35	3
Clinic or dispensary	12	3	1		3	1	4	
Health education	1							1
Convalescent care	7	1		2	1	1	1	1
Other health services	8	2		1		2	3	
Temporary shelter	13	1			4	2	6	
Residence	40		1	2	5	13	15	4
Other residential services	2					1	1	
Neighborhood hse. or settle.	139	7	7	6	22	52	40	5
Camp or vacation	16	6	2	1		2	5	
Other group work	22	4	4			6	8	
Other recreational services	15	4	2	3		3	2	1
Maternity home	1					1		
Protective services	4						4	
Family welfare	11	1	1	1	1	4	3	
Employment and vocational	1					1		
Rehabilitation	5			1		2	2	
Sheltered workshop²	2							2
Social education and action	10	1	3		1	2	3	
Chaplaincy: in prisons	2						2	
Chaplaincy: in hospitals	19				2	8	8	1
Other chaplaincy service	4			1		1	1	1
Other major service	42	15	3	2	2	8	10	2
Not ascertainable	19	5	2	2	2	1	4	3

1. Not including ten-states and New York city samples.
2. Includes Goodwill Industries of America, Inc., which consists of 110 autonomous local units.

Table S-4   Population Size of Place in Which Agencies Serve — By Denominational Relationship

Denominational relationship	All sizes	Number of agencies located in places of						Not given
		Less than 2,500	2,500-9,999	10,000-24,999	25,000-99,999	100,000-499,999	500,000 or more	
All denominations	986¹	171	124	79	118	206	247	41
Assemblies of God	3	2				1		
Amer. Baptist Convention	67	7	7	6	8	19	17	3
Church of the Brethren	17	5	6	1	2		1	2
Cong. Christian Church	7	3		1	1		2	
Disciples of Christ, Int. Con.	19	4	2	1	2	5	4	1
Evang. & Reformed Church	32	9	2	3	3	3	12	
Evang.FreeChurchofAmer.	1			1				
Evang. United Brethren	4	2		1			1	
Amer. Evang. Luth. Church	1					1		
American Lutheran Church	12	4	3		2	3		
Aug. Evang. Luth. Church	40	8	1	3	4	15	9	
Evang. Lutheran Church	24	7	2	6	3		5	1
Luth. Church—Miss. Syn.	30	3	4	7	2	2	12	
Lutheran Free Church	2		1					1
Inter-Lutheran²	113	34	24	8	8	13	22	4
Un. Luth. Church of Amer.	27	3	3	2	3	4	10	2
Un. Evang. Luth. Church	5	4	1					
Methodist Church	292	40	37	19	48	75	61	12
Moravian Church	4	3	1					
Presby. Church in the U. S.	12	2	3	3		2	1	1
Presby. Church in the U.S.A.	120	13	14	9	12	26	41	5
Un. Presby. Church of N. A.	6	4			1	1		
Protestant Epis. Church	99	6	5	5	13	20	42	8
Reformed Church	2	2						
Re. Soc. of Fr., Phila. & vic.	9	3	2	1	1	1	1	
Salvation Army	1						1	
Seventh Day Adventists	14	3	6	2	1		1	
Volunteers of America	23				4	14	4	1

1. Not including ten-states and New York city samples.
2. Several Lutheran bodies co-operatively sponsoring.

Table S-5 Year of Establishment of Agencies — By Type of Agency

Type of agency	All years	Number of agencies established in								Not given
		Prior to 1865	1865 to 1899	1900 to 1909	1910 to 1919	1920 to 1929	1930 to 1939	1940 to 1949	1950 to 1955	
All types	986[1]	34	175	133	118	132	69	135	143	47
Home for the aged	211	7	41	29	17	30	18	33	30	6
Other service to the aged	12		1	2					3	1
Institutional care of children	126	10	49	25	17	12	2	8	2	1
Child placement and adoption	30	3	5	7	2	3	3	3	2	2
Day nursery	22	1	4	3	2	6	1	3		2
Other services to children	24		2	4	2	5	2	4	2	3
Hospital	166	7	28	14	24	16	12	15	45	5
Clinic or dispensary	12		1	1	1	3	1	4	2	1
Health education	7		1		2	1			1	1
Convalescent care	8		1	3	2	1	1	2	1	1
Other health services	13	1	5	4	2	4	3	1		1
Temporary shelter	40		8		7	7		7	1	3
Residence	2									
Other residential services	139	1	10	25	25	23	10	24	15	6
Neighborhood house or settlement	16		1	1	2	4	2	2	3	2
Camp or vacation	22	1	1	1	2	1	5	6	4	1
Other group work	15	1	1	1	1	3	1	2	5	
Other recreational services	4				1					
Maternity home	11		1	1	1	1	1	2	3	1
Protective services	5				1	2	1			2
Family welfare	2				1					
Employment and vocational	10		3	1	1	1	1	2	1	
Rehabilitation	2								6	
Sheltered workshop[2]	19	1		1	1	1	1	1		1
Social education and action	4		2	2	3	2	4	2	3	
Chaplaincy: in prisons	42		2	1	1	1		1		
Chaplaincy: in hospitals	19	1	7	7	2	5	2	7	11	3
Other chaplaincy service		1	1					4	6	4
Other major service										
Not ascertainable										

1. Not including ten-states and New York city samples.
2. Includes Goodwill Industries of America, Inc., which consists of 110 autonomous local units.

187

Table S-6 Year of Establishment of Agencies — By Denominational Relationship of Agencies

Denominational relationship	All Years	Number of agencies established in								Not given
		Prior to 1865	1865 to 1899	1900 to 1909	1910 to 1919	1920 to 1929	1930 to 1939	1940 to 1949	1950 to 1955	
All denominations	986[1]	34	175	133	118	132	69	135	143	47
Assemblies of God	3									1
American Baptist Convention	67	1	8	11	7	9	5	11	12	3
Church of the Brethren	17	1	2	4	3	2			2	
Congregational Christian Church	19		1	1	2		1	2	2	
Disciples of Christ, International Convention	32	3	4	5	2	3	1	3	3	1
Evangelical and Reformed Church	1									1
Evangelical Free Church of America	4		8	3	4	6	1			
Evangelical United Brethren			1	1	1	1	1			
Lutheran Bodies:										
American Evangelical Lutheran Church	1				1					1
American Lutheran Church	12		4		8	2			2	1
Augustana Evangelical Lutheran Church	40		9	9	5	5	3	3	2	
Evangelical Lutheran Church	24		5	3		2	1		6	2
Lutheran Church—Missouri Synod	30	1	9	5	5	2	2		6	
Lutheran Free Church	2		3		1					1
Inter-Lutheran[2]	113	2		7		7	23	20	45	4
United Lutheran Church of America	27	3		4	1	2	1	3	3	1
United Evangelical Lutheran Church	5							1		18
Methodist Church	292	6	39	46	49	43	20	35	36	
Moravian Church	4		6	1		1		1	1	
Presbyterian Bodies:										
Presbyterian Church in the U. S.	12	1	2		2	3		2	1	2
Presbyterian Church in the U. S. A.	120	4	24	15	13	22	9	21	10	
United Presbyterian Church of N. America	6		2		1	14	2	7	1	6
Protestant Episcopal Church	99	10	30	13	9			1	8	
Reformed Church	2			1	1			1		
Religious Society of Friends, Phila. and Vic.	9	1	4		1	2		1	1	
Salvation Army	1				1	1				
Seventh Day Adventists	14					1		10	3	
Volunteers of America	23		11	2	2	2	1			5

1. Not including ten-states and New York city samples.
2. Several Lutheran bodies co-operatively sponsoring.

188

Table S-7

Year of Establishment of Agencies — By Geographic Division[1]

Geographic division	All years	Number of agencies established in								Not given
		Prior to 1865	1865 to 1899	1900 to 1909	1910 to 1919	1920 to 1929	1930 to 1939	1940 to 1949	1950 to 1955	
All divisions	986[2]	34	175	133	118	132	69	135	143	47
New England	27	1	7	3	4	3	1	5	2	1
Middle Atlantic	184	16	51	21	20	26	8	15	18	9
East North Central	200	5	40	30	33	36	13	21	12	10
West North Central	180	6	31	26	19	16	16	23	38	5
South Atlantic	113	3	19	15	10	13	6	24	16	7
East South Central	58	2	11	8	7	7	4	9	7	3
West South Central	59	.....	2	6	8	9	6	9	12	7
Mountain	62	.....	2	7	5	6	6	8	25	3
Pacific	86	1	11	14	10	15	8	17	8	2
Outside the Continental U.S.	17	.....	1	3	2	1	1	4	5	.....

1. Standard geographic divisions of the U.S. Census.
2. Not including ten-states and New York city samples.

189

Table S-8   Services Offered — By Type of Agency, Number of Agencies Offering Services

Types of agency	All agencies	All services	Home for aged	Other serv. to aged	Inst. care of child.	Child placement and adoption	Day nursery	Other serv. to child.	Hospital	Clinic or dispensary	Health education	Convalescent care	Other health services	Temporary shelter	Residence
All types	1082(115)[1]	3406(348)	269(17)	135(15)	187(22)	84(10)	101(11)	175(14)	220(26)	145(22)	87(10)	60(9)	45(5)	70(7)	125(6)
Home for aged	226(15)	368(30)	226(15)	15(1)	8(2)	5(1)	5(1)	3	8(2)	9(1)	1(1)	24(2)	1	8(2)	13(2)
Other serv. to aged	14(2)	37(8)	8	14(2)		1			2		1(1)	2	1(1)		
Inst. care of child.	139(13)	297(28)	4	1	139(13)	33(1)	5	15(2)	2(1)	8(2)	4(1)	2(1)		15(3)	6(1)
Child plcment & adop.	33(3)	142(15)	3	5(1)	12	33(3)	1(1)	12	2(1)	3(1)	1	1		4	2
Day nursery	25(3)	99(4)		4	2		25(3)	5		3	4(1)				2
Other serv. to child.	26(2)	131(5)		3	4	1(1)	3	26(2)		3	5		2	5	4
Hospital	187(21)	392(48)	5(2)	4(1)	2		2	5(3)	187(21)	55(13)	19(4)	12(3)	12		11
Clinic or dispensary	12	52		1			1	5	1	12	5			1	
Health education	2(1)	16(7)									2(1)		1		
Convalescent care	9(2)	14(3)	3	1	1(1)			2(1)				9(2)			
Other health services	8	26	1	2	2	1				1	1	1	8		
Temporary shelter	13	69	2	2	1					1	1	2		13	[3]3
Residence	41(1)	100(2)	9	47(2)		1	1	1	3	1	1	3		5	41(1)
Other res. services	3(1)	19(2)			1									1	1
Neighborhood hse. setl.	147(8)	707(33)	1	1	3	1(1)	44(4)	54(1)	3	32(1)	20		8(1)	2	22
Camp or vacation	18(2)	51(6)			1(1)	1	4(1)	9		7(2)	2				
Other group work	24(2)	146(13)	1	5	1		4	6		1(1)	7		2(1)	1	1
Other rec. services	15	93		3		1	4				2	1	2		1
Maternity home	7(6)	20(14)			1(1)			1	2(1)						1(1)
Protective services	4	14					2	8(3)						2	
Family Welfare	19(8)	90(29)		7(3)	3(2)	4(3)			1		1	1			2
Employment & vocation.	3(2)	10(8)						2(1)							1
Rehabilitation	10(5)	46(18)		2	1(1)									3(1)	3(1)
Sheltered workshop[2]	15(13)	61(55)		5(5)			1(1)	1			2		1(1)		2
Social educ. & action	10	56		1										3	
Chaplaincy: in prisons	2	11				1		3						1	
Chaplaincy: in hosp.	19	79	3	4					4	1	1	1			1
Other chaplaincy serv.	4	25		1							1				
Other major service	47(5)	235(20)	2	4	5(1)	2	4(1)	15(1)	3(1)	6(1)	8(1)	1(1)	5(1)	5(1)	6

Table S-8—(Continued)

Type of agency	Other res. services	Neigh. hse. or settlement	Camp or vacation	Other group work	Other recrea. services	Maternity home	Protective serv.	Family welfare	Employment & vocational	Rehabilitation	Sheltered workshop	Social education & action	Chaplaincy: in prisons	Chaplaincy: in hospitals	Other chaplaincy service	Other major service
All types	29(3)	204(14)	189(16)	157(7)	148(12)	24(8)	20(2)	142(14)	84(22)	90(23)	48(20)	106(8)	44(3)	102(1)	78(7)	238(14)
Home for aged	2	1	3	3	2			4	1(1)	5	1(1)	1(1)	3	3	14(1)	1
Other serv. to aged		1						1	3	1(1)	1	1(1)	1	1		4
Inst. care of child.			10	6(1)	1(1)	5	4	8	1(1)	5	1				5	18(1)
Child plcment & adop.	1		3(1)		7(1)	4(1)		11(1)	2	1(1)				9	5	11
Day nursery	1		5	7	7		2(2)	6	5	2				2		16
Other serv. to child.	1	7	7	9	6(1)	1	1	7	2	4	1	3		4	5(1)	1
Hospital	5	10(1)	3	6	7				2	8	3	3	6	38	2	
Clinic or dispensary								1		1(1)			1	2	1	2
Health education		2			2(1)			2	6	1				3	1	
Convalescent care		2								6				1		4
Other health services		1(1)	3	1	1		1	2	3	5	2	1	3	1	3	3
Temporary shelter	8(1)	1	2(1)		2	1	1	6			2				4	
Residence	3(1)	1	4	3	4			1		7		3	1	5		
Other res. services	1				1											46
Neighborhood hse. setl.		146(8)	1(1)	2	44(3)			27(1)	14(2)	2	1	2(1)	2	1	1(1)	1
Camp or vacation		3	84(6)		5				1	2		2				8
Other group work		11(1)	6(1)	51(2)	16(2)				5(1)		4	39(2)			3	13
Other rec. services	2	4	13(2)	6(1)	15			2	2	1(1)	1		2	1	3	2(2)
Maternity home		2	8	24(2)	4(1)	7(6)		9(1)	2(1)	2(1)	3				4	2(3)
Protective-services		1(1)		13		2	2	5	1		1					5(2)
Family welfare	1	2(2)	5	3(1)	2(2)	2	1	19(8)	5(2)	1(1)	1	8	3(1)		4	2(1)
Employment & vocation	1(1)	1						2	3(2)	10(5)	2(2)	2			1(1)	9
Rehabilitation	1	1	1(1)	1	6	1(1)	4	4(3)	3(2)	13(12)	6(4)	7(2)	1	1(1)	1(1)	2
Sheltered workshop²			2						9(9)		15(13)					2
Social educ. & action			2(1)	5				1		1		10	2		2(2)	5
Chaplaincy: in prisons	1		4	1	1		1	5					12	1		
Chaplaincy: in hosp.				1										19	1	
Other chaplaincy serv.			2							3		3			9	
Other major service		7(1)	10(1)	12	15	1	3	12	8(1)	7	3	13(1)	3(1)	3	7(1)	66(5)

1. Numbers in parentheses indicate agencies in ten-states sample included in preceding figure.
2. Includes Goodwill Industries of America, Inc., which consists of 110 autonomous local units.

191

Table S-9

Persons Served — By Type of Service

Type of service	All agencies	Under 25	25-49	50-99	100-249	250-499	500-999	1000-2499	2500-4999	5000-9999	10000-14999	15000-29999	30000 & over	Not given
Total all type service	2,156[1]	24	356	320	413	428	171	137	126	58	66	33	18	1,307
Home for the aged	227		57	53	73	40	3		2			1		44
Other service to aged	87		25	26	18	10	2	4						50
Institutional care of children	147		21	36	53	33	4							41
Child placement and adoption	59		19	10	14	10	2	4	1		1			26
Day nursery	71		14	20	27	7			1		1			33
Other services to children	126		21	33	34	21	8	6	26	22	37	13	5	49
Hospital	173	16	4	1	2	4	14	29	16	5	11	7	5	47
Clinic or dispensary	82	3	2	3	5	13	4	8						63
Health education	35		9	6	4	5	3	1	5	1		1		53
Convalescent care	28		3	8	2	5	3	4	4					33
Other health services	29	1	4		5	9	5	4	4	1			1	17
Temporary shelter	44	1	13	8	19	2	6	3						26
Residence	81		30	15	3	8	1	1	26	6	2			46
Other residential services	19	1	7	3	3	3	26	29	3			1		10
Neighborhood house or settlement	127		1	13	6	29	10	5	3	5	1		1	81
Camp or vacation	107	1	13	13	32	31	16	6	2	1	1		1	87
Other group work	102		10	12	13	35	16	6	5	1				57
Other recreational services	80		3	6	15	27								68
Maternity home	15		2	3	5	5				1	1			9
Protective services	10		4	1	1	3			1	1				10
Family welfare	92		22	11	12	25	9	9	3	1		1	5	53
Employment and vocational	41		12	6	5	10	4	2	1					45
Rehabilitation	42		18	8	6	6	3	1						50
Sheltered workshop[2]	41		5	6	3	8	2	2	1	1		1		20
Social education and action	41	1	4	7	11	10	3	2	1			2		68
Chaplaincy: in prisons	23		5	2	3	5	3	2	8	6		4	3	22
Chaplaincy: in hospitals	43		3	3	3	2	3	2	7		10	1		59
Other chaplaincy service	28		4	3	2	8	5		7	6	3			50
Other major service	163	1	21	19	34	46	15	11	7	7			2	90

1. Includes ten-states and New York city samples.
2. Includes Goodwill Industries of America, Inc., which consists of 110 autonomous local units.

Table S-10 Persons Served — By Total, Number Not Protestant,[1] and Type of Agency

Type of agency	Total		Not Protestant	
	Agencies reporting	Persons	Agencies reporting	Persons[2]
All types..................................	963[3]	4,141,232	863[3]	1,299,067
Home for the aged...........................	212	22,057	201	2,670
Other service to the aged....................	11	7,879	11	196
Institutional care of children.................	127	16,191	124	784
Child placement and adoption................	27	74,489	25	318
Day nursery.................................	21	51,553	19	26,158
Other services to children....................	24	22,116	21	6,966
Hospital....................................	163	1,634,801	130	896,282
Clinic or dispensary.........................	9	57,617	6	3,873
Health education............................	1	5,000	1	1,200
Convalescent care...........................	3	107	2	....
Other health services........................	6	1,907	4	280
Temporary shelter...........................	11	39,792	9	11,310
Residence...................................	34	8,504	36	2,716
Other residential services....................	2	5,110	1	....
Neighborhood house or settlement............	134	345,212	116	77,444
Camp or vacation...........................	17	140,409	14	28,793
Other group work...........................	21	90,490	22	17,277
Other recreational services...................	15	6,234	12	1,020
Maternity home.............................	6	1,158	4	125
Protective services..........................	3	9,184	3	130
Family welfare..............................	17	24,179	13	4,593
Employment and vocational..................	3	572	3	86
Rehabilitation...............................	9	357,551	7	2,824
Sheltered workshop[4]........................	12	36,157	12	17,188
Social education and action..................	7	7,265	8	321
Chaplaincy: in prisons.......................	1	29,522	1	1,500
Chaplaincy: in hospitals.....................	16	196,097	9	2,300
Other chaplaincy service.....................	2	570	2	1
Other major service.........................	36	936,522	36	192,268
Not ascertainable...........................	13	12,987	11	444

1. Also not Anglican and Eastern Orthodox.
2. The figures for "total number of persons" and "number of persons not Protestant" are not comparable in that the same agencies did not necessarily report both.
3. Includes ten-states and New York city samples.
4. Includes Goodwill Industries of America, Inc., which consists of 110 autonomous local units.

Table S-11   Persons Served — By Total, Number Not Protestant,[1] and Denominational Relationship of Agencies

Denominational relationship of agencies	Total		Not Protestant	
	Agencies reporting	Persons	Agencies reporting	Persons[2]
All denominations...................	963	4,141,232	863	1,299,067
Assemblies of God........................	3	128	3	....
American Baptist Convention...............	59	66,965	58	610,765
Church of the Brethren....................	13	5,519	10	24
Congregational Christian Church...........	7	55,163	6	40,505
Disciples of Christ, International Convention....	15	8,693	16	3,900
Evangelical and Reformed Church............	29	396,032	29	31,890
Evangelical Free Church of America..........	1	47	1	....
Evangelical United Brethren................	4	538	3	....
Lutheran Bodies				
American Evangelical Lutheran Church......	1	50	1	....
American Lutheran Church.................	11	1,418	9	396
Augustana Evangelical Lutheran Church.....	37	103,865	31	11,288
Evangelical Lutheran Church..............	21	9,717	20	3,179
Lutheran Church—Missouri Synod.........	25	117,208	22	587
Lutheran Free Church....................	2	12,265	1	10
Inter-Lutheran[3].........................	99	229,921	90	24,763
United Lutheran Church of America........	23	53,573	22	2,431
United Evangelical Lutheran Church........	5	1,374	5	402
Methodist Church.........................	247	876,396	226	137,719
Moravian Church.........................	4	715	3	2
Presbyterian Bodies				
Presbyterian Church in the U. S.............	11	7,222	9	106
Presbyterian Church in the U. S. A..........	111	483,764	104	90,296
United Presbyterian Church of North America	5	1,094	5	222
Protestant Episcopal Church.................	90	328,648	84	108,714
Reformed Church.........................	2	214	2	25
Religious Society of Friends, Philadelphia & Vic.	8	939	7	95
Salvation Army...........................	1	3,600	1	2,500
Seventh Day Adventists.....................	9	33,853	4	58
Volunteers of America......................	20	419,903	13	21,088
Ten States General Sample..................	93	419,352	72	72,940
N. Y. C. Sample...........................	7	503,106	6	135,162

1. Also not Anglican and Eastern Orthodox.
2. The figures for "total number of persons" and "number of persons not Protestant" are not comparable in that the same agencies did not necessarily report both.
3. Several Lutheran bodies co-operatively sponsoring.

Table S-12   Persons Served — By Total, Number Not Protestant,[1] and Geographic Division[2]

Geographic division	Total		Not Protestant	
	Agencies reporting	Persons	Agencies reporting	Persons[3]
All divisions...........................	963[4]	4,141,232	863[4]	1,299,067
New England..............................	39	153,397	32	34,671
Middle Atlantic............................	198	1,668,253	176	340,119
East North Central.........................	192	1,058,505	175	123,856
West North Central.........................	166	346,731	148	34,859
South Atlantic.............................	98	162,731	89	611,413
East South Central.........................	55	227,790	49	6,324
West South Central.........................	51	85,335	49	22,551
Mountain..................................	59	94,461	55	30,004
Pacific....................................	89	285,679	74	48,649
Outside Continental U. S....................	16	58,350	16	46,621

1. Also not Anglican and Eastern Orthodox.
2. Standard geographic divisions of the U.S. Census.
3. The figures for "total number of persons" and "number of persons not Protestant" are not comparable in that the same agencies did not necessarily report both.
4. Includes ten-states and New York city samples.

Table S-13   Types of Agency Employees — By Full-time and Part-time and Type of Agency

Type of agency	Agencies reporting	All employees Full time	All employees Part time	Social workers Full time	Social workers Part time	Medical doctors Full time	Medical doctors Part time	Registered nurses Full time	Registered nurses Part time	Other professionals Full time	Other professionals Part time	Nonprofessionals Full time	Nonprofessionals Part time
All types	1,102[1]	54,283	12,838	1,255	406	4,015	3,247	8,193	2,206	5,860	1,092	34,960	5,887
Home for the aged	225	3,755	862	42	26	76	191	270	50	438	68	2,929	527
Other services to the aged	15	577	89	18			13	10	12	24	3	525	61
Inst. care of children	137	2,234	411	145	25	12	114	44		274	53	1,759	211
Child place. and adopt.	34	529	112	160	26		23	5	8	48	17	316	44
Day nursery	26	682	133	21	6	60	55	53	9	122	20	426	43
Other children's services	26	140	82	26	13			1		32	13	81	51
Hospital	83	41,848	8,873	146	27	3,811	2,637	7,565	2,014	3,943	487	26,383	3,708
Clinic or dispensary	12	93	188	14	4	7	19	20	15	9	12	43	138
Health education	2	2	3	2	3	1							
Convalescent care	9	157	24	2	1		4	15	5	18	3	121	11
Other health services	8	162	39	1		1	7	27		11	3	123	29
Temporary shelter	13	116	46	11	2	3	3	7	6	12	7	85	28
Residence	40	221	65	12			2	10	2	35	7	161	54
Other resid. services	3	91	5	4			1			26		60	3
Neigh. house or settlement	148	711	828	337	201		29	10	11	175	151	189	436
Camp or vacation	18	68	177	11	26	1	2	1	9	43	10	13	130
Other group work	24	101	87	35	10		4	2	3	37	25	26	45
Other rec. services	15	54	26	15	3		3		1	14	5	25	14
Maternity home	7	64	21	9	3	14	4	6	2	10		25	12
Protective services	4	30	10	19	8		2					10	
Family welfare	19	171	53	72	7		11	1		10	11	89	24
Employment and vocational	3	66	1							3		61	
Rehabilitation	10	235	67	12	2	15	6	24	1	56	19	165	39
Sheltered workshop[2]	15	768	93	50	1		79	1		163		516	12
Social educ. and action	11	27	13	7				1		17	3	2	10
Chaplaincy: in prisons	2	84	91	4	1	5	2	101	1	50	29	29	58
Chaplaincy: in hospitals	18	375	244	9	3		15		53	105	89	155	84
Other chaplaincy service	4	43	3			9		14	1	11		32	1
Other major service	49	760	154	59	8		14	14	1	147	37	531	94
Not ascertainable	23	119	39	11			14	1	1	27	18	80	20

1. Includes ten-states and New York city samples.
2. Includes Goodwill Industries of America, Inc., which consists of 110 autonomous local units.

195

Table S-14 Types of Agency Employees — By Full-time and Part-time and Denominational Relationship of Agencies

Denominational relationship	Agencies reporting	All employees Full time	All employees Part time	Social workers Full time	Social workers Part time	Medical doctors Full time	Medical doctors Part time	Registered nurses Full time	Registered nurses Part time	Other professionals Full time	Other professionals Part time	Nonprofessionals Full time	Nonprofessionals Part time
All denominations	1,102	55,282	12,838	1,255	406	4,014	3,247	9,193	2,206	5,860	1,092	34,960	5,887
Assemblies of God	3	30	2	9				1	1			20	1
American Baptist	66	986	424	57	15	8	26	183	85	116	39	622	259
Church of the Brethren	17	299	133	11	5	2	62	30	16	25	3	231	47
Cong. Christian	7	136	27	4		5	6	11		24	1	92	20
Disciples of Christ	19	340	82	15	11	8	17	24	4	45	16	248	34
Evang. & Reformed	32	2,202	391	16	11	70	18	456	112	142	44	1,518	206
Evang. Free Church	1	10	6					1		2		7	6
Evang. United Breth.	4	112	30				4	3	4	9	3	100	19
Lutheran bodies													
Amer. Evangelical	1	6	4		1		2	2		1		3	1
American	12	224	60	6	1		4	38	10	28	2	152	43
Augustana Evang.	40	2,583	716	11	6	184	28	526	206	292	75	1,570	401
Evang. Lutheran	24	534	334	5	4		105	40	16	180	20	309	189
Missouri Synod	28	1,158	196	60	2	50	25	166	44	219	66	663	59
Lutheran Free	2	361	157			68		174	90	10		109	67
Inter-Lutheran[1]	112	4,247	868	108	14	20	73	820	231	443	100	2,856	450
United L. in Amer.	27	453	140	32	27	2	23	32	4	57	26	330	60
United Evangelical	5	22	14				1	1		3	3	18	10
Methodist Church	286	17,733	3,798	334	116	1,195	1,360	2,767	638	1,654	212	11,783	1,472
Moravian Church	4	3	10									3	10
Presbyterian bodies													
Presbyterian, U. S.	12	107	154	3	7		13	3	2	11	1	90	131
Presbyterian, U. S. A.	120	10,971	1,672	184	94	1,203	517	1,765	253	1,380	213	6,439	595
United	6	77	14				3	5		12		60	11
Protestant Episcopal Church	97	5,009	1,559	131	28	607	236	938	227	452	100	2,881	968
Reformed	2	16	2							2		14	2
Friends, Phila. and Vic.	8	339	59	14	4	7	1	21	2	18	1	279	51
Seventh Day Adventist	14	325	52	1	1	27	2	48	18	30	3	219	28
Salvation Army	1	16	9		5					5		7	4
Volunteers of America	9	388	111	33	4		3	4	1	60	26	291	77
Ten-States Sample	117	6,365	1,744	175	47	557	710	1,132	240	572	98	3,929	649
N. Y. C. Sample	12	230	70	42	3	1	8	2	2	68	40	117	17

1. Several Lutheran bodies co-operatively sponsoring.

Table S-15 Types of Agency Employees—By Full-time and Part-time and Geographic Division

Geographic division	Agencies reporting	All employees		Social workers		Medical doctors		Registered nurses		Other professionals		Nonprofessionals	
		Full time	Part time	Full time	Part time	Full time	Part time	Full time	Part time	Full time	Part time	Full time	Part time
All divisions	1,102[1]	55,282	12,838	1,255	406	4,014	3,247	9,193	2,206	5,860	1,092	34,960	5,887
New England	43	1,587	292	67	19	124	118	213	14	92	26	1,091	115
Middle Atlantic	229	14,017	3,397	354	86	782	969	2,353	419	1,528	275	9,000	1,648
East North Central	227	16,225	3,810	299	136	1,393	1,030	2,417	675	1,455	361	10,661	1,608
West North Central	179	8,461	2,323	109	24	537	268	1,769	646	1,034	183	5,012	1,202
South Atlantic	117	2,751	655	107	24	61	181	314	88	430	23	1,839	339
East South Central	64	1,605	463	55	46	66	331	173	4	317	28	994	54
West South Central	59	2,239	396	72	35	33	33	353	91	170	28	1,611	209
Mountain	64	2,573	821	49	6	364	280	465	157	376	66	1,319	312
Pacific	104	5,296	658	135	27	639	30	1,036	112	402	100	3,084	389
Outside Continental U.S.	17	528	23	8	3	15	7	100	.....	56	2	349	11

1. Includes ten-states and New York city samples.

Table S-16 Total Operating Expenses[1] of Agencies — By Type of Agency

Type of agency	Total operating expenses	
	Agencies reporting	Amount (in thousands)
All types	978[2]	$256,506
Home for the aged	197	15,282
Other service to the aged	12	1,505
Institutional care of children	128	12,774
Child placement and adoption	31	3,694
Day nursery	21	1,980
Other services to children	25	807
Hospital	176	173,029
Clinic or dispensary	10	521
Health education	1	8
Convalescent care	5	468
Other health services	6	619
Temporary shelter	12	482
Residence	35	1,022
Other residential services	3	336
Neighborhood house or settlement	130	3,047
Camp or vacation	20	170
Other group work	11	395
Other recreational services	6	151
Maternity home	4	250
Protective services	4	187
Family welfare	16	718
Employment and vocational	2	470
Rehabilitation	8	1,359
Sheltered workshop[3]	13	23,341
Social education and action	10	179
Chaplaincy: in prisons	1	414
Chaplaincy: in hospitals	18	3,056
Other chaplaincy service	3	51
Other major service	45	9,609
Not ascertainable	15	582

1. Last fiscal year ending in 1954 or 1955.
2. Includes ten-states and New York city samples.
3. Includes Goodwill Industries of America, Inc., which consists of 110 autonomous local units.

Table S-19 Total Operating Income[1] of Agencies — By Type of Agency

Type of agency	Total operating income	
	Agencies reporting	Amount (in thousands)
All types	1,011[2]	$262,782
Homes for aged	196	16,699
Other services to the aged	13	1,760
Institutional care of children	131	11,887
Child placement and adoption	32	3,647
Day nursery	24	2,081
Other services to children	26	703
Hospital	175	179,039
Clinic or dispensary	10	389
Health education	1	8
Convalescent care	6	538
Other health services	6	632
Temporary shelter	13	477
Residence	35	1,035
Other residential services	3	342
Neighborhood house or settlement	142	3,342
Camp or vacation	14	251
Other group work	22	440
Other recreational services	13	185
Maternity home	7	259
Protective services	4	190
Family welfare	18	745
Employment and vocational	2	468
Rehabilitation	10	1,616
Sheltered workshop[3]	14	22,732
Social education and action	11	165
Chaplaincy: in prisons	1	414
Chaplaincy: in hospitals	19	2,899
Other chaplaincy service	4	92
Other major service	44	9,161
Not ascertainable	15	586

1. Last fiscal year ending in 1954 or 1955.
2. Includes ten-states and New York city samples.
3. Includes Goodwill Industries of America, Inc., which consists of 110 autonomous local units.

Table S-17 Total Operating Expenses[1] of Agencies — By Denominational Relationship of Agencies

Denominational relationship of agencies	Total operating expenses	
	Agencies reporting	Amount (in thousands)
All denominations	978	$256,506
Assemblies of God	3	71
American Baptist	56	6,245
Church of the Brethren	14	937
Cong. Christian	7	533
Disciples of Christ	17	1,586
Evang. and Reformed	28	7,697
Evang. Free Church	1	44
Evang. United Brethren	3	486
Lutheran Bodies		
Amer. Evangelical	1	39
American	12	979
Augustana Evang.	37	12,272
Evangelical	22	2,124
Missouri Synod	30	5,925
Lutheran Free	2	1,376
Inter-Lutheran[2]	106	20,817
United Lutheran of America	26	2,556
United Evangelical	5	177
Methodist	261	93,217
Moravian	3	25
Presbyterian Bodies		
Presbyterian, U.S.A.	9	506
Presbyterian, U.S.A.	108	41,647
United Presbyterian	6	298
Protestant Episcopal	86	21,490
Reformed, Phila. and Vic.	2	38
Friends, Phila. & Vic.	6	1,138
Salvation Army	10	1,399
Seventh Day Adventist	17	1,333
Volunteers of America	89	29,757
N. Y. C. Sample	11	1,794

1. Last fiscal year ending in 1954 or 1955.
2. Several Lutheran bodies co-operatively sponsoring.

Table S-20 Total Operating Income[1] of Agencies — By Denominational Relationship of Agencies

Denominational relationship of agencies	Total operating income	
	Agencies reporting	Amount (in thousands)
All denominations	1,011[2]	$262,782
Assemblies of God	3	75
American Baptist	60	4,471
Church of the Brethren	12	841
Cong. Christian	7	470
Disciples of Christ	15	1,316
Evang. and Reformed	29	9,352
Evang. Free Church	1	45
Evang. United Brethren	3	498
Lutheran Bodies		
Amer. Evangelical	1	50
American	12	1,042
Augustana Evang.	37	13,203
Evangelical	22	2,408
Missouri Synod	30	6,013
Lutheran Free	2	1,475
Inter-Lutheran[3]	108	21,873
United Lutheran in America	26	2,658
United Evangelical	5	173
Methodist	270	94,748
Moravian	4	40
Presbyterian Bodies		
Presbyterian, U. S.	10	621
Presbyterian, U. S. A.	112	45,097
United Presbyterian	5	237
Protestant Episcopal	88	19,878
Reformed, Phila. and Vic.	1	34
Friends, Phila. and Vic.	6	1,046
Salvation Army	....	
Seventh Day Adventist	11	1,430
Volunteers of America	22	1,691
Ten States Sample	98	30,040
N. Y. C. Sample	11	1,885

1. Last fiscal year ending in 1954 or 1955.
2. Includes ten-states and New York city samples.
3. Several Lutheran bodies co-operatively sponsoring.

Table S-18 Total Operating Expenses[1] of Agencies — By Geographic Division[2]

Geographic division	Total operating expenses	
	Agencies reporting	Amount (in thousands)
All divisions	978	$256,506
New England	34	5,683
Middle Atlantic	195	58,183
East North Central	204	67,814
West North Central	169	39,022
South Atlantic	103	28,441
East South Central	55	7,759
West South Central	53	12,187
Mountain	60	8,886
Pacific	89	26,526
Outside Continental U. S.	16	2,005

1. Last fiscal year ending in 1954 or 1955.
2. Standard geographic divisions of the U.S. Census.

Table S-21 Total Operating Income[1] of Agencies — By Geographic Division[2]

Geographic division	Total operating income	
	Agencies reporting	Amount (in thousands)
All geographic divisions	1,011[2]	$262,782
New England	36	5,733
Middle Atlantic	202	61,135
East North Central	210	71,352
West North Central	169	39,099
South Atlantic	105	29,613
East South Central	59	8,550
West South Central	57	10,382
Mountain	63	9,137
Pacific	94	25,749
Outside the Continental U. S.	16	2,032

1. Last fiscal year ending in 1954 or 1955.
2. Includes ten-states and New York city samples.

Table S-22   Sources of Operating Income[1] of Agencies — By Per Cent of Total Operating Income and Type of Agency

Type of agency	Total operating income		Per cent of total operating income											
	Amt. in thou. of dollars	Percent of all types	Contributed from								Earned from			
			Religious organizations				Community Chests	Public funds	Individuals	Other sources	Service fees from indiv.	Service fees from public funds	Income from Investments	All other
			Local Churches	Local organ.	State or reg. org.	Nat'l organ.								
All types (except hospitals)	$262,782[2]	100.0	3.1	.3	.9	1.1	2.0	.5	6.3	9.5	66.3	2.3	4.4	4.4
Home for the aged	16,699	6.4	10.0	1.0	3.2	.7	1.1	1.9	7.8	3.7	44.1	3.1	13.4	6.4
Other services to the aged	1,760	.7	12.2		.6	.3	3.4		17.9	6.0	30.6		14.1	14.8
Inst. care of children	11,887	4.5	27.3	.8	5.8	4.8	4.0	2.3	11.9	5.4	6.5	6.3	14.1	5.0
Child place. and adopt.	3,647	1.4	21.7	.3	6.3	2.7	9.0	1.1	7.7	5.5	8.5	28.1	6.1	2.7
Day nursery	2,081	.8	7.7	2.8	.3	2.5	4.5		3.3	6.2	63.2	.2	8.3	.6
Other children's services	703	.3	10.4	4.1	3.4	14.8	15.1	17.2	11.4		5.4	1.3	2.3	4.4
Hospital	179,039	68.1	.2	.1	.2	.2	4.8	.2	.8	1.5	84.4	1.8	3.1	3.0
Clinic or dispensary	389		2.8	1.3	4.6	21.3	1.0		.5	.3	64.8		.3	2.8
Health education	8	.003					75.0		12.5	12.5				
Convalescent care	538	.2	4.3	.2	.3	.6	3.0		7.8	2.6	38.5	7.4	4.8	3.2
Other health services	632	.2	8.2	.6			23.3	.2	6.8	15.0	61.7		1.9	1.9
Temporary shelter	477	.2	10.3		5.7	3.1	2.7	1.1	6.5	6.9	10.3	2.7	6.7	23.7
Residence	1,035	.4	16.3	1.6	.4	5.8	25.7	17.5	1.7	5.6	42.7	.5	6.3	15.2
Other resid. services	342	.1					32.0	1.9	2.3	1.2	25.7			16.1
Neigh. hse. or settlement	3,342	1.3	11.8	4.6	5.4	18.3	8.0	2.5	7.1	5.3	9.0	.3	1.7	1.4
Camp or vacation	251	.09	15.5	2.5	.8	5.6	21.8		32.7	.8	35.5	.4		
Other group work	440	.2	23.0	6.5	9.8	21.1	11.9		4.8	2.0	7.5	.7	4.8	2.0
Other rec. services	185	.07	11.4		4.9	24.3	39.8	2.7	2.7	1.5	11.4			23.2
Maternity home	259	.09					53.7		5.4	12.0	23.2	8.1	3.1	2.1
Protective services	190	.07	14.7	1.1	1.1	1.1	60.0	2.3	11.1	1.1	1.6	4.7	7.9	3.5
Family welfare	745	.3	7.2	1.5	.8		2.8		3.0	6.0	10.5	5.8	.7	94.9
Employment and vocational	468	.2				3.8	2.1	.1		.4	15.4	2.4	.2	53.3
Rehabilitation	1,616	.6	.9	.8	2.2		3.2	.004	21.0	38.3	2.3	.06	3.2	7.2
Sheltered workshop[3]	22,732	8.7				33.9			45.2	18.8	1.8	.01	9.7	1.8
Social educ. and action	165	.06	20.6	1.4	10.9		2.4		.6	4.1	7.8		13.5	2.2
Chaplaincy: in prisons	414	.2	1.4	.06	10.9	2.0	.8		22.7	1.5		34.1	.6	.2
Chaplaincy: in hospitals	2,899	1.1	7.0	3.3	2.4	38.0	12.0		12.1	1.1	57.7	.2		
Other chaplaincy services	92	.03	12.0	.4	30.4	6.0	2.1		2.2	93.7			16.9	
Other major service	9,161	3.5	4.2	1.4	1.1	3.1	4.1	.3	10.7	5.5	49.5	.8	8.4	11.1
Not ascertainable	586	.2	12.3		13.7				5.8		10.6			39.2

1. Last fiscal year ending in 1954 or 1955.
2. Includes ten-states and New York city samples.
3. Includes Goodwill Industries, Inc, which consists of 110 autonomous local units.

Table S-23 — Contributed Income[1] of Agencies — By Source and Type of Agency

Number of Agencies reporting and amounts (in thousands) received from

Type of agency	All sources	Religious Organizations — Local churches	Other local	State or regional	National	All religious	Community chest	Public funds	Individuals	All other
All types	934 $58,057	583 $8,049	147 $796	240 $2,390	300 $2,801	748 $15,234	251 $5,140	69 $1,217	490 $16,444	407 $24,999
Home for aged	177 5,047	128 1,676	17 162	42 523	22 115	151 2,477	19 187	8 323	97 1,310	77 620
Other service to aged	12 710	10 214	· ·	1 10	2 5	11 228	3 60	· ·	10 315	4 106
Inst. care of children	127 7,526	96 3,246	16 · 98	34 693	29 565	116 5,747	31 470	22 272	91 1,415	53 643
Child placement & adopt.	32 1,982	23 790	3 12	13 228	12 97	28 1,131	17 330	2 41	24 280	20 199
Day nursery	24 576	15 160	7 58	3 6	7 52	18 280	9 93	3 · ·	11 69	8 129
Other serv. to children	26 611	18 73	5 29	9 24	16 104	21 233	7 106	4 121	16 80	9 69
Hospital	144 6,612	46 419	19 180	20 290	16 428	73 1,321	28 859	13 275	64 1,392	77 5,069
Clinic or dispensary	8 124	5 11	1 5	3 18	7 83	8 118	1 4	· ·	1 2	1 2,761
Health education	1 8	· ·	· ·	· ·	· ·	· ·	1 6	· ·	1 · ·	1 · ·
Convalescent care	4 95	3 23	1 1	· ·	· ·	3 23	1 16	· ·	3 42	2 14
Other health services	6 219	2 52	1 3	1 2	3 4	5 81	· ·	· ·	3 43	4 95
Temporary shelter	13 269	10 49	2 · ·	1 27	1 15	11 94	6 111	1 11	9 31	4 33
Residence	31 368	25 169	3 17	6 4	17 60	31 250	2 28	1 60	13 18	12 58
Other res. services	2 161	· ·	· ·	· ·	· ·	· ·	1 88	1 62	1 8	2 4
Neighborhood hse. or settlement	142 2,919	105 396	45 155	47 181	94 613	131 1,368	64 1,068	4 62	71 236	68 178
Camp or vacation	11 161	12 39	1 · ·	1 · ·	3 14	11 54	2 20	1 5	8 82	5 9
Other group work	22 373	7 101	2 11	9 43	18 93	21 247	7 96	· ·	9 21	4 2
Other recre. services	13 120	1 21	3 12	6 9	8 45	12 86	2 22	· ·	5 5	4 9
Maternity home	7 170	· ·	· ·	· ·	· ·	· ·	7 103	· ·	3 14	4 1
Protective services	4 158	3 28	1 · ·	1 2	· ·	3 32	4 102	4 7	8 21	4 31
Family welfare	18 590	10 54	6 11	5 6	3 8	11 79	14 447	· ·	8 22	2 2
Employment & vocational	9 13	· ·	· ·	· ·	· ·	· ·	4 13	1 17	· ·	10 45
Rehabilitation	9 500	4 14	3 13	2 36	1 61	4 116	4 34	· ·	7 340	1 · 7
Sheltered workshop[3]	11 19,696	2 34	1 · ·	5 18	· ·	3 108	8 725	2 1	2 10,266	1 8,703
Social education & action	11 141	4 5	1 6	1 45	9 56	11 56	· ·	1 1	1 94	2 31
Chaplaincy: in prisons	19 177	1 · ·	3 · ·	12 70	6 57	18 329	1 10	· ·	9 35	1 17
Chaplaincy: in hospitals	4 1,187	13 202	3 8	3 28	3 35	4 78	2 24	· ·	1 · ·	6 44
Other chaplaincy service	4 92	3 11	3 8	10 45	16 273	32 521	1 11	1 19	12 265	1 · ·
Other major service	39 7,238	21 190	1 8	5 80	6 18	12 177	4 83	1 · ·	6 34	15 6,163
Not ascertainable	13 214	9 72	· ·	· ·	· ·	· ·	4 24	· ·	· ·	5 32

1. Last fiscal year ending in 1954 or 1955.
2. Includes ten-states and New York city samples.
3. Includes Goodwill Industries, Inc., which consists of 110 autonomous local units.

Table S-24 Contributed Income[1] of Agencies — By Source and Denominational Relationship of Agencies

Number of Agencies reporting and amounts (in thousands) received from.
Each cell shows: number of agencies / amount (in thousands of dollars).

Denominational relationship of agencies	All sources	Local churches	Other local	State or regional	National	All religious	Community chest	Public funds	Individuals	All other
All denominations	934[2] / $58,057	583 / 8,049	147 / 796	240 / 2,390	300 / 2,801	748 / 15,234	251 / 5,140	69 / 1,217	490 / 16,444	407 / 24,999
Assemblies of God	3 / 60	2 / 19			1 / 3	3 / 52			2 / 8	
American Baptist	58 / 1,379	46 / 304	15 / 33	24 / 53	35 / 164	55 / 566	16 / 175	4 / 111	26 / 356	25 / 166
Church of the Brethren	11 / 123	6 / 31	2 / 1	3 / 20	1 / 4	8 / 55		1 / 18	6 / 26	2 / 23
Cong. Christian	6 / 141	5 / 55			1 / 14	5 / 69		2 / 25	5 / 42	2 / 5
Disciples of Christ	14 / 1,136	12 / 529	5 / 45	2 / 3	6 / 266	14 / 872	3 / 33		7 / 103	6 / 127
Evang. and Reformed	26 / 921	21 / 386		6 / 58	6 / 65	25 / 598	3 / 57	1 / 6	16 / 99	13 / 160
Evang. Free Church	1 / 16	1 / 16				1 / 16				
Evang. United Brethren	3 / 336	3 / 204				3 / 204		1 / 13	3 / 115	1 / 3
Lutheran Bodies										
Amer. Evangelical	1 / 30			1 / 8	1 / 11	1 / 19			1 / 8	1 / 2
American	12 / 569	8 / 95	3 / 38		8 / 76	10 / 162	2 / 14		8 / 159	11 / 235
Augustana Evang.	32 / 804	29 / 189	3 / 7	17 / 154	7 / 13	32 / 394	12 / 94	1 / 47	19 / 173	11 / 95
Evangelical	22 / 425	18 / 156	5 / 70	5 / 15	16 / 98	20 / 276	2 / 13	1 /	11 / 54	15 / 34
Missouri Synod	29 / 2,389	17 / 443		12 / 189	4 / 113	23 / 805	7 / 183	4 / 73	20 / 244	15 / 133
Lutheran Free Church	2 / 11	2 /			1 / 2	2 /			2 / 1	2 / 6
Inter-Lutheran[3]	89 / 3,173	39 / 1,016	15 / 38	10 / 38	24 / 128	44 / 1,218	16 / 264	2 / 37	30 / 460	63 / 1,210
United Lutheran in Amer.	26 / 1,391	18 / 255	5 / 16	11 / 410	2 / 39	26 / 719	3 / 24	1 / 46	3 / 390	1 / 155
United Evangelical	5 / 112	5 / 10	2 /		2 / 24	4 / 35		1 / 61	3 / 6	1 / 10
Methodist Church	256 / 26,109	176 / 2,253	39 / 171	84 / 696	134 / 1,166	247 / 5,296	51 / 1,581	16 / 160	114 / 10,849	86 / 9,266
Moravian Church	4 / 8	4 / 6		1 /	1 / 2	4 /			1 /	1 /
Presbyterian Bodies										
Presbyterian, U. S.	10 / 426	7 / 194		4 / 102	1 / 105	10 / 401	1 / 7	1 / 4	5 / 33	5 / 36
Presbyterian, U. S. A.	106 / 4,053	72 / 945	24 / 115	10 / 107	38 / 415	91 / 1,599	29 / 489	2 / 81	54 / 709	32 / 1,175
United	5 / 135	4 / 97	2 / 21		1 / 16	5 / 135			1 /	
Protestant Episcopal	82 / 2,932	45 / 196	15 / 60	43 / 388	4 / 39	66 / 710	32 / 856	11 / 139	55 / 741	38 / 488
Reformed in Amer.	1 / 24	1 / 12				1 / 12				
Friends, Phila. & Vic.	4 / 12								4 / 9	1 / 3
Salvation Army										
Seventh Day Adventist	2 / 21	2 / 1				2 / 1				2 / 19
Volunteers of America	21 / 789	5 / 12	2 / 64			6 / 77	12 / 240	2 / 17	15 / 379	6 / 5,065
Ten States Sample	92 / 9,884	27 / 610	7 / 113	5 / 137	5 / 30	30 / 893	57 / 1,071	15 / 323	56 / 1,113	48 / 6,424
N. Y. C. Sample	11 / 648	6 / 14	3 / 4	2 / 12	2 / 8	8 / 39	5 / 39	2 / 56	8 / 355	9 / 159

1. Last fiscal year ending in 1954 or 1955.
2. Includes ten-states and New York city samples.
3. Several Lutheran bodies co-operatively sponsoring.

203

Table S-25   Contributed Income[1] of Agencies — By Source and Geographic Division[2]

Geographic division	All sources	Religious Organizations					Community chest	Public funds	Individuals	All other
		Local churches	Other local	State or regional	National	All religious				
All divisions	934 $58,057	583 $8,049	147 $796	240 $2,390	300 $2,801	748 $15,234	251 $5,140	69 $1,217	490 $16,444	407 $24,999
New England	32 890	18 111	3 9	10 72	8 51	18 246	14 233	1 6	20 265	15 137
Middle Atlantic	196 14,441	129 2,121	33 169	39 490	27 184	154 2,975	55 967	23 637	111 2,437	83 7,420
East North Central	192 8,595	120 1,528	42 389	47 434	54 472	154 2,934	79 1,482	14 208	119 1,544	97 1,409
West North Central	157 4,324	102 1,165	17 37	38 215	40 288	115 1,739	32 561	7	71 793	77 1,053
South Atlantic	98 2,994	66 1,755	12 42	36 566	43 403	92 3,764	9 745	8 77	51 10,347	39 9,043
East South Central	57 1,622	35 465	8 29	23 355	25 292	53 1,144	8 129	7 36	27 143	20 172
West South Central	54 1,356	39 541	8 57	18 69	34 357	52 1,063	8 88	3 67	26 123	17 122
Mountain	51 774	21 76	5 27	8 10	23 275	31 392	9 180	....	17 172	23 34
Pacific	82 2,786	48 277	19 37	20 171	33 266	64 746	37 744	4 53	46 613	35 5,609
Outside Continental U.S.	15 275	5 10	....	1 8	13 213	15 231	1 11	2 27	2 7	1 ......

Number of Agencies reporting and amounts (in thousands) received from

1. Last fiscal year ending in 1954 or 1955.
2. Standard geographic divisions of the U.S. Census.

Table S-26

Earned Income[1] of Agencies — By Source and Type of Agency

Type of agency	Number of agencies reporting and amounts (in thousands) earned from									
	All earned income		Service fees from individuals		Service fees from public funds		Income from investments		All other	
All types	823[2]	$204,544	660	$174,296	132	$5,950	421	$11,564	389	$11,441
Home for the aged	184	11,169	153	7,363	23	510	134	2,236	78	1,064
Other services to the aged	9	1,049	7	539			3	249	5	261
Institutional care of children	114	3,811	71	777	39	746	92	1,676	66	591
Child placement and adoption	30	1,657	21	311	15	1,026	21	222	12	97
Day nursery	21	1,507	19	1,316	1	5	6	172	7	12
Other children's services	17	93	12	38	1	9	5	16	8	31
Hospital	173	172,776	172	158,307	21	3,285	62	5,464	72	5,370
Clinic or dispensary	8	264	8	252			2	1	4	11
Health education	6	442	5	207	1	40	3	26	1	17
Convalescent care	5	413	4	390			4	12	2	12
Other health services	9	205	9	49	2	13	2	32	5	113
Temporary shelter	31	668	26	442	1	5	15	65	15	157
Residence	2	143	2	88						
Other residential services	97	418	89	302	8	10	22	56	41	55
Neighborhood house or settlement	10	91	10	89	1	1	2		3	48
Camp or vacation	9	68	8	33	1	3	3	21	5	9
Other group work	6	66	3	21					5	43
Other recreational services	5	89	4	60					1	4
Maternity home	3	32	2	3	2	21	4	8		
Protective services	7	154	5	78	2	9	3	15	3	26
Family welfare	2	455	4	249	3	43	2		2	444
Employment and vocational	10	1,115	4	533	1	11			8	862
Rehabilitation	14	2,886	2	3	1	4	1	4	10	1,629
Sheltered workshop[3]	6	22	1	32	2		6	720	4	3
Social education and action	1	237	5	1,673			3	16	1	9
Chaplaincy: in prisons	1				1	141	1	56	4	6
Chaplaincy: in hospitals					2	6	9	18		
Other chaplaincy services	9	2,468	12	1,079	1					
Other major service	27	1,898	2	62	3	61	13	425	20	336
Not ascertainable	7	348					3	49	4	230

1. Last fiscal year ending in 1954 or 1955.
2. Includes ten-states and New York city samples.
3. Includes Goodwill Industries of America, Inc., which consists of 110 autonomous local units.

Table S-27 Earned Income[1] of Agencies — By Source and Denominational Relationship of Agencies

Number of agencies reporting and amounts (in thousands) earned from

Denominational relationship of agencies	All earned income (No.)	All earned income (Amount)	Service fees from individuals (No.)	Service fees from individuals (Amount)	Service fees from public funds (No.)	Service fees from public funds (Amount)	Income from investments (No.)	Income from investments (Amount)	All other (No.)	All other (Amount)
All denominations	823	$204,544	660	$174,296	132	$5,950	421	$11,564	389	$11,441
Assemblies of God	3	15	2	5	1	6	1		1	2
American Baptist	38	3,012	32	2,690	3	59	19	227	14	33
Church of the Brethren	12	718	9	495	2	17	8	27	7	180
Cong. Christian	7	327	5	242			5	66	3	19
Disciples of Christ	9	165	5	15	1	6	4	10	3	116
Evang. and Reformed	27	8,402	22	7,770	8	159	18	300	14	171
Evang. Free Church	1	29	1	29			1			
Evang. United Brethren	3	162					3	103	2	60
Lutheran Bodies										
Amer. Evangelical	1	19	1	19						
American	12	475	12	338			12	30	1	106
Augustana Evang.	35	11,841	32	11,324	4	48	23	51	7	415
Evangelical	20	2,017	17	1,902	5	36	11	50	18	26
Missouri Synod	26	4,383	19	3,156	10	348	16	52	7	62
Lutheran Free	2	1,464	2	1,425			1		10	39
Inter-Lutheran[2]	97	18,682	93	17,411	12	255	22	128	2	511
United Lutheran in Amer.	21	1,266	16	532	6	272	17	311	20	151
United Evangelical	5	61	5	54			3	2	14	6
Methodist	207	68,557	173	61,894	21	1,443	81	2,521	121	2,471
Moravian	4	31	4	27			2	5	1	
Presbyterian Bodies										
Presbyterian, U. S.	9	139	4	24	1	8	7	92	3	16
Presbyterian, U. S. A.	84	41,137	63	34,143	11	1,121	53	4,185	42	1,977
United	5	102	4	76			2	23	1	3
Protestant Episcopal	73	16,938	56	12,537	20	1,197	57	1,906	37	1,146
Reformed in Amer.	1	10	1	9					1	
Friends, Phila and Vic.	5	1,034	5	971	1	4	3	60		
Salvation Army										
Seventh Day Adventist	11	1,409	11	1,409	1	4	2	2	11	620
Volunteers of America	14	899	11	245						
Ten States Sample	80	20,014	49	15,406	22	401	41	973	43	3,227
N. Y. C. Sample	11	1,236	6	148	3	566	9	437	5	84

1. Last fiscal year ending in 1954 or 1955.
2. Several Lutheran bodies co-operatively sponsoring.

Table S-28   Earned Income[1] of Agencies — By Source and Geographic Division[2]

Number of agencies reporting and amounts (in thousands) earned from

Geographical division	All earned income		Service fees from individuals		Service fees from public funds		Income from investments		All other	
All divisions	823[3]	$204,544	660	$174,296	132	$5,950	421	$11,564	389	$11,441
New England	32	4,693	26	2,914	3	78	19	824	15	879
Middle Atlantic	154	46,739	115	33,674	38	3,691	121	6,496	85	3,017
East North Central	176	63,610	144	57,214	37	806	106	2,019	85	2,797
West North Central	150	34,287	138	32,840	17	243	61	508	50	691
South Atlantic	77	6,381	54	4,395	9	109	35	1,094	43	760
East South Central	45	6,980	31	5,995	2	1	20	194	28	793
West South Central	44	8,939	29	8,267	3	1	16	84	27	582
Mountain	54	8,275	51	7,916	4	117	7	82	13	160
Pacific	78	22,887	61	20,019	15	286	31	260	36	1,690
Outside the Continental U. S.	13	1,753	11	1,062	4	618	5	3	7	72

1. Last fiscal year ending in 1954 or 1955.
2. Standard geographic divisions of the U.S. Census.
3. Includes ten-states and New York city samples.

Table S-29

Types of Capital Assets of Agencies — By Type of Agency[1]

Type of agency	Number of agencies reporting and value of capital assets (in thousands of dollars)						
	Total capital assets		Endowments and investments		Bldgs., land and equipment		All other
All types	832[2]	701,279	453	$265,148	761	$376,908	363	$47,166
Home for the aged	190	121,155	145	50,823	179	63,490	74	4,836
Other services to the aged	10	9,208	4	7,473	9	1,611	4	124
Institutional care of children	113	69,946	90	31,038	106	35,810	46	3,009
Child placement and adoption	28	10,302	24	4,525	25	5,444	13	331
Day nursery	16	7,588	4	2,491	15	4,853	5	246
Other children's services	16	1,869	6	515	14	1,251	4	102
Hospital	171	387,307	71	146,483	159	204,581	119	28,051
Health education	6	510	1	18	6	491		1
Convalescent care	5	5,157	4	2,684	5	2,030	4	346
Other health services	11	1,411	5	191	5	1,195	2	25
Temporary shelter	11	1,605	4	734	11	856	4	15
Residence	27	6,191	17	1,629	26	3,864	15	475
Other residential services	3	847			2	686	1	37
Neighborhood house or settlement	92	9,892	25	1,102	82	8,448	21	159
Camp or vacation	9	575	3	24	9	532	3	19
Other group work	13	1,106	3	83	11	905	4	117
Other recreational services	11	622	1	4	10	574	4	43
Maternity home	6	545	4	103	5	436	2	6
Protective services	4	357	3	345	2	5	2	7
Family welfare	13	1,322	3	489	9	798	5	29
Employment and vocational	9	325	2	41	9	253	1	31
Rehabilitation	2	3,732	2	205	8	2,263	4	725
Sheltered workshop[3]	12	25,667	5	1,587	12	17,450	8	6,639
Social education and action	3	745	2	222	2	523		
Chaplaincy: in prisons	1	2,324	1	1,317	2	1,007		
Chaplaincy: in hospitals	14	4,729	8	486	10	3,863	5	379
Other chaplaincy services	2	154	1	3	1	151		
Other major services	34	22,317	10	9,521	29	11,363	9	830
Not ascertainable	6	3,771	4	1,012	6	2,175	3	584

1. Last fiscal year ending in 1954 or 1955.
2. Includes ten-states and New York city samples.
3. Includes Goodwill Industries of America, Inc., which consists of 110 autonomous local units.

Table S-30 Types of Capital Assets of Agencies — By Denominational Relationship of Agencies[1]

Number of agencies reporting and value of capital assets (in thousands of dollars)

Denominational relationship of agencies	Total Capital assets (No.)	Total Capital assets ($)	Endowments and investments (No.)	Endowments and investments ($)	Bldgs., land and equipment (No.)	Bldgs., land and equipment ($)	All other (No.)	All other ($)
All denominations	832[2]	$701,279	453	$265,148	761	$376,908	363	$47,166
Assemblies of God	3	189			3	181	1	8
American Baptist	45	15,856	18	4,213	41	9,850	11	1,655
Church of the Brethren	15	3,196	8	631	14	2,474	6	80
Cong. Christian	6	2,672	4	1,384	6	1,094	3	193
Disciples of Christ	13	6,680	8	1,894	11	4,442	4	343
Evang. and Reformed	27	28,379	19	8,890	26	17,182	13	2,314
Evang. Free Church								
Evang. United Brethren	3	4,100	3	2,292	3	1,653	2	152
Lutheran Bodies								
Amer. Evangelical	1	293	1	93	1	200		
American	11	3,393	10	703	11	2,691	14	2,385
Augustana Evang.	36	23,489	25	2,031	35	18,885	11	341
Evangelical	21	7,581	14	696	18	6,045	13	666
Missouri Synod	28	16,267	16	1,493	26	12,700	2	129
Lutheran Free	2	1,369			2	1,239		
Inter-Lutheran[3]	98	26,553	25	3,031	88	18,870	80	4,638
United Lutheran in Amer.	21	16,424	16	6,244	20	9,667	10	514
United Evangelical	4	520	3	55	4	465		
Methodist	191	167,239	92	39,418	178	110,502	80	14,556
Moravian	4	293	3	75	4	183	2	35
Presbyterian Bodies								
Presbyterian, U. S.	10	4,554	8	2,080	10	2,310	3	165
Presbyterian, U. S. A.	89	187,369	52	105,379	84	71,026	19	9,903
United	3	475	2	34	3	431	1	10
Protestant Episcopal	76	101,316	58	56,454	60	38,100	29	3,368
Reformed in Amer.	2	250	1	20	1	200	1	7
Friends, Phila. and Vic.	6	3,682	4	766	4	2,380	2	536
Salvation Army	11	1,388			10	1,136	5	238
Seventh Day Adventist	19	3,288	2	14	18	2,277	11	294
Volunteers of America			5	78				
Ten States Sample	79	65,135	49	20,325	73	38,769	35	4,118
N. Y. C. Sample	8	9,329	6	6,854	7	1,956	5	518

1. Last fiscal year ending in 1954 or 1955.
2. Includes ten-states and New York city samples.
3. Several Lutheran bodies co-operatively sponsoring.

209

Table S-31

Types of Capital Assets[1] of Agencies — By Geographic Division[2]

Geographical division	Number of agencies reporting and value of capital assets (in thousands of dollars)							
	Total capital assets		Endowments and investments		Bldgs., land and equipment		All other	
All divisions	832[3]	$701,297	453	$265,148	761	$376,908	363	$47,166
New England	31	21,284	23	13,021	31	7,244	16	852
Middle Atlantic	163	283,203	124	161,274	145	108,160	67	13,095
East North Central	171	168,820	110	54,827	161	100,220	71	12,386
West North Central	155	75,608	66	12,693	140	51,739	80	5,021
South Atlantic	78	57,413	42	9,236	71	37,561	26	7,435
East South Central	46	16,715	22	3,280	43	12,303	17	1,129
West South Central	39	17,662	16	2,510	36	14,532	15	992
Mountain	54	13,923	11	1,466	49	10,975	30	1,147
Pacific	80	43,886	36	6,832	72	31,879	34	4,647
Outside the Continental U. S.	15	2,765	3	9	13	2,295	7	462

1. Last fiscal year ending in 1954 or 1955.
2. Standard geographic divisions of the U.S. Census.
3. Includes ten-states and New York city samples.

Table S-32

Types of Expansion Planned by Agencies — By Type of Agency[1]

Number of agencies reporting and expansion plans (in thousands of dollars)

Type of agency	Total expansion		Bldgs. & land		Equipment		Staff & program		Other	
All types	362[2]	$162,406	279	$133,891	193	$44,927	181	$5,661	27	$3,596
Home for aged	74	22,710	67	19,772	39	2,523	25	416	1	20
Other service to the aged	4	1,499	3	730	3	135	1	34	1	600
Institutional care of children	50	9,733	42	8,702	22	373	29	402	2	6
Child placement and adoption	15	1,711	9	1,272	7	181	13	257		
Day nursery	9	809	6	645	6	139	6	26		
Other children's services	7	743	6	656	4	33	4	51	1	3
Hospital	65	103,375	63	89,836	40	9,812	15	2,463	6	2,263
Clinic or dispensary	1	25	1	20	1	5				
Health education										
Convalescent care	2	104	1	75	2	29	2	40	1	30
Other health services	3	1,735	2	1,650	2	15	4	38		
Temporary shelter	5	229	4	155	4	36	2	28	2	8
Residence	7	779	6	688	2	55	2	30		
Other residential services	2	373	2	318	1	25				
Neighborhood house or settlement	46	3,505	33	2,515	25	10,305	26	216	7	371
Camp or vacation	5	175	3	135	4	31	2	9		
Other group work	10	761	5	677	7	39	9	43	1	1
Other recreational services	5	273	4	196	3	13	4	64		
Maternity home	1	25	1	25						
Protective services	2	14			1		2	12	1	2
Family welfare	7	71					7	71		
Employment and vocational	7	100			1	20,000	1	35	1	30
Rehabilitation	8	1,798	5	835	1	35	5	620	1	100
Sheltered workshop[3]	8	3,784	6	2,636	7	243	5	496	2	162
Social education and action	6	65	2	32	5	490	1	30		
Chaplaincy: in prisons	1	98	1	43	1	3	1	55		
Chaplaincy: in hospitals	6	125	1	60			5	65		
Other chaplaincy services	3	138	2	115	1	2	3	19		
Other major service	11	7,645	4	2,103	5	405	7	137		
Not ascertainable	1	4					1	4		

1. To 1956.
2. Includes ten-states and New York city samples.
3. Includes Goodwill Industries of America, Inc., which consists of 110 autonomous local units.

Table S-33   Types of Expansion[1] Planned by Agencies — By Denominational Relationship of Agencies

Number of agencies reporting and expansion plans (in thousands of dollars)

Denominational relationship	Total expansion		Bldgs. & land		Equipment		Staff & program		Other	
	No.	$	No.	$	No.	$	No.	$	No.	$
All denominations	362[2]	$162,406	279	$133,891	193	$44,927	181	$5,661	27	$3,596
Assemblies of God	1	40	1	40						
American Baptist	25	3,811	18	3,359	15	336	13	97	1	20
Church of the Brethren	3	108	4	471	3	29	1	7		
Cong. Christian	1	265	1	200	1	50	2	15		
Disciples of Christ	6	1,230	5	746	3	455	2	29		
Evang. and Reformed	17	9,666	16	8,448	9	1,088	4	110	1	20
Evang. Free Church										
Evang. United Brethren										
Lutheran Bodies										
Amer. Evangelical										
American	9	980	6	840	2	15	8	125		
Augustana Evang.	12	3,716	9	3,118	5	505	6	92	1	2
Evangelical	6	779	6	736	4	32	2	10		
Missouri Synod	14	5,642	11	5,109	6	282	8	251		
Lutheran Free										
Inter-Lutheran[3]	38	14,588	27	13,495	14	700	17	287	1	1
United Lutheran in Amer.	9	2,093	7	1,787	5	253	6	53		
United Evangelical	1	42	1	30	1	5	1	4	1	3
Methodist	75	66,925	58	58,409	44	15,710	38	2,441	10	365
Moravian	1	40	1	40						
Presbyterian Bodies										
Presbyterian, U.S.	8	1,079	6	745	2	60	3	24		
Presbyterian, U.S.A.	48	23,711	42	19,704	30	2,173	20	172	4	1,660
United	2	81	1	75	1	3	1	3		
Protestant Episcopal	28	11,041	15	3,837	10	1,444	17	257	2	1,128
Reformed in Amer.										
Friends, Phila. and Vic.	1	15			1	15				
Salvation Army										
Seventh Day Adventist	2	107	2	82	1	25				
Volunteers of America	11	1,025	10	667	10	155	7	173	1	30
Ten States Sample	42	15,327	30	11,913	25	21,577	23	1,471	5	367
N. Y. C. Sample	2	95	2	40	1	15	2	40		

1. To 1960.
2. Includes ten-states and New York city samples.
3. Several Lutheran bodies co-operatively sponsoring.

Table S-34   Types of Expansion¹ Planned by Agencies — By Geographic Division²

Number of agencies reporting and expansion plans (in thousands of dollars)

Geographic division	Total expansion		Bldgs. & land		Equipment		Staff & program		Other	
All divisions	362³	$162,406	279	$133,891	193	$44,927	181	$5,661	27	$3,596
New England	4	1,154	2	961	2	10,045	4	73	1	75
Middle Atlantic	66	30,494	45	21,279	31	22,127	33	505	5	1,582
East North Central	80	34,079	64	30,094	49	3,120	39	1,129	6	181
West North Central	66	37,175	59	32,511	29	2,888	30	1,624	3	150
South Atlantic	34	19,296	27	17,132	21	1,499	19	598	3	67
East South Central	16	11,266	12	8,270	9	1,707	9	1,062	1	2
West South Central	21	7,383	18	6,094	15	769	14	318	2	203
Mountain	26	4,831	19	4,521	14	220	12	90	......	......
Pacific	42	13,982	27	11,282	18	2,387	17	178	5	586
Outside the Continental U. S.	7	2,746	6	1,747	5	165	4	84	1	750

1. To 1960.
2. Standard geographic divisions of the U.S. Census.
3. Includes ten-states and New York city samples.

Table S-35   Nature of Religious Involvement of Agencies[1] — By Major Types of Agencies

Percentage of agencies in

Nature of religious involvement	All types	Homes for aged	Inst. care for children	Child placement	Hospital	Residence	Neighborhood house	All other agencies
All agencies	100%	100%	100%	100%	100%	100%	100%	100%
(Number of Agencies)	(986)[2]	(211)	(126)	(30)	(166)	(40)	(139)	(274)
Recognition of Relationship								
a. Officially recognized by a religious organization as related	87.1	88.2	95.2	100.0	60.3	95.0	97.1	91.2
b. With *officially stated* relationship	78.2	76.8	88.1	86.7	49.4	90.0	90.6	83.2
I. Nature of Religious Control								
a. Directly responsible to a religious organization, with *no* Board of its own	8.3	3.3	6.3		4.8	5.0	13.7	13.9
b. Have own Board where:								
all members are chosen by religious organization	38.4	54.5	49.2	50.0	22.3	45.0	31.7	32.1
½ or more are chosen by religious organization	5.7	.9	4.8	10.0	5.4		12.2	6.9
less than ½ are chosen by religious organization	3.7	4.3	4.0	3.3	1.2		4.3	4.7
c. Have own Board which requires certain religious affiliation of members:								
all Board members *must be* of a certain affiliation	57.3	78.2	63.5	83.3	46.4	72.5	33.8	51.8
½ or more of its members must be of a certain affiliation	12.2	3.8	9.5	6.7	21.1	5.0	25.9	9.1
less than ½, but some of its members must be of a certain affiliation	1.1	1.4	.8		1.8	2.5	1.4	.4
d. Make official reports to religious organization	80.7	72.0	84.9	83.3	78.9	75.0	90.6	82.1
e. Number where religious organization has final authority	51.7	46.9	59.5	33.3	24.7	60.0	69.8	59.9
Control and Character of Services								
In practice, require certain religious affiliation of:								
director	81.3	87.7	82.5	93.3	63.3	87.5	87.1	81.8
all other professional staff members	32.3	21.3	40.5	6.7	2.4	40.0	45.3	43.8
½ or more of other professional staff members	6.0	4.7	8.7		1.8	2.5	10.1	6.6
less than half of other professional staff members	.9	1.4	.8		.6		.7	1.1
II. Character of Services								
a. With religious objective, whether or not services are secular	87.4	85.3	89.7	96.7	81.9	87.5	91.4	88.3
b. Provides distinctly religious services	65.8	73.5	73.8	63.3	71.7	40.0	48.9	65.3
1. Worship services	47.4	65.9	59.5	26.7	24.7	32.5	33.8	52.6
2. Religious instruction	5.4	.9	12.7	16.7	.6	2.5	10.8	5.8
3. Evangelistic programs	.3			3.3			.7	1.8
4. Chapel facilities	8.1	4.3	.8	13.3	38.0	5.0	.7	2.9
5. Chaplaincy services	2.4	1.9	.8	3.3	6.6		.7	.4
6. Pastoral services	1.2	.5			1.8		2.2	2.6
7. Others								
c. Officially limiting services to persons of certain religious affiliation	16.6	38.9	15.9	26.7	.6	27.5	4.3	13.1
d. In practice, serves persons of a certain affiliation	28.4	56.9	36.5	66.7	.6	30.0	5.8	26.6
e. Consider themselves Christian agencies in tradition and spirit	96.5	94.8	99.2	100.0	97.0	97.5	96.4	95.6
III. Nature of Assistance								
a. Agencies originated under auspices of a religious organization	78.2	71.1	84.9	80.0	53.0	85.0	93.5	87.2
b. Uses building owned by religious organization which is:	50.9	39.8	49.2	23.3	25.3	80.0	84.2	57.7
1. Provided rent free	41.9	27.5	42.1	16.7	21.7	72.5	72.7	47.8
2. Provided below market rental	1.7	.1	1.6	3.3	1.2		2.2	2.9
3. Provided at full market rental	1.5			3.3			2.9	1.8
c. Receives significant financial support from religious sources	66.1	67.3	85.7	93.3	16.3	65.0	87.8	72.6
1. All of income	22.3	12.8	16.7	10.0	.6	17.5	38.8	39.1
2. More than ½ of income	24.2	21.3	51.6	60.0	3.0	17.5	25.2	23.4
3. Less than ½ of income	19.2	31.3	16.7	23.3	12.7	30.0	22.3	11.3
d. Receives assistance (other than financial) from religious organization	62.1	58.8	85.7	83.3	38.0	47.5	71.9	62.8
1. Volunteer training or recruitment	20.2	6.6	23.0	26.7	13.9	2.5	35.3	27.4
2. Promotion or fund-raising	34.4	37.4	50.0	43.3	16.9	17.5	41.0	44.5
3. Consultation services	25.6	27.5	34.1	46.7	14.5	17.5	29.5	23.7
4. Ministerial or pastoral services	30.9	43.1	40.5	46.7	21.7	22.5	19.4	28.1
5. Gifts in kind (food, clothes, etc.)	48.9	41.7	79.4	60.0	24.1	35.0	63.3	48.9
6. Others	8.8	7.5	14.3	6.7	4.2	7.5	10.1	9.9